A hieroglyphic of the signs of Heaven, at the eclipse of the moon, November 3, 1827.

The female zodiac, 1812.

the HISTORY
of ASTROLOGY
ZOLAR

TARPON HOUSE PUBLISHING
USA • UNITED KINGDOM • SWEDEN

Printed in the United States by Marrakech Express
Tarpon Springs Fl 34689

ISBN 1-886500-00-2

First published 1972 under the title
The History of Astrology
by Arco Publishing Company, Inc
New York

Second edition 1980 by
Samuel Weiser, Inc
New York,

Third edition 1997 by
Tarpon House Publishing
P.O Box 771
Tarpon Springs, Fl 34688

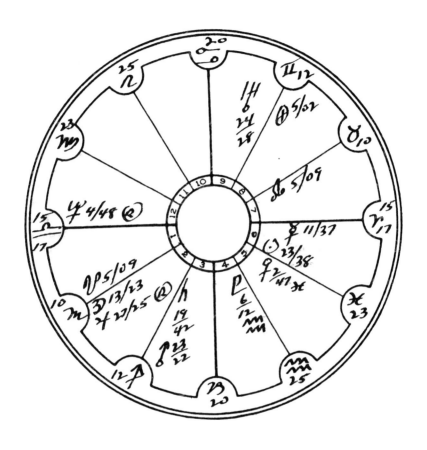

Birth of Modern Astrology
Discovery of Uranus
March 13, 1781
Approximately 8:00 P.M.

PREFACE TO THE THIRD EDITION
A CHAT WITH ZOLAR

Almost a quarter of a century has now passed since the very first edition of THE LURE OF THE HEAVENS...A HISTORY OF ASTROLOGY was published. From the Chaldean astrologers who five thousand years ago sought clues to the future in the position of the planets, to its present day revival in the many "900" lines advertised on late night television, astrology continues to fascinate and amuse us all.

In 1980 when I wrote the Foreword to the first paperback edition of this work I predicted that the widespread use of personal computers by astrologers would totally revolutionize the practice of astrology, which has indeed happened.

At the time little did I imagine, however, that it would be television, and not the computer, that would bring interest in the stellar and the psychic world to an all time high, generating millions of dollars in sales for those offering such quick fix services.

Why has this happened? Simply because in the finality all popular interest in astrology ends in what has always been called "fortune telling" no matter how we seek to spell the word!

Today, despite the soundings of Washington spin doctors and the media, times ARE tough and are getting tougher and tougher!

Hardly a day passes when I don't find written in the press news of the closing of yet ANOTHER business and the loss of additional jobs. Clearly, downsizing is something here to stay.

Added to this is the general acceleration of consciousness brought about by the movement worldwide due to our passage from the idealistic sign Pisces to the high-tech Internet that accompanies Aquarius.

Perhaps for the first time since the Great Depression, people no longer know "where" they are going, "how" they are getting there, or "who's going with them." This is scary.

And when people are afraid, coming from a place of fear rather than love, they have always turned to the psychic world for answers! (Thousands of Ouija boards were sold during the World War.)

Unfortunately, with the easy access of "900" telephone psychics, the highly personal and professional attention people received in the past from their very special "astrologer" may all too sadly soon become a relic of the past.

Why? Because the general public can no longer afford their services!

It has now become much quicker, and easier, to dial a telephone number and get sound bite answers to a few specific questions than to meet in person with a trained counselor who can help you "grow" through your horoscope chart, not just "go" through it!

But as all things that go around come around, the day will surely return when Astrology returns to its divine role as a source of psychological understanding.

I have often likened an accurately cast horoscope chart to an x-ray of the Soul since it indicates the whys and wherefores of this and ALL THE LIVES we have lived before! (Yes, Astrology does embrace Reincarnation!)

In the pages that follow readers will find told an extraordinary story that truly has no beginning and ending.

Tarpon House Publishing has done us a great service in making this ZOLAR classic once again available.

I know you will enjoy reading it as much as I did bringing it to you.

> ZOLAR
> Tarpon Springs, Florida
> Winter 1996

FOREWORD TO THE SECOND EDITION

Eleven years have passed since the first manned spaceship that we know of landed on the Moon heralding in a new age of outer space. Considering this event in the light of Jung's synchronicity, such could only occur synonymously with the re-evaluation of the influence of outer space bodies on inner space beings.

Only the actual birth of an earthling on the Moon's surface, or that of another planet, would cause us to discard our current geocentric (earth at the center) system of astrological calculations.

As this is yet to happen, we remain relatively secure in our use of astrological systems which have a time-honored tradition.

But what of the future of these systems and astrology itself?

Tradition would tell us that an astrological chart may be cast for any event having an existence in time-space, hence a chart for the birth of modern astrology falls well within this conception.

Giving credence to the belief that the planet Uranus rules Aquarius and astrology, its discovery in 1781 would likely mark its probable history in the same way a chart for the birth of a nation would predict its annual events.

Although it is somewhat doubtful as to the exact moment on March 13, 1781 that Uranus was first seen, from the facts surrounding its discovery an accepted time of 8:00 P.M. seems likely.

What can we glean from an examination of this chart and its transits?

Leaving aside a discussion of this chart as to the 'nature of astrology' itself and turning instead to an analysis of its transits we find that as all that exists in the Cosmos, astrology, too, has its cycles of expansion and contraction.

As of the moment of this writing, the planet Jupiter is transiting the eleventh house (the house of friends and aspirations), one would expect many to turn to astrology at this time seeking universality for their ideals.

After September 1980, however, Jupiter will leave the eleventh house and enter the twelfth. Most likely this will give rise to great astrological research and a thrust towards the further marriage of astrology and psychology (ruled by Pisces and the twelfth house).

This trend will continue until the end of September 1981, at which time one would expect a renewed interest in astrology among the general public as Jupiter enters the first house.

It was not until the end of December 1984 that Jupiter reaches the very bottom of the chart. Most likely at this time there will be some attempt once again (not new to astrology) to discredit the stellar art.

Certainly we could go on and on tracing the movement of Jupiter through this chart, but let us look to other transits as well.

Again, at the moment of this writing, Uranus is placed in Scorpio at the 25th degree which places it near to the second house Jupiter.

Most recently, conversations with fellow professional astrologers have elicited the response "business stinks." Of course it would as transiting Uranus conjunct second house Jupiter would produce financial unpredictability.

After November 1984, transiting Uranus will enter into the third house which in a mundane chart is related to books, news papers and literary undertakings. One could easily predict that this passage will mark a great increase in astrological publishing and its acceptance by the populace as a whole.

Assuming the use of this chart as a valid way to ascertain the growth and movement of modern astrology, it is easy to understand the current trend towards unification of astrology and humanistic psychology.

The original research of Carl G. Jung in this area cannot be stressed enough for it was he who first suggested that an astrological chart might provide psychologists with insights not readily available elsewhere. It is said of Jung that whenever he was stuck with discerning the cause of a psychological aberration in one of his patients he would do one (or both) of two things: have the horoscope of the patient cast and/or send for and interview his/her parents!

In viewing the many astrological conferences which have taken place in recent years, a definite growing trend toward uniting psychology and astrology can be clearly seen. Not only are psychologists who practice astrology often the featured speakers, but seminar topics themselves address the growing need for a useful unification of these two arts.

One would only hope, however, that astrology can somehow maintain its independence from psychology and not find itself swallowed up and predigested as happened to the osteopathic teaching after its assimilation by the American Medical Association.

A recent conference of the New York Chapter of the National Council of Geocosmic Research (N.C.G.R.), 200 West 20th Street, New York City, included such topics as: Astrological Counseling—A Psychotherapist's View; Homosexuality—Astrological Indicators and Counseling Techniques; and Astro-Dynamics Between Parents and Children.

This program is but a skimming of the cream off the milk of countless conferences which are taking place worldwide.

Certainly, any attempts to bridge these two arts must cause a re-evaluation of the education prerequisites and training of the professional astrologer. In this area, too, the N.C.G.R. and similar organizations have taken the lead to legitimize astrological education and certification.

Here again, however, one would hope that those who are already engaged in the professional practice of astrology might find themselves admitted to certification through the time honored 'grandfather' clause as is the case with other professions such as chiropractic and podiatry. Not to do this would seem a big mistake and an act intended only to cause alienation and division among the currently existing astrological community.

So too, it is possible to envision the continuation and expansion of academic courses and programs in astrology in our universities. The writer was privileged a number of years ago to teach two such courses offered for full academic credit at The New School for Social Research in New York City.

Yes, it would seem that astrology must once again return to the university if it is to gain the respect of its sister science, astronomy.

A more political football lies in the area of local licensing of astrological practitioners and the removal from the books of vestige 'fortune telling' statutes which make its practice a crime.

As of this writing, far too little has been done to clear the slate for the recognition of astrology as a valid technique of evaluating human dynamics. While astrologers may attempt to deduce a future cause of action from a present state of being, there is nothing magical or mystical about such a practice.

Government astronomers annually publish sunrise and sunset tables 'predicting' the times of such events, yet no one seeks to question whether the sun will indeed rise as predicted.

In still another area, the use of astrological charts for medical diagnosis seems a future reality as soon as the myths and superstitions of the past can be cleanly severed from the body of astrological tradition. Research projects in the astrology of asthma, suicides, nutrition and birth control have in recent years given credence to the belief where there's smoke there's fire.

With billions of dollars spent on cancer research annually, no one has thought to offer the astrologer his turn at bat. If astrology is valid, should it not be valid herein as well?

When one talks of research, one cannot fail to mention the current and upcoming use of the computer by the professional astrologer. No single development in an allied field has so colored astrology as the employment of the computer both for the random calculation of charts and for detailed statistical research.

For a few thousand dollars any astrologer can now have access and availability, in his own office, to charts for any time-space occurrence from 3000 B.C. to 7000 A.D.

Within the next ten years' one would expect home astrological computers to be commonplace with their selling price under a thousand dollars, thus placing them well within the means of any one so interested.

In a nutshell, what is being said here is really quite simple: Astrology is now in its adolescence.

Paraphrasing Paul: When astrology was a child, it spoke as a child...But now it's just growing up and much like Topsey will grow its own way with whatever pains it must endure.

Just as one cannot discount heredity, however, it is important that the roots and origin of astrology be clearly understood for one cannot appreciate the present without knowing the past.

To this end, the work following clearly and accurately addresses itself.

Read it and prophet!

ZOLAR
March 1980
New York City

xiv

10,000–25,000 B.C.

10,000–25,000 B.C.	Notches on the bones of reindeer and tusks of mammoths represent the phases of the moon.
6000 B.C.	The beginning of the observation of the sky by the Sumerians.
3500 B.C.	*The Book of the Dead* of Egypt.
2470–2430 B.C.	Astrological predictions of Sargon the Old, perhaps the first ever written.
2400 B.C.	Babylonian tables of the royal astrologers.
2073 B.C.	Chounn, the first emperor of China, makes a sacrifice to the "seven rectors," the planets.
2000 B.C.	Hermes Trismegistus (Thrice-Great Hermes). Legendary father of magic and alchemy of ancient Egypt.
1800 B.C.	Construction of the megaliths of Stonehenge, near Salisbury, southern England.
1375 B.C.	Hymn to the sun written by Pharaoh Ikhnaton.
Fourteenth Century B.C.	The great Sumerian gods are Sin, the Moon god; Shamash, the Sun god; and Ishtar, the goddess of Venus.
800 B.C.	Hebrew prophets write many predictions.
700–400 B.C.	Discovery and description of the zodiac by the Babylonians.
660–583 B.C.	Zoroaster (or Zarathustra) of Persia.
624–550 B.C.	Thales of Miletus. Greek. The first philosopher-scientist.
512–497 B.C.	Pythagoras of Samos. Doctrine of the harmony of the spheres.
Fifth Century B.C.	First astrological maxims in Chaldea on the birth of the king.
495–435 B.C.	Empedocles of Agrigentum. Greek physician. Doctrine of the four elements.
460–361 B.C.	Hippocrates. Physician and father of medicine. Doctrine of critical days.
429–348 B.C.	Plato (Aristocles). The notion of the divinity of the stars.
409 B.C.	Date of the oldest known Babylonian horoscope.

409–356 B.C.	Eudoxos of Cnidus. Credited with calculating the solar year.
384–322 B.C.	Aristotle of Stagyra. The motions of the stars rule the world below.
331 B.C.	Conquest of Chaldea by Alexander the Great.
280 B.C.	Publication of *Babyloniaca,* a treatise on astrological medicine, by Berossus, priest of Marduk, in Babylon.
280 B.C.	Aristarchus of Samos writes on the heliocentric universe.
230 B.C.	Eratosthenes of Cyrene. Measures the circumference of the earth.
220 B.C.	The Greek Carneades criticizes astrology in the name of reason.
180–125 B.C.	Hipparchus of Nicaea. First writer on the geocentric universe.
70 B.C.	The first Greek horoscopes that take precisely into account the hour of birth.
40 B.C.	Cicero publishes *On Divinations,* in which he discusses some scientific criticisms of astrology.
30 B.C.	Octavius, the future Emperor Augustus, of Rome, has his horoscope read by the astrologer Thrasyllus.
4 B.C.–A.D. 65	Seneca (Lucius Annaeus). Early writer on comets.
A.D. 10	Publication of the *Astronomica* by Manilius, an early work on astrology.
14	Celsus (Aulus Cornelius). Roman encyclopedist. Writes many books on astrological medicine.
23–79	Pliny the Elder (Gaius Plinius Secundus). Author of the encyclopedic *Natural History.*
46–125	Plutarch, Greek author. Writes the lives of the great Greeks and Romans.
120–190	Ptolemy (Claudius Ptolemaeus). Author of *Almagest* and creator of the Ptolemaic system. Publishes (in 140) *Tetrabiblos,* the famous work on astrology.
130–200	Galen of Pergamum, physician. Writes over eighty-three books on medicine and the doctrine of the four humors.

300	Hermes Trismegistus (Spurious). A body of mystical writings written at Alexandria, claimed to be written by the original Hermes.
354–430	St. Augustine (Aurelius Augustinus). Neoplatonist and author of *The City of God*. Criticizes astrology in his *Confessions*.
700–1200	Islam perpetuates the ancient astrological tradition.
1135–1204	Moses Maimonides. Jewish philosopher. Writes on complex metaphysical problems.
1160–1240	Sacrobosco (John of Holywood). Writes the *Sphere*, a treatise on astrology.
1193–1280	Albertus Magnus. Aristotelian philosopher. Writes the *Summa Theologiae* to reconcile astrology with Christianity.
1214–1294	Roger Bacon. Scientist and writer on natural science and astrology.
1225–1274	Thomas Aquinas. Philosopher and Aristotelian writer on the theology of one earth-centered universe.
1250–1316	Peter of Abano. Physician who taught astrological medicine at Padua.
1265–1321	Dante Alighieri. Poet and author of the *Divine Comedy*.
1270–1308	John Duns Scotus. Philosopher who said truth comes from God in heaven.
1303–1415	Nicholas Flamel. Alchemist and astrologer.
1400–1600	In the Aztec religion of Mexico, Quetzalcoatl, the feathered serpent, is regarded as the lord of the planet Venus.
1412–1461	Georg Peuerbach (Purbach). Mathematician and astrologer.
1436–1476	Regiomontanus (Johann Müller). Systematic observer of the heavens.
1452–1519	Leonardo da Vinci. Artist and engineer.
1463–1494	Giovanni Pico della Mirandola. Opponent of astrology on humanistic grounds.
1473–1543	Nicholas Copernicus (Koppernigk). Describes the sun as the center of the universe.

1483–1553	Girolamo Fracastoro. Writes about comets and how their tails are always turned away from the sun.
1486–1535	Cornelius Heinrich Agrippa. Seer and occultist.
1493–1541	Paracelsus (Theophrastus Bombastus von Hohenheim). Physician and cynical critic of Galen.
1495–1552	Apianus (Peter Bienewitz). Professor of astrology at Ingolstadt.
1501–1576	Girolamo Cardano (Jerome Cardan). Physician and mathematician.
1503–1566	Nostradamus. Physician and seer. First edition of prophecies published (in 1555) in Lyons, France.
1543–1549	Pope Paul III of Rome. Supporter of astrology.
1543	With the publication of Copernicus' *De Revolutionibus Orbius Coelestium*, the earth is no longer regarded as the center of the universe.
1546–1601	Tycho Brahe. Paves the way for Kepler.
1564–1642	Galileo Galilei. Constructs the first astronomical telescope and confirms the Copernican theory.
1564–1617	David Fabricus. Friend of Kepler and observer of sun spots.
1570–1624	Simon Marius (Mayr). Among the first to use a telescope for astrological studies.
1571–1630	Johannes Kepler. Discovers the laws of motion of the planets and actively pursues the creation of a new astrology.
1574–1637	Robert Fludd (or Flud). Rosicrucian and student of the ancient secrets of Egypt.
1596–1650	René Descartes. Mathematician and philosopher.
1602–1681	William Lilly. Prophet and author of *Christian Astrology*.
1616–1654	Nicholas Culpeper. Physician and student of herbal medicine and astrology.
1627–1691	John Gadbury. Author of *Doctrine of Nativities*.
1631–1700	John Dryden. English poet who writes astrological verse.
1642–1727	Sir Isaac Newton. Philosopher, mathematician, and astrologer.

1646–1719	John Flamsteed. First astronomer royal of England and compiler of star catalog.
1656–1742	Edmund Halley. Second astronomer royal of England and predictor of the return of a comet (Halley's Comet).
1666	Official condemnation of astrology by Colbert, minister of Louis XIV, in France. Astrology is banished from the Academy of Sciences and from the university.
1693–1762	James Bradley. Third astronomer royal of England.
1738–1822	Sir William (Friedrich Wilhelm) Herschel. Discovers the planet Uranus in 1781.
1743–1795	Cagliostro (Giuseppi Balsamo). Mystic and astrologer.
1749–1832	Johann Wolfgang von Goethe. German poet who pursued astrology.
1828	The English astrologer Raphael publishes his *Manual of Astrology*.
1835–1906	Richard Garnett. English author (pseudonym, A. G. Trent). Author of "The Soul and the Stars."
1875–1961	Carl Gustav Jung. Psychiatrist. Studies the horoscopes and nativities of people.
1898	The scholarly Swede Svante Arrhenius (later to win the Nobel prize for chemistry) undertakes the first statistical work on the influence of the moon on the weather and on living beings.
1920	Renewal of the horoscope and rebirth of astrology, helped by the development of communications media.
July 20, 1969	First manned spaceship lands on the Moon.

Contents

ONE

The Lure of the Heavens

The story of man's quest for an understanding of the heavens begins long before the time records were written, about 3000 B.C. Astrology is often said to be the oldest of all sciences. We are not far from wrong when we assume that astrologers were among the first wise men in even the most primitive civilizations. Where did astrology originate? The answer is, everywhere on earth. When did it actually begin? It must be as old as man or possibly even older. When the sun goes into total or partial eclipse, animals become restless and anxious; they seem to fear an imminent danger. Birds cease to sing and apes leave their trees, banding together for safety and keeping deathly silent.

Astrology was born from the encounter between an intelligence only dimly capable of representing the world to itself and the fear inspired by that unknown and misunderstood world. For primitive man, the sky was filled with marvelous and awesome wonders. Our knowledge of the Neolithic (new Stone Age) cultures is far more complete than that of the Paleolithic (old Stone Age). All over the world, and particularly among the natives of both Americas, these cultures are still in existence, greatly modified, but still retaining their basic religious tendencies. We can state that the sun, moon, planets, stars and star groups are all closely associated by these peoples with both their mythologies and the rituals of their religions.

To find a reason for this, and to discover why the astrologer was a valued and powerful member of even the earliest civilizations, we must try to put ourselves in their place. We must make an effort to imagine the way of life of the days when men wandered in nomadic tribes over the lands of the Near East and lived on what they could find in the land around them and on the animals they could either snare or kill in the hunt. To think back into the times before written history and before life settled down into some form of civilization is not an easy task. We must strip ourselves of our cherished modern ideas and our even more treasured prejudices. We must cast away our very mode of thinking, since this is based on the work and teaching of all others before us. We must try to stand in the prehistoric world and let the bare sensory experiences of that world be the sole sources of our knowledge.

The first and most obvious fact we notice is the alternation of night and day. We soon find, however, that this is not purely a matter of equal periods of daylight, and no daylight, following one upon another with unceasing regularity. No, there is much more to it than that. Daylight is warmer than no daylight, and its brightness as well as its warmth comes from something that rises every day in the same general direction and moves slowly across the sky. Daylight ends when this "thing" reaches a direction opposite to that from which it started. What this something is we do not know. Normally it is too bright to look at, although sometimes we can make out that it is round. At any rate we can give it a name and call it "Sun."

Clearly it is a thing of great power. It gives us warmth and provides us with each period of daylight, and in addition it is the brightest of all the things that shine down from above. If we think of it as a god of life and power, who is to say we are wrong? Who can deny that Sun is not a god?

At night, the time of no daylight, things are very different. The Sun is gone, but the heavens are studded with bright specks of light. The great majority of these always stay in the same places relative to each other. The same patterns appear in the sky night after night. These we shall call stars, and they can be recognized again if we fit them into patterns. The patterns to choose are those shaped like the animals and the gods and the goddesses we understand.

There are some stars that do not fit into these patterns because they never stay really still in the sky but continually weave and wander in and out among the rest. There is a very bright star that sometimes can be seen just after the sun has completed his daily trip across the sky and another that often can be seen just before he starts out again in the morning. Obviously there are very, very important stars. They have lives of their own quite independent of the other stars that move around the sky together, and no doubt they are very powerful gods and so must have special names.

At night there is in the sky another thing that appears very regularly. Like the sun it begins its journey at one side of the earth and ends up on the other. While it is in the sky this strange body moves among the star patterns and changes its shape. Clearly it is another powerful god. Although it does not help to keep us warm, it does provide light at night and assists us in our night hunting trips that it must bless and favor. Again, we must find a name for it and we shall call it "Moon." And we must worship it and the sun with the proper deference due to such important gods of the sky.

The earliest human civilizations relied on herding, farming, fishing, or hunting and were at the whim of the vagaries of nature. The sky would fill with clouds, lightning would dart through space, and thunder would roll. Rain would follow the wind and harvests would be destroyed. If the skies remained serene, drought would dry the crops and invite the plague of hungry migrant locusts. In winter the freezing air would turn the quenching drops of rain into little dancing crystals that covered the countryside with a thick white mantle.

As far back in time as we can go, we find some records of man's efforts to watch the skies. Alexander Marshack, writing in the November 6, 1964, issue of *Science*, thought that the nicks cut in certain reindeer bones and in mammoth ivory during the Upper Paleolithic period represent notations of lunar sequences. Thus, some ten thousand to twenty-five thousand years ago man was observing and reporting the cycles of the moon.

But to return to our main point. Even primitive man required some kind of calendar, and this was the chief problem to which he turned his attention. What he really wanted was some kind of natural time interval that could be remembered in the days before writing was invented. The day itself was, of course, a simple natural interval, but it was certainly too short for use in anything but the briefest time reckonings. At the other end of the scale there was the time between one rainy season and the next, but this was useful only for the reckoning of age or of experience.

It was the changing shape of the moon that really offered the most satisfactory answer, for the 29½-day interval between one new moon and the next was neither too long nor too short. It was easy to remember and yet useful for counting comparatively long periods of time. Furthermore, the moon's changes of shape were gradual and gave a simple visual indication of how the 29½-day period was progressing.

The use of the moon's phases as a calendar helped those who went on night hunting expeditions, for it told them when to expect light nights and when to expect dark ones. This 29½-day period coincided with the cyclic menstrual changes in women, and these were the basis of certain taboos in many early societies. Thus the moon interval, or "month," assumed a supernatural significance. It was just as reasonable that all religious festivals and ceremonies should be determined by a lunar calendar.

However, when more settled communities were established and men began to till the ground and sow seeds and then look forward to a harvest, the lunar calendar began to cause difficulties. The needs of agriculture, the demands of the farmer, and the administration of a settled community required a calendar based on something besides the phases of the moon and independent of seasonal changes. Another regularly recurring phenomenon was needed that bore at least some relationship to the cycle of tilling, sowing, and reaping the harvest. The passage of the sun across the sky was the obvious indicator to use for finding the time of day. It also seemed to affect the growth of crops and the breeding times of animals.

Man now put his mind to the very real and serious problem of finding how to use the sun as an indicator of long periods of time. The problem was essentially a simple one. All that was needed was to replace the lunar calendar by a solar calendar, but the solution presented a multitude of difficulties. The age of the moon was always found from its phases, and the month was the period from the thin crescent of the new moon to new moon again. The trouble was that the sun presented no phases and no obvious interval between one month's end and the next. Then again, its use as a time indicator, desirable though it might be to the farmer, did not seem a practicable proposition to the earliest astrologers.

Yet at some time, at some place, a genius among primitive astrologers hit upon the all-important fact that the sun, besides rising and setting each day, also moved among the fixed pattern of stars in the sky. Indeed, this was a monumental discovery and one that must have demanded a great deal of very careful thinking before it could be made. Whenever the sun is visible, its light is so powerful that it blots out the lesser light of the stars. With the sun in the sky, nothing else, except perhaps the moon, was seen by these early astrologers. We may well ask ourselves how any Magi, however clever he was, could be sure the stars were in the sky all through the day as well as the night. He could have thought that perhaps the stars shone only at night and even fled at the appearance of the mighty Sun god each dawn.

Although we do not know what led the early astrologers to the realization that the sun and the stars do shine together, we may attempt a pretty good guess—a total eclipse of the sun. This was the one awesome time when, during the few minutes the sun's light was completely blotted out by the moon, the stars could be seen shining in the sky.

So we see that astrology is of great antiquity. As practiced by us today it derives originally from ancient Mesopotamia. The Greeks and Romans tended to call all astrologers Chaldeans or Babylonians, while their name for a horoscope was simply "Babylonian numbers." In these early beginnings astrology was still intertwined with astronomy, which came into being when people began to ask for long-period, accurate time reckoning. Such a time reckoning was required for their agricultural purposes but even more for their religion. Religious ceremonies were required to take place at fixed dates, and so the astrologers were the priests. A Babylonian priest in the early days was also a landlord: The land belonged to the gods, and the priests were the gods' stewards. In other countries farther to the east these priestly astrologers retained their powers till recent times. (The Brahmin *purohitas* of India, for instance, who published the Hindu almanac, could with a word make Hindu parents abandon their babies.)

Later we shall see how the Babylonian priests assigned constellations, planets, zodiacal signs and a few major stars to particular countries and to specific gods. The events they forecast were limited, but included invasions, war, crop failure, or a fine harvest. Also, any catastrophe that might befall the royal personage or those near to him was foretold by the study of Babylonian astrology. The well-being of the king was of great national interest. The Babylonians were quite content with their system, for their knowledge of astrology was in the hands of the learned priests.

But the Middle East was not the only scene of astrological observations. Two thousand years ago some Roman legionnaires visited Stonehenge, ten miles from present-day Salisbury in the southern part of England, and wondered who erected the circle of megaliths. The puzzle remains, although radiocarbon dating has now shown that the mysterious stone group was started over four thousand years ago. It was long believed that Stonehenge was some kind of Druidic temple for the performance of religious rites, but it is now established that the ring was built at least a thousand years before there were any Druids.

Most archeologists believe that it was some sort of temple, put there by the mysterious people who erected similar patterns of huge stones at other sites in the British Isles and on the Continent. Most startling is a new theory propounded by a Harvard astronomer, Dr. Gerald Hawkins, which is that Stonehenge was an astrological observatory and a computer for predicting the movements of the sun and the moon.

Fascinated by a tradition that the Stonehenge axis points to the midsummer sunrise with a megalith called the heelstone marking the exact spot, Dr. Hawkins put the plan of Stonehenge on a plotting machine and had the positions of the stones punched on IBM cards. He ran these cards through a computer to determine whether any combination of stones or archways at Stonehenge lined up with the rising or setting points of any heavenly bodies at the time Stonehenge was built.

The answer: No correspondence with positions of stars or planets, but ten alignments matching rising and setting points of the sun, fourteen more for the moon, all fitting in precisely with the calculations that the sun rose directly over the heelstone at midsummer.

The historian Diodorus of Sicily wrote in 50 B.C. that from a circular temple on the island of Hyperborea the moon appeared to be close to the earth and that "the god visits the island every nineteen years." Wondering whether Hyperborea could have been England, an archeologist asked Professor Hawkins whether there might be some lunar phenomenon visible from Stonehenge every nineteen years. Guessing at an eclipse, perhaps over the heelstone, the professor discovered that the midwinter full moon is eclipsed over the heelstone at intervals of nineteen, nineteen, and eighteen years: a fifty-six-year cycle.

There are fifty-six chalk-filled holes, called Aubrey holes after their discoverer, around the outer circle of Stonehenge. Professor Hawkins plotted on a diagram of Stonehenge and discovered that a set of marker stones placed in certain Aubrey holes and shifted one hole per year would indicate alignments of megaliths, slots, and arches that predicted eclipses of the moon.

Other astronomers challenged the theory, insisting that the sun has never risen over the heelstone and would not do so until the year 3260. To prove or disprove the Hawkins theory, the Columbia Broadcasting System set up cameras at Stonehenge before dawn one midsummer day: The sun rose with micrometric precision over the peak of the heelstone. Professor Hawkins' calculations were exact within a tenth of a degree.

The Stonehenge computer predicted an eclipse of the moon on December 19, 1967; the cameras recorded it, right over the heelstone as scheduled. Midwinter sunrise and sunset were filmed a few days later; the sun rose as predicted in the center of a slot between two megaliths and set in the arch of the great trilithon, also as predicted. Stonehenge was an observatory and astrological calculator. This does not necessarily mean it was not a temple; the sun and moon were considered gods by the builders, and their observatory would have served a religious purpose as well.

Stonehenge shows the concern of our early ancestors as they looked up into the skies. Primitive man needed to understand the world, for it was indispensable even if hostile and unfriendly. He must control it somehow! Astrology was discovered as a way of combining worship and science. The sun, moon, and stars became objects of worship, of hope, and of fear. Their influence affected not only the fate of man, but also the future of the world, since there is ceaseless interaction between the cosmos and the world below.

In Egypt, Pharaoh Amenophis IV took the name of Ikhnaton in honor of the sun and called the sun the only god in 1375 B.C. Long before this the Egyptians saw that the paths of the sun and stars above the horizon were extremely unequal: The path of the sun was different at different times of the year and the paths of the stars depended upon their position near the equator or toward the pole. This may explain a curious change in the drawing of the goddess Nu-t, in which she is represented double, as a larger figure stretching over a smaller one.

Not only the sun gods but the stars were supposed to travel in boats across the heavens from one horizon to the other. The underworld was the abode of the dead; and daily the sun, and the stars that set each morning, died on passing to the regions of the west (or Amenti) below the western horizon. They were born again on the eastern horizon with each new day. In this we have the beginning of the early Egyptian idea of immortality.

We can now begin to glimpse the early Egyptian cosmology. Seb, the earth, was the husband of Nu-t, the sky. The gods and goddesses of the sun and dawn were their children; as also were Shu, representing sunlight; and Refnut, representing the flames of dawn. Maat, the goddess of law, was the daughter of Ra, the great god of the sun.

We know several points regarding Egyptian customs besides those found in astrological inscriptions. We know there were sacrifices at daybreak; we know the stars were watched before sunrise and heralded the dawn; and we know that these observations were among the chief duties of the sacrificial priests. It is obvious that a knowledge of star places, as well as star names, was imperative to these morning watchers, who eventually compiled the first lists of decans—that is, the lists of belts of stars extending around the heavens, the risings of which followed each other by ten days or so. These are the exact equivalents of the moon stations that the Indians, Arabians, and other peoples discovered and used for the same purpose. We also know from inscriptions in some graves at Thebes that the daily risings of the chief stars were observed very carefully throughout the entire year.

Paul Christian, in 1870, explained these observations in more detail. The civil year of the Egyptian Magi was composed of twelve months, each with thirty days; the total sum of the days corresponded to the three hundred and sixty degrees of the circle of the zodiac. But as the annual revolution of the sun actually takes three hundred and sixty-five days and about six hours, the Magi added, at the end of the twelfth month, five days called epacts or complementary days.

The Egyptian year began on the first day of the month of "Thoth," and this month, corresponding to the thirty degrees of Virgo, began on August 23rd, using our calendar. "Paophi," the second month, similarly corresponding to Libra, began on September 22nd; "Hathor" (or "Hathry"), the third month (Scorpio), on October 22nd; "Choiak" (or "Choiakh"),

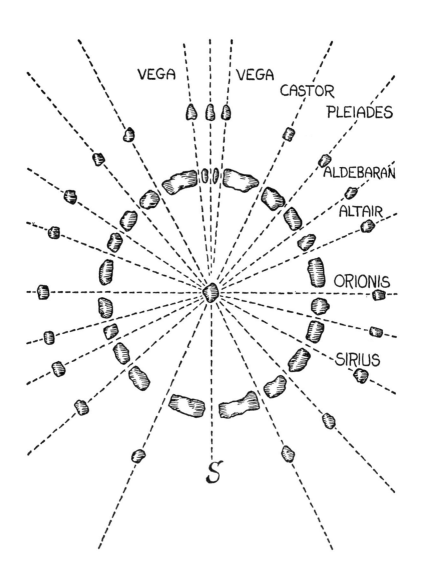

Megalithic Stonehenge, in addition to the solar and lunar alignments discussed in the text, was used to observe the heliacal rising and setting of certain bright stars. These were Vega, Castor, Pleiades, Aldebaran, Altair, Orionis, and Sius—if we are to believe Sir Norman Lockyer, who studied the megalithic relics of northern Europe for many years.

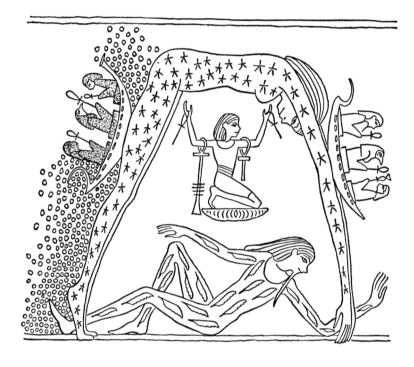

In Egyptian cosmology the sky is called Nu or Nu-t and is represented as a female figure bending over Seb, the earth. Her feet are on one horizon and her fingertips are on the other. Seb is recumbent and separated from Nu-t by Shu, the god of air and sunlight. The journey of the sun is represented by a boat crossing the sky from east to west.

the fourth month (Sagittarius), on November 21st; "Tybi," the fifth month (Capricorn), on December 21st; "Mechi" (or "Mechir"), the sixth month (Aquarius), on January 20th; "Pharmuthi" (or "Pharmuti"), the eighth month (Aries), on March 21st and the vernal equinox; "Pachon" (or "Pachons"), the ninth month (Taurus), on April 20th; "Payni," the tenth month (Gemini), on May 20th; "Epiphi," the eleventh month (Cancer), on June 19th; "Mesore," the twelfth month (Leo), on July 19th, and was followed by the five epacts or unallotted days.

Besides this division of the year into months, the ancient Egyptian Magi observed, in their secret temple traditions, another division of the year that was called the "fatidic" (or "sacred") year and began at the vernal equinox. The adoption of the modern calendar has not altered the correspondence of the first degree of Aries with the vernal equinox and with the ancient order of the twelve signs of the zodiac.

The political history of Egypt was turbulent and difficult but the economic basis of life was simple. It depended on the annual flooding of the Nile, which delivered water to the fields and fertilized them with deposits of silt.

In addition to fertilizing the fields, the Nile floods brought about two things: They forced development of a strong central government very early in Egypt's history and they advanced the science of astrology.

The Egyptians, living under a normally cloudless sky from which the stars shone brilliantly, evolved their own set of constellations. Some of them were the same groups of stars as ours, though with different names (Big Dipper is the Bull, Little Dipper the Hippopotamus); while others, like the Crocodile and the Sparrow Hawk, were not the same as ours. But to make interpretation difficult, their tomb paintings of the constellations show only the Crocodile or the Bull without indication of the stars that made up these constellations.

The Egyptians did construct some astrological tables similar to those of the Chaldeans, but during the day they used sundials and for the night hours they had water clocks. The only star to which they paid careful attention was Sothis (Sirius). Sirius, as observed from Memphis, the capital of ancient Egypt, became visible in the morning twilight just above the eastern horizon when the Nile started to rise in its annual flood. This means that the ancient Egyptians were well versed in astrological knowledge and lore along with their worship of the sun.

Other people in other lands also looked to the heavens, and the setting of the sun god was a sad event. The rising sun gave life and the setting sun took it away. The moon, however, was always linked to fertility. The moon was the principle of life and the mother of human, animal, and plant vigor—perhaps, as noted before, because the cyclic waxing and waning of the moon corresponded so closely with the menstrual cycle of fertile women.

In other ancient lore, various star clusters were worshiped: The Great Bear (Big Dipper) was worshiped in China as a propitious god. To the Aztecs of Central America, the seven stars of the Pleiades crossing the meridian signaled the start of human sacrifices. Man had begun to realize that the cosmic rhythms reveal harmony, order, and fertility, as well as being a sacred macrocosm. Man had started to formulate the first great astral law: As it is in the macrocosm (heavens), it is below in the microcosm (man).

The great Chinese religions were filled with astrological ideas, as was the emperor (son of the heavens) himself. About this Confucius says, "He who rules by means of virtue is like the Pole star that stays motionless in its place, while all the other stars turn around it." A proverb of the Chinese is, "Love everything in the universe, because the sun and the earth are but one body." The Taoist religion advises, "The Tao is revealed by the sun's course through the heavens and inside a man's heart." And again, "The sun is the vital energy that lends existence to being. On earth it makes the crops grow; while on high it orders the paths of the stars." The Chinese were very aware of the sun and its mysteries.

The earliest record of a solar eclipse is found in an ancient Chinese manuscript pertaining to the reign of Chung-k'ang, the fourth emperor of the Hsia dynasty, who lived about forty centuries ago. This eclipse took place on October 22, 2137 B.C. Two royal astrologers, Hsi and Ho, were supposed to be prepared to perform the customary rites of beating drums, shooting arrows, and so forth, to scare away the dragon that was devouring the sun. But Hsi and Ho got thoroughly drunk hours before the beginning of the eclipse and when it occurred they were in no state to carry out the expected public performance that was part of their duties. Intense confusion resulted and Emperor Chung-k'ang was so irritated by the unreliability of these two astrologers that he ordered their heads chopped off.

Nowadays, eclipses pass without such ceremonies on the part of people, with the possible exception of those living in some dark corners of Africa. It was entirely different in ancient times when the world was ruled by fear and superstition. High priests and court astrologers of even such advanced countries as ancient China and ancient Egypt taught the people that an evil spirit was attacking the sun or the moon and that would vanish forever from the sky unless special prayers and noisy demonstrations were organized to scare away the devil.

This teaching was, of course, pure trickery, designed to maintain the prestige of temple attendants in the eyes of the naive populace. The perpetrators of those hoaxes knew very well that eclipses occur periodically every eighteen years and eleven and a half days (the so-called Saros period, discovered by the ancient Chaldeans) and that they would happen again and again no matter what the people did or did not do.

Not many years ago, right here in the United States, some Oklahoma Indians saw a total eclipse of the moon and became greatly frightened. Some threw themselves down on their knees and prayed to their gods to save them. Others flung themselves flat on the ground, face downward, so that they could not see the dreadful thing that was happening to their beautiful moon. Many of them cried and yelled in excitement and terror.

At last an old Indian stepped from the door of his lodge and mumbled a few words no one could understand. Then he fired a shot from his gun at the darkened moon. As the eclipse was just about over, the moon once more peeped forth. Then there was rejoicing. The frightened Indians really believed that the old Indian brave fired his shot just in time to drive away the unholy shadow and save the moon from being put out.

The Indians of ancient India were concerned with the heavens from the first dawn of their history. Of course, human thought has always been dominated by the belief that astral movements are related to earthly phenomena, ruling farming, husbandry, health, and the social order of man. The great religions of mankind are still permeated by such astral thought. One can easily discover the astrological ideas in Hindu religious writing. The Vedas set the dates for sacrifices at the new and at the full moon. The celestial bodies are the guardians of *rita*, or the union of the cosmic and the social orders. The Vedas say, "Across the sky runs the twelve-fold path of *rita*, which never grows old." And Brahma is called "the ruling breath of the cosmos."

In all religion the main concern is to harmonize man with the cosmos, and with space and time; and all systems of worship are as strangely similar in substance as they are varied in form. This is why one has to speak not of one astrology, but of many: the Chaldean, the Egyptian, the Mexican, the Indian, the Chinese. But none of these really deals with astrology as we know it—that is, as a prediction by means of the stars. Of all these ancient religions, only one that embodied what we now call astrology has survived. This is the Chaldean view of the universe, and its history will be covered in the following chapters.

But before we go on, we need to discuss the forms of astrology. Traditionally, astrology was divided into "natural" astrology, which foretold the motions of the heavenly bodies, and "judicial" astrology, which interpreted these phenomena in terms of life on earth. The most important form of judicial astrology today is "genethliacal" astrology, which is the art of erecting and interpreting an individual's horoscope.

Medicine was quick to assign astrological meanings to illnesses, and "medical" astrology developed in ancient Greece. "Mundane" astrology was the chief interest of the Babylonians because it was concerned only with affairs of state and the king. "Horary" astrology, or the answering of questions by erecting a horoscope at the moment of a question, was popular in the seventeenth century. At about the same time, "electional" astrology was used to choose the right moment for any enterprise. Flamsteed, the first astronomer royal of England, used this form of astrology in the design of Greenwich Observatory. Physiognomy, palmistry, and the Tarot are other methods of astrally predicting the future.

The lure of the heavens has been with us since the first man. Adam was most probably the first astrologer, for surely he looked up into the heavens for guidance. And however fanciful the early ideas of astrology were, they were the starting point for the long history of astrology. We shall see in the next chapter how the first primitive ideas were developed into a semblance of science by the Babylonians and Egyptians.

TWO

Babylonia and Egypt

In the first chapter we told how, throughout the world, primitive man has always been conscious of the lure of the heavens. They always meant much to his well-being, for he observed and respected their reality, seeking to comprehend it. The stars circled overhead nightly from east to west and changed positions with time and seasons. Men were well aware of the brightly shining sun and the ever-changing moon as these two proceeded across the heavens above.

Men also noticed the wandering, brightly shining planets, to say nothing of the fearful and awe-inspiring eclipses and tailed comets that became even more meaningful events. Such things deeply concerned the observers and thinkers of ancient times. The wise men responded to this concern by further inquiry and speculation. The events of the heavens were followed day after day with great suspense and anxiety.

In the ancient land of Mesopotamia, high above the hustle and bustle of city streets, were watchtower observatories. There the priests studied the movement of the heavens continuously without interruption. These towers were about 270 feet high and were called ziggurats (cosmic mountains). In Ur, Uruk, and Babylonia they had seven terraces, one on top of the other to represent the seven known planets. The Bible tells of such a tower in the legend of the Tower of Babel (Genesis 11:1–9), which was to reach the summit of the universe.

Thus astronomy and astrology were studied first in Chaldea and Babylonia and were established very early as sciences—about 5000 B.C. Actually to date the beginnings of astrology is not as easy as it might appear, for the calendar of the ancients' was a lunar one and consisted of twelve lunar months of 29½ days each. This gives a year of only 354 days. To make the year come out right with the seasons a thirteenth month was added every second or third year. It was not until the eighth century B.C. that a sun calendar was introduced. This required regular, exact observations and records.

The Babylonians prepared the stage for such a set, for the entire culture of Babylonia was concentrated upon divination. Medically, the diagnosis and treatment of all earthly ills was determined by studying the sizes and shapes of the livers of various sacrificial animals, and the mystical lure of the stars found a warm response in these Babylonian physician-priests. It was not long before they discovered that the ever-changing heavenly occurrences could be utilized for their prognostications.

The Babylonians' main contribution soon became a system of organized observation and interpretation with occult predictions. This called for meanings and symbols for the various relations and motions of the planets and stars. The brightly shining planets were given the status of gods, but the greatest attention was given to the moon. The moon was the basis for the month, and the appearance of the new moon was actually observed each and every month.

The role of Venus as a morning and evening star was associated with the goddess Ishtar. Ishtar, the mistress and goddess of vegetation during the season of growth, was imprisoned deep within the bowels of the earth during the rainy winter months. Jupiter was also singled out for special honors. The planets Mercury, Mars, and Saturn were grouped together into a threesome of gods.

Soon different months of the year were assigned to represent the different neighboring political states. The presence or absence of a planet during any particular month was interpreted carefully. The planets were considered either favorable or ominous; thus their positions were carefully and persistently charted and followed closely.

It was this careful charting of the planets that led to the discovery of the ecliptic (pathway of the sun). It was mapped out among the stars and its circle was divided into three separate large regions. Each region was devoted to a divinity as well as to a neighboring country.

The bands of stars contained within the path of the sun gained greater and greater prominence. These stars soon occupied exceptional positions of splendor and importance in the heavenly display.

The creativeness of man responded to the mystery of the solar belt, for it was divided into twelve subdivisions—the signs of the zodiac. The designation zodiac was given to these groups of stars because eleven represented animal figures. Only Libra (the scales) was not an animal figure, since it had a special significance of its own and was thought to represent heavenly harmony or balance. These twelve groups were used to tell the exact position of a planet at any particular time. This concept broadened the scope of Babylonian astrological predictions, and later on the mathematical Greeks placed these constellations within equal arcs of thirty degrees.

The concept that events in the heavens foretold events on earth was deep rooted and implicitly accepted. Events in the sky represented Natural Law. They were the products of the doings and workings of the gods. It was not until the Graeco-Roman Empire and the days of the great Ptolemy that astrology blossomed to a stature great in its own right.

The path of the sun was soon mapped out, and four separate points attracted attention. These were the two equinoxes and the winter and summer solstices. The equinoxes were days of equal darkness and light in the spring and fall. The summer solstice was the day the sun at noon was at its highest point in the heavens. The winter solstice, the day the sun was lowest in the sky at noon, was of great importance. These points gave astrologers a means of dividing time into years, which could be divided into four seasons. Each season was marked by the sun's distinctive position in the ecliptic of the zodiac.

The unit of the week was developed, and probably came from the custom of assigning an hour of the day to each of the seven planets. The planet for the first hour of daylight gave its name to the entire day, and a seven-day cycle (or week) came into being. The last day of the week, the day of Saturn, was one of evil. Bad luck prevailed, and it was soon converted into a holy day by the people. The Jews referred to it as the day of the Sabbath; other people of the period termed it Saturn's day (Saturday).

The final Babylonian calendar was a combination of both solar and lunar cycles. The year consisted of twelve lunar cycles, with a 29-day month followed by a 30-day month, presided over by a different deity. This resulted in a year of 354 days, which did not agree with the solar year of 364¼ days. The Babylonians compensated for this by adding an extra month every second or third year.

How did they view the universe? Did they consider the earth to be flat? What did they have to say regarding the reasons for the motion of the sun, moon, and planets? After all, they were amazingly scientific in their approach to these problems, and in some ways their ideas have a modern slant.

They pictured the sky as shaped like a dome, and certainly there was no good reason why they should not do so. Go out into the countryside on a clear night and look up at the heavens. You will find yourself hard put to disagree with the Babylonians. They not only recognized a dome, but also realized that it would need some support. To them the earth was flat, higher in the center than at the edges, and floating on water. This water separated the earth from the wall that supported the dome of heaven.

Under the dome the various celestial bodies went through their paces, entering the dome through doors in the dome itself. Outside the dome was more water, in drop form, as evidenced by the rains. Yet in spite of all their careful observations the Babylonians came to no conclusions about what caused the movement of the sun, moon, and planets. They were able to calculate where the planets would be at any time, but did not formulate a theory of planetary motion. They viewed comets and shooting stars simply as weather phenomena. However, eclipses were noted with terror and dismay.

From records kept on baked clay tablets that have survived the ravages of time, we know that the Babylonians:

1. Traced the ecliptic and divided it into four parts, corresponding to the seasons.
2. Drew up a list of constellations whose heliacal rising corresponded to the twelve months of the year.
3. Determined the synodical movements of the planets with respect to the sun.
4. Knew that eclipses occurred regularly and tried to foretell them.
5. Knew that a lunation is nearly 29½ days.
6. Divided the day into hours, minutes, and seconds. At first the hours were not the same length, but merely one twelfth of the period of daylight and one twelfth of the period of night.

The Babylonians accumulated data and developed certain cherished ideas and interpretations. The first written astrological maxims we possess date back to about 3000 B.C. The most famous are the predictions of Sargon the Old (2470–2430 B.C.) and are concerned almost entirely with the appearance of the sun and the moon:

If the moon can be seen the first night of the month, the country will be peaceful; the heart of the country will rejoice. If the moon is surrounded with a halo, the king will reign supreme.

If the setting sun seems twice as large as usual, and three of its rays are bluish, the king of the land is lost.

If the moon is visible on the thirtieth, good tidings for the land of Akkad, bad for Syria.

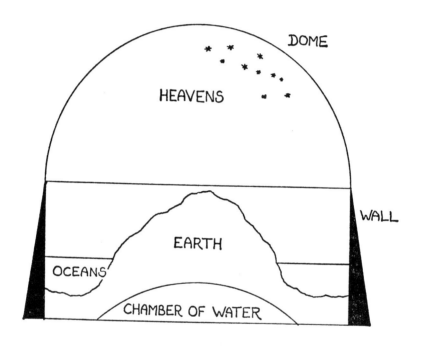

The Babylonian concept of the universe has the earth enclosed beneath the dome of the heavens, surrounded by oceans, and resting on a chamber of water (see text).

Later these predictions became codified and the Babylonian collection has an entire section—called "Adad," from the name of the god of mountains—devoted to various weather predictions:

If a dark halo surrounds the moon, the month will be cloudy and rainy.

If there is thunder in the month of Shebat, there will be a plague of locusts.

Local politics and the economy were not forgotten, but were recorded in another section:

If Mars comes close to Gemini, a king will die and there will be rivalry.

If Jupiter seems to enter into the moon, prices will go down.

However, it is only in the light of much more knowledge amassed over the centuries that we now take a different view. The Babylonians were very logical in the maxims they adopted.

The Egyptians, with whom the Babylonians traded, have a long history going back to before 3000 B.C., when King Menes united the north and south kingdoms along the Nile. Indeed, the Nile was the main artery of their life. Its annual flooding marked the beginning of their year, for only after this flooding did the ground become irrigated and the crops begin to prosper. During their first thousand years as a united nation, or the period usually known as the Old Kingdom, the Egyptians progressed in many practical arts and crafts.

Egyptian physicians were highly respected all over the ancient world for thousands of years. Homer regarded them as the best of his time. They were called to the courts of Persian emperors and other Eastern potentates; and not until the sixth century B.C. were they replaced by Greek physicians. Beyond the psychotherapeutic values of magic and religion, Egyptian physicians made solid advances in observation and rational treatment. Their contributions are worthy of a place beside other accomplishments of this great ancient civilization.

There was a close association in Egyptian medicine of astrology, religion, and magic. Egyptian physicians used many drugs, but thought their effect primarily magical. The papyri (so called because they were written on sheets prepared from the papyrus plant) that dealt exclusively with medicine abound with magic formulas and prayers. In some cases where human help seemed to be unavailing, a last attempt was made to get help from a supernatural source—a practice not incompatible with that of the astrological or religious minded physician who sought aid and guidance.

It was during the last half of the Old Kingdom that the great pyramids were built. In the undulating desert sands near Giseh rise three mighty pyramids, the tombs of three great kings—Khufu, Khafre, and Menkure. At the foot of the pyramids crouches the Great Sphinx with talons outstretched over the City of the Dead, guarding the ancient secrets gathered therein. "In front of the pyramids," wrote Pliny, "is the Sphinx, a still more wondrous object of art, but upon which rests a spell of silence, as it is looked upon as a great deity."

In his book *Isis and Osiris*, Plutarch said, "The Sphinx symbolizes the secret of all occult wisdom." He described it as a magnificent creature having wings of ever-changing hue. When they were turned toward the sun, they glittered like gold; when toward the clouds, they shone with the reflection of a rainbow of colors. But even Plutarch failed to penetrate the mystery of the mighty Sphinx. For countless ages, the Sphinx remained the guardian of all Egyptian magic. Plutarch assures us that Solon, Thales, Pythagoras, Eudoxus, even Lycurgus himself, undertook the arduous journey to Egypt just to visit the Sphinx.

The thirteenth-century Arab writer, Abd-al-Latif, says, "The true reason why all mention of this great monument was avoided was the silent terror it inspired." As late as the Middle Ages, its face and figure were still beautiful. And its mouth, Abd-al-Latif relates, bore "the imprint of grace and beauty, as if it were smiling." The huge head with its red varnish was still unblemished, and he named it "Abulhawl," or "Father of Terror."

In Egypt all images from ancient times are treated as living, active beings. From the beginning, Egypt was the land of magical statues whose great occult powers could affect the physical world. The awesome figure of the guardian Sphinx did a lot more than frighten away the profane. It could reward and punish. The Sphinx, when it opened its stone mouth, revealed the true will of the gods. The king and the assembled people were often present, and the scribes wrote down the words on their papyri.

The Sphinx, crouching a little distance from the foot of the Great Pyramid, is carved out of the solid granite of the plateau. There is no break between its base and the original bedrock. Its height of about 75 feet gives some idea of the enormous labor needed to free it of unwanted stone and to level the base.

Its total length is 190 feet; its height from breast to chin is 50 feet; and from the chin to the top of the head 25 feet. The circumference of the head, taken around the temples, is 80 feet; the face is 14 feet wide; and the head 30 feet long. The layers of granite from which it has been carved divide the face into horizontal bands in a very mysterious way; its mouth actually is formed by the space between two of the layers of stone.

A hole several feet deep was drilled in the head by the ancients and this was used as a receptacle for the priestly tiara or the royal crown.

This great carved rock, reddish in color, has a tremendous effect on one as it silently overlooks the desert sands. It seems to be a keenly attentive phantom—one could almost say it listens and looks! Its great ear seems to hear all the sounds of the past and its eyes, turned toward the east, seem to look toward the future. Its gaze has a depth that fascinates and confounds the spectator.

There is in this figure, half statue and half mountain, a peculiar majesty, a great serenity, and even a certain gentleness.

In Greek mythology, the living Sphinx was a monster, part man, part beast, whose practice it was to ask terrified travelers a riddle. They had to solve it under pain of being eaten alive.

Oedipus, the Greek, took up the challenge. The Sphinx asked, "What walks on four feet at sunrise, on two feet at noon, and on three feet at sunset?"

Oedipus replied without hesitation, "It is a man!"

The Sphinx was overcome with amazement, and Oedipus, taking advantage of its unguarded surprise, killed it and turned it to stone.

The Sphinx, as it stands in front of the Great Pyramid, was reproduced on the thresholds of all the great temples. It forms the true key to the occult of Egypt. A description of its major parts and their meanings is as follows:

The Sphinx expresses the idea of holding tightly and is composed of four parts taken from four occult symbols. These are the head of a *Woman*, the body of a *Bull*, the paws of a *Lion*, and the wings of an *Eagle*. This combination loses its monstrosity and mystery as soon as the true meaning of the symbols is clearly understood.

The Woman's head means human intelligence—the aim of all aspirations, the means of attaining goals, the obstacles to be avoided, and the barriers to be broken in the search.

The Bull's body means man—armed with science, goaded by a tireless will, and bearing the yoke of trial with patience. Thus man must travel slowly by his special road toward success or failure.

The Lion's paws mean that to attain the aim set by intelligence, man must desire and also must venture. It is not enough merely to work, it also is necessary to fight and to make a place for oneself by force if necessary.

The Eagle's wings, folded back over the Sphinx's powerful mass, mean that man must hide his plans beneath a thick veil of secrecy until the moment comes to act with firm and steadfast resolution. If need be, the resolution may reach the heights of absolute audacity.

The "Heirophat" (Guide to Mystery) tells the novice: "Learn to see clcarly, to desire judiciously, to attempt everything your conscience allows. Learn to keep your plans secret. And if, on the following day, your perseverance results only in the continuation of the preceding day's effort, go on. Go until your end is achieved!"

The Sphinx is the Alpha and Omega, the first and last word of the great initiation, for as the Sphinx said, "I am the child of yesterday; the twin lion gods have made me come into being."

Along with their occultism, the Egyptians were intensely practical, and their achievements in civil engineering are enshrined in the pyramids. Their concept of the universe, discussed in Chapter One, was, of course, quite unscientific. Yet their practical genius showed itself in their calendar, which was a model one. Because they depended on the annual flooding of the Nile, they adopted a solar calendar that gave them seasonal information. They plotted the path of the sun among the stars at a very early date and were adept at observing the stars that rose just after sunset.

The rising of the bright star Sirius (Sothis) nearly coincided with the annual flooding of the Nile, and so became the marking point for the new year. The year had 365 days and was divided into twelve months of thirty days each, with the extra five days added separately. Indeed, the Egyptians also realized that the year was really 365¼ days long and that neglecting the one-fourth day would make the Nile floods more and more out of phase with the sunset rising of Sirius. They made allowance for the error and noted that every 365 x 4 years things would come back in step. This long period they called the *Sothic cycle.*

But where was their astrological knowledge hidden, since it was not in the various papyri discovered?

At first nobody was disturbed, assuming that astrological texts would soon be discovered on papyri. But as time and discoveries went on, there was no sign of a recorded Egyptian astrology.

A great deal of speculation developed. If the ancient priests considered astronomical knowledge sacred, they would probably not have entrusted it to a papyrus anyone might find. The logical conclusion was that the priests recorded their astrological knowledge in some other manner.

John Taylor, bookseller and publisher in London, found the answer and wrote about it in his book *The Great Pyramid, Why It Was Built and Who Built It,* published in 1859. His main idea was that the sacred knowledge was hidden in open and plain sight, in a form that would say nothing to the uninitiated but everything to the initiated. The knowledge, he thought, was hidden in those large but really unknown structures, the pyramids, especially in one of them. This was the so-called Great Pyramid, also known as the Pyramid of Cheops (or Khufu).

Cheops is the Greek version of the name: It was pronounced sounding the "ch" as a guttural sound. The Egyptian name of the ruler comes from the hieroglyphics as Hwfw, which—in order to pronounce it at all—is pronounced Khufu. As for the word pyramid, the Egyptian term was pir-em-us, which actually referred to the height of the structure.

The pyramid of Khufu is located about six miles west of Cairo. (Because other small pyramids were built near it at a later date the area is now called the pyramid plateau.) Khufu chose the site for several reasons: It was near enough to his summer palace for him to watch the actual construction; the area would be covered with water during the annual Nile flood, so that blocks of stone quarried nearby could be floated to the site on log rafts; and peasants idle during the flood season could be forced into service without any loss to the national economy. Still another reason for Khufu's choice, stressed by students of Egyptology, is that there was a natural, solid, rocky outcropping on the plateau. This is now hidden by the Great Pyramid itself, but its existence saved a good deal of work when the solid structure was built over and around it. It was obvious to John Taylor that King Khufu built the pyramid as his tomb and monument, as well as to conceal Egyptian astrological secrets. Taylor started looking for them. What, for example, did the actual height of the pyramid signify? From a statement about the pyramid's original height, he concluded it was 1/270,000 of the circumference of the earth itself.

Taylor must have felt that such a ratio did not carry much meaning, so he continued with his probing and looking. In England, in Taylor's time, a measure for wheat was called a quarter. But there was no *whole* for this quarter. Taylor discovered that the English measure corresponded precisely to one quarter of the cubic volume of the large stone chest (mistakenly called the sarcophagus) in the King's chamber. He also found that the square of the height of the pyramid, compared to the area of one of its triangular faces, was a demonstration of the golden section. This is the division of a straight line into two unequal parts in such a manner that the ratio of the shorter to the longer is the same as the ratio of the longer to the whole. Mathematicians, Taylor wrote, credited Euclid with this principle, but here was a much older example.

Fortunately Taylor found a disciple who was a fine mathematician and scientist. Charles Piazzi Smyth, son of an English admiral, was born at Naples on January 3, 1819. His godfather, Professor Giuseppe Piazzi, S.J., discoverer of the planetoid Ceres, expressed hope that the baby would grow up to be an astronomer, and so he did. Smyth rose to become astronomer royal for Scotland, making very valuable contributions to the new science of spectroscopy. John Taylor convinced him that Khufu's pyramid was a place that concealed wonderful secrets. The result of the two men's work was a great success.

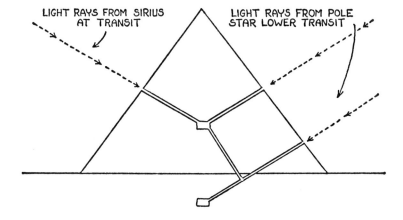

LIGHT RAYS FROM SIRIUS
AT TRANSIT

LIGHT RAYS FROM POLE
STAR LOWER TRANSIT

The Pyramid of Cheops is constructed on a geometrical plan common to that of Sneferu. At its transit across the meridian, the rays of Sirius—the dog star whose heliacal rising announced the beginning of the Egyptian year with the flooding of the sacred river Nile—were at right angles to the south face of the Great Pyramid. These rays shone straight down the ventilating shaft into the royal chamber, illuminating the head of the dead pharaoh. The main opening, as well as the second shaft leading to the lower chamber, conveyed the rays of the polestar to the royal chamber. The polestar was then a star in the constellation Draco, and three degrees below the true celestial pole.

Having far greater astronomical knowledge than Taylor and much more practice in finding mathematical relationships, Smyth had no trouble in penetrating mysteries Taylor had overlooked. The book Smyth wrote was called *Our Inheritance in the Great Pyramid*. It appeared in 1864 and ran to over six hundred pages. The major discovery he revealed was that the Egyptians had known how to *square the circle*. As applied to the Great Pyramid, this was demonstrated by the fact that the bottom square was equal in area to a circle drawn with the height of the pyramid as its radius.

The base of the pyramid was 3055.24 feet long, according to the most accurate measurements. Neither height nor slope angle could be measured directly. Originally the pyramid was built of huge limestone blocks, and the blocks were covered with a casing of white limestone. When new, the pyramid had smooth, even slopes and was blinding white under the hot desert sun. Herodotus saw it that way, but later on the white limestone casing was removed for other building projects. Pieces of the pyramid casing now form major parts of mosques in Cairo.

Because the height could not be measured exactly, Smyth approached the problem from the slope angle. This was somewhere near 52°. Smyth found that it must have been exactly 51° 51′14.3″, which made the height of the pyramid exactly 486.256 feet. Therefore, the ratio of height to circumference was exactly 2 π . Smyth, after these careful mathematical manipulations, had discovered this amazing ratio.

One side of the pyramid, at its base, measured 763.81 feet; dividing this figure by 365.2422, Smyth obtained a unit of length of about 2 feet. He called this unit the "pyramid meter." Then he found that the Egyptians, by making the base 365.2422 pyramid meters long, knew the exact number of days in a year. He then divided the pyramid meter into 25 parts to obtain the "pyramid inch." By a coincidence it was nearly the same as the English inch. But this was not a coincidence, according to Smyth! The pyramid inch simply had remained in use even though the carelessness of later workers shortened it by a tiny fraction. This proved the inch measure sacred and stable. (A group of people in Boston, in 1879, started a movement for outlawing the metric system and they had the full support of President James Garfield.)

The pyramid inch led Smyth to many more discoveries. Multiply it by 10^7 and you have the length of the polar axis of the earth. Express the height of the pyramid in pyramid inches and multiply this figure by 10^9 and you have the distance of the sun from the earth. The result is 91,-840,000 miles, which is neither the maximum distance at aphelion nor the minimum distance at perihelion, but very close to the mean distance.

As for the stone chest, it was not only the original whole for the English quarter, but it was even more. Express its volume in cubed pyramid meters (5.7) and you have the specific gravity of the earth itself. As for the whole volume of the pyramid, it gave, when expressed in cubic pyramid inches, the total number of all the people who have walked on the earth since man's creation.

Later pyramidologists claimed that all the great events in history are indicated by cracks in the granite slabs forming the inclined tunnel called the main gallery. Even those cynics who rejected Smyth's manipulations admitted that the slope angle, which could be accurately measured, was close to the slope required for the golden section and also to that required for expressing π. Nobody could say the Egyptians had not tried to measure these.

However fanciful much of this may sound, it cannot be denied that the Egyptians were a people who could make careful observations and precise calculations. Even if they did not contribute a large fund of scientific facts to astrology, they impressed and influenced those Greeks who visited them from about 600 B.C. onward.

Let us turn our attention briefly to a neighbor of both Babylonia and Egypt—Israel. The Italian astronomer Giovanni Virginio Schiaparelli published in Milan in 1903 a work entitled *L'astronomia nell' Antico Testamento* (*Astronomy in the Old Testament*).

The examples of old Babylonia, where the lights in the sky were considered the seats of the gods (and by the common man, no doubt, the gods themselves), and of Assyria, where astrology from precedent rather than from rules dominated life, were horrible examples to the Jews. Zephaniah (1:5) said the Lord told him He would "cut off all those that worship the host of heaven upon the housetops, and yet swear by Milcom."

The most violent of all the prophets was Isaiah (47:12–14):

> You are wearied with your many counsels; let them stand forth and save you, those who divide the heavens, who gaze at the stars, who, at the new moons predict what shall befall you.

> Let now the astrologers, the stargazers, the monthly prognosticators [of the new moon] stand up, and save thee from these things that shall come upon thee.

> Behold, they shall be as stubble; the fire shall burn them; they shall not deliver themselves from the power of the flame.

Isaiah was so furious about the influences of Assyrian thought that he predicted the end of the starry sky itself (34:4):

And all the host of heaven shall be dissolved, and the heavens shall be rolled together as a scroll: and all their host shall fall down, as the leaf falleth off from the vine, like leaves falling from the fig tree.

Astrology, which rejected the study of the sky as both "foreign" and "godless," could not develop among the Jews.

Schiaparelli puts it: "Small wonder that astronomy among the Hebrews remained at about the level which, as we know, has been reached by some nonliterate people of the Americas and in Polynesia."

The ancient Jewish picture of the world was that of a flattened sphere with a plane through its center. The plane was the land and the surface of the waters; below was the abyss; and above, the air that supported the clouds. Apparently the top of this sphere was pictured as being clear and transparent, for the sun and the moon were above the upper part of the sphere itself.

The astronomical phenomena known to the Jews were mainly the sun, the moon, and the eclipses. Not knowing what caused the eclipses, they regarded them as omens of punishments to come. Joel (2:31):

The sun shall be turned into darkness and the moon into blood, before the great and the terrible day of the Lord comes.

As almost everybody knows, the eclipsed moon often looks dark red; therefore, this line in Joel must certainly refer to the eclipses. It is quite possible that Joel even saw an eclipse himself, for eclipses were visible at Palestine on August 15, 831 B.C.; April 2, 824 B.C.; June 15, 763 B.C.; March 2, 832 B.C.; and October 6, 825 B.C.

Only two planets are mentioned in the Old Testament, Venus and (probably) Mars. Isaiah (14:14):

How you are fallen from heaven, O Day Star, Son of Dawn! How you are cut down to the ground, you who laid the nations low!

Amos (5:26):

You shall take up Sakkuth your king, and Kaiwan your star god, your images, which you made for yourselves . . .

"How you are fallen from heaven, O Day Star . . ." can only mean Venus as the morning star. It is not as certain what the other planet is. The word rendered as Kaiwan in this translation can be read either as Kijjun or as Kewan, depending on which vowels are inserted into the vowel-less original text. Kewan was the name of the planet Saturn among the ancient Syrians and the ancient Persians. Schiaparelli pointed out, however, that a German biblical expert had reason to believe that the word Kaiwan, at the time of Amos, meant the planet Mars. As Mars is much easier to see and more conspicuous than Saturn, it seems the likelier choice.

Although Isaiah ranted against stargazers, in Job (38:5) the Lord asked: "Who hath laid the measures thereof, if thou knowest? or who hath stretched the line upon it?" This indicates that to the Jews the measuring of the earth was a superhuman task. The simple fact is that the Jews could not have functioned without a calendar of some kind. That calendar was a lunar calendar! Even the word for month, *herach*, is closely related to the word for moon, *jareach*, just as the two words are in present-day English.

Although there can be no doubt that the first astrologers were the Chaldeans, during the latter part of their history they were no longer the only ones. The new month for the Jews began—as for their despised Babylonian neighbors—when the crescent moon first became visible. Even the names of the months were similar to the heathen Babylonian names. It is interesting and significant how the Jewish Bible almost always simply referred to "the third month" or "the fifth month." Because these were purely lunar months, an extra month was needed from time to time. This was made to follow the twelfth month and, when named, was called *we-Adar*—literally, *and Adar*, meaning only the second month of Adar.

Of the fixed stars and constellations only a few are named in the Bible, and the references are in the Book of Job. The stars *Kimah* and *Kesil* (Job 38:31) are the Pleiades and Orion, while *Ajish* (Job 38:32) must be the Hyades. Two other constellations are easy to identify, but a third mentioned in the same passage is a surprise. Job 37:9 is usually translated as "Out of the south cometh the whirlwind; and cold out of the north." But in the original Jewish the words "north" and "south" are names of constellations. The northern one is written either *mizrajim* or *misrim*—plural forms of the word *mizreh*, which means "winnowing shovel." The *mizrajim* are, therefore, the two winnowing shovels. Today we call them the Big and the Little Dipper.

South in the original is *chadre theman*, or "chambers of the south." Today we do not know all the stars included in the chambers of the south during the time of Job. We do know that among them were the upper few stars of the Southern Cross, which was visible just above the horizon at Palestine in those early days. In spite of Job, Isaiah, and Amos, the Jews of 500 B.C. did look to the stars and moon, if only to measure the days of the week and the month. The biblical feast of Passover occurs on the fourteenth of Nisan (spring equinox). This raises the possibility that an ancient spring festival might have been given a new meaning by assigning to it the commemoration of the Jewish exodus from Egypt.

The last day of the week, the day of Saturn, was always one of evil and bad luck. It was referred to by the Jews as the day of the Sabbath; others called it "Saturn's day." The Jews consecrated this day and held religious observances on it. Our weekly calendar of today is merged with the Jewish or sabbatical week in many ways. It still depends on your own personal belief as to whether Saturday or Sunday is the true Sabbath.

Now let us turn to the first scientist to discuss the universe at large. To anyone interested in astrology and alchemy and their implications, the name of Hermes Trismegistus is most intriguing. However, when one sets out to track down definite information about the life and activities of this man, one is doomed to bitter disappointment. Much has been written about Hermes but practically all of it is based upon legend, and today he is always thought of as a chemist. More correctly, it should be said he was a cosmologist, to whom chemistry was only one part of science as a whole.

There is little or no reliable information as to the date of his birth or even where he was born. According to some authorities, he was an Egyptian priest who lived about 2000 B.C. He was the inventor of all useful arts and was elevated to the rank of a god. The Egyptian origin of alchemy is credited to Hermes Trismegistus, or Hermes the Thrice-Great, the alleged father of the "Hermetic Art" and the patron of the self-styled "Sons of Hermes." Hermes was also regarded as the Greek equivalent of the ibis-headed moon god, Thoth, who was the Egyptian god of healing, intelligence, and letters. Hermes wrote the "Emerald Table of Hermes," which gives us about all the information available concerning this man. As the messenger of the gods, Hermes wore winged boots and carried a caduceus, or herald's staff, which is shown as a winged wand entwined by two serpents. The Greeks called him Mercury.

The precepts of Hermes comprised the Emerald Table of Hermes, or the Smargadine Table, and consisted of a series of pronouncements inscribed upon the emerald stone. It is most interesting to consider them:

1. I speak not fictitious things, but that which is certain and true.
2. What is below is like that which is above, and that which is above is like that which is below, to accomplish the miracles of one thing.
3. And as all things are produced by the one word of one Being, so all things were produced from this one thing by adaptation.
4. Its father is the sun, its mother the moon; the wind carries it in its belly, its nurse is the earth.
5. It is the father of perfection throughout the world.

6. The power is vigorous if it be changed into earth.

7. Separate the earth from the fire, the subtle from the gross, acting prudently and with judgment.

8. Ascend with the greatest sagacity from the earth to heaven, and then again descend to the earth, and unite together the powers of things superior and things inferior. Thus you will obtain the glory of the whole world, and obscurity will fly far away from you.

9. This has more fortitude than fortitude itself, because it conquers every subtle thing and can penetrate every solid.

10. Thus was the world formed.

11. Hence proceed wonders, which are here established.

12. Therefore, I am called Hermes Trismegistus, having three parts of the philosophy of the whole world.

13. That which I had to say concerning the operation of the sun is completed.

These oracular pronouncements were held in the greatest veneration by medieval astrologers and alchemists, who appear to have regarded them as the alchemical creed, or profession of faith in the Divine art. The second and third precepts conceive that all forms of matter have a common origin, a common soul, or essence, which alone is permanent; that the outward form, or body, is merely the temporary abode of the imperishable soul; and that substances are produced by evolutionary processes and are capable of undergoing transmutation. In the fourth precept, the sun and moon (gold and silver, or sulphur and mercury) are interpreted as the sources of the Stone. The eighth precept is suggestive of the *kerotakis,* or the later Vase of Hermes, in which the Stone—"the father of perfection throughout the world"—was held to be prepared.

The name Hermes Trismegistus is in itself significant of the capabilities of the man in that it means Hermes the Thrice-Great—prince, poet, and philosopher. "And this is that Hermes which after the flood was the first finder-out and setter-forth of all arts and disciplines both literal and mechanical." His Table appears to contain no chemistry, yet it asserts the essential unity of the world and perhaps refers to spiritual things, intending a monistic metaphysics. On the other hand, perhaps it asserts the fundamental unity of matter within the cosmos, as Hortulanus understood it and as modern physics is coming to believe.

In closing this chapter, I suggest you follow along with a zodiacal belt you can set up for yourself. All the twelve signs are depicted and should be traced or photocopied so as not to destroy the book. They should be cut to a convenient size and placed sign inward around the brim of an open umbrella. The horizontal dotted line labeled "ecliptic" should be even with the edge of the cloth. This places the signs correctly with the path of the sun. They also should be equally spaced using the vertical date line for this purpose.

When you stand beneath the umbrella as shown in the diagram and revolve it slowly, you can see the procession of the signs: Aries, Taurus, Gemini, Cancer, Leo, Virgo, Libra, Scorpio, Sagittarius, Capricorn, Aquarius, and Pisces.

Owing to the movement known as the precession of the equinox, the zodiac is gradually shifting backward through the constellations. The point of the spring equinox, with which the zodiac begins (0° Aries), is now in the constellation Pisces. The zodiacal signs coincided with the constellations at about the time of Christ. Authorities are not really agreed about this date; some fix it at up to two hundred years later, because astrology as we know it in the West today started with Ptolemy.

As explained before, the zodiacal belt with its constellations, was known in Babylonia as early as 700 B.C. The first tablet of the series *MulApin* lists "the constellations in the path of the moon" as follows:

the hair brush = Pleiades
the bull of Anu = Taurus
Anu's true shepherd = Orion
the old man = Perseus
sickle sword = Auriga
the great twins = Gemini
Prokyon or Cancer
lion or lioness = Leo
furrow = Spica
the scales = Libra
scorpion = Scorpio
archer = Sagittarius
goatfish = Capricornus
great star or giant = Aquarius
the tails = Pisces
the great swallow = Pegasi
the Goddess Anunitum = Pisces + middle part of Andromedes
the hireling = Aries

The fixed stars, which of course are only apparently fixed in position as contrasted with the planets, are so numerous it is necessary to group them in some way. Even today they are grouped in arbitrary constellations, derived from the ancient world with only minor alterations through the course of centuries. Most are labeled with names derived from Greek mythology, but the same figures are found with very little alteration in the ancient astrology of Egypt, India, Persia, Phoenicia, Chaldea, and Ac-

ECLIPTIC

ECLIPTIC

MAY 1ST

JUNE 1ST

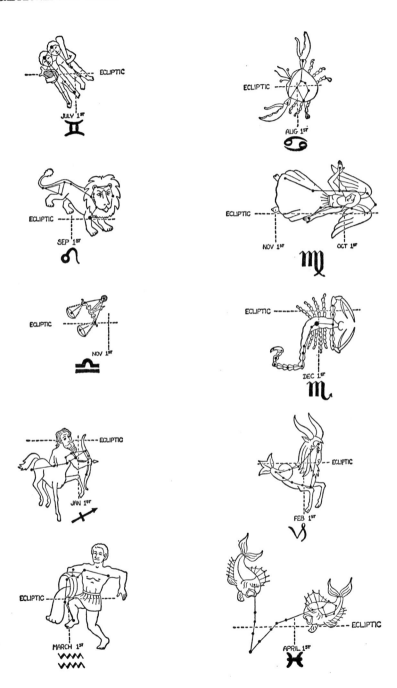

cadia. Among the Chinese and Tibetans other symbols were in use, but there are analogies. Most of these cultures also had the twenty-seven or twenty-eight mansions of the moon that overlie the zodiacal constellations. They were used particularly in the astrology of India, Persia, and Arabia.

The majority of constellations are very old. Forty-eight of them were catalogued by Ptolemy in his *Catalogue*, A.D. 137, in which he gives the latitude and longitude of 1022 fixed stars. In the Far East, in Japan, China, and Tibet, a different set of symbols was being crystallized. The twelve corresponding to the zodiacal are: rat, ox, tiger, hare, dragon, snake, horse, sheep, monkey, cock, dog, boar. This all may sound a little confusing at present, but will become clearer as we discuss the ancient Greeks in the next chapter.

THREE

Ancient Greece

In Greece the science of astrology was regarded as a direct gift from the gods, as mathematics was accepted as the outward expression of divine conduct. The Greek scientists accepted the new science without hesitation. The Pythagoreans believed that man should respond to the beauty of the "heavenly harmony" by trying to comprehend it. Belief in the heavens was wisdom and virtue, according to Plato to be sought after diligently. The notions of stellar determinism and star worship were enthusiastically received by the intellectual Greeks.

In the eastern Mediterranean about five thousand years ago, along with the flourishing Babylonians and Egyptians, a civilization developed on the island of Crete. The earliest traditions of Greek culture are attributed by some to this land. Their greatest king was Minos, who built the labyrinth to house the Minotaur. This half-bull, half-man was born to Minos' wife after her union with a bull sent to the king as an occult sign by the sea god Poseidon. It is probably from the Cretans that we received the names of the star constellations we still use. Among them is the constellation of Taurus the bull.

The cultural ideas of Crete were taken north to Greece by sailors who journeyed across the Aegean Sea. Later these legends were well and truly told by Homer in the *Iliad* and the *Odyssey*. The significance of these epic poems to us is that they enshrine a world that had a profound influence on the Greeks. They also contain the only evidence we have of the very early Greek opinions about the nature of the cosmos.

In the vividness of their fancy, intensified by glorious scenery and sunny skies, the ancient Greeks believed that the gods dwelt on the summit of Mount Olympus and that strange and lovely beings roamed about the land. They heard the raging of the wind gods, the dancing feet of wood nymphs, the nimble trip of satyrs, and the music of the pipes of the merry god Pan. They knew that naiads peeped from the mist in fountains and dryads lived in the hearts of trees, while down in the sea Neptune tossed up the billows with his trident and little sea maids sat in them and rocked and sang. Heroes, semidivine, rid the earth of its monsters, while gods in golden chariots attended to the welfare of mankind. So deeply sincere was this faith that great temples and beautiful shrines were built in honor of the gods. One can scarcely find a spot in all of Greece, or in all the sky that hangs over Greece, that is not hallowed by some wonderful legend.

This country was thought to lie around the center of the earth, which was marked by the oracle of Apollo at Delphi. The earth was supposed to hang like a disk in the great hollow globe of the world, its land divided into two parts by the Mediterranean Sea and its edges washed by the turbulent stream of the ocean. The upper part was illuminated by the sun, moon, and stars and was called Heaven, but the lower part extended below the earth disk and formed a terrifying pit of utter darkness. The Milky Way was the road that led to the home of the gods, but the pit was a place of dire punishment.

In brief, the earth, flat disk though it might be, was fixed in the middle of the whole sphere of creation. Indeed, this was a truly revolutionary outlook! The single dome of heaven of primitive man, as accepted by the Babylonians and Egyptians, was not adequate for the Greeks. They invented the larger extension to satisfy their aesthetic ideals. Still it was not all aesthetics—the idea of how and why was creeping into the concepts. Things and actions were explained in more detail.

One of the many duties of the gods was to see that the earth was properly lighted by the sun and the moon and that the stars were "penned in" at dawn and "unpenned" at night. The sun, moon, and stars rose and sank in the stream of the ocean, but the sun, instead of being submerged, was carried around the stream from west to east in a golden boat made by the god Vulcan. It was at first thought that Vulcan, with a mighty heave, threw the hot sun ball over the Caucasus mountains in the east to the Atlantic ocean in the west, and then hastily paddled around the world stream to catch it as it fell. Later it was believed that Apollo, the sun god, drove it across the sky in a chariot; the return journey to the country of the sunrise was accomplished by placing both chariot and sun in Vulcan's remarkable boat.

The ancient Greeks imagined that before the earth was smoothed out flat in its present form, the whole world was tumbled together in great confusion—land, air, sea, sky, hot, cold, soft, hard, light, and heavy all mixed in a desolate mass presided over by the god Chaos. Chaos was dethroned by the God of Darkness, who in turn was dethroned by Light and Day. Light and Day industriously sorted the earth from the sea and extracted the heavens from both. The fiery part was cast into the sky where it splintered into stars, while the earth, "a lifeless lump, unfashion'd and unfram'd," was heaped in a big, broad mound with a deep and terrifying stream of waters flowing around it.

Then Uranus, or Heaven, noting his superior position, took the scepter away from Light and Day and became the first ruler of the created world. Love was born and Earth hemmed in her valleys and extended her plains, made paths for the rivers and beds for the lakes. The seeds, relieved of weight, burst their coverings, and the hills became green with foliage and the meadows brilliant with flowers. The world was now beautiful, and Heaven looked down on the colorful earth, and Earth looked up into the starry eyes of Heaven and love grew, and Earth became Heaven's bride. And it was below as it was above.

Such Homeric tradition laid the foundation for first Thales and then Pythagoras. Thales, the first of the great Greek philosopher-scientists, flourished at the seaport of Miletus from 624–550 B.C. Miletus was in an ideal position as a trading port for the entire Aegean area, with ships and men from Egypt, Babylonia, and Phoenicia coming and going, trading and spreading ideas.

Now the idea of the universe that Thales taught differed only a little from the spherical universe of Homer, but he concluded that the earth floated on water. Yet this was not sufficient, and he began to speculate on how things on earth came into being. (This attitude of mind shows clearly the spirit of scientific enquiry we find in Greek philosophical thinking.) Thales then suggested that water was the primeval substance from which everything was formed.

Thales did not drop suddenly from the sky and shout, "Everything must be made from water!" He had traveled in Egypt and was familiar with Babylonian mythology—and in both these river cultures water played a preponderant part. (Aristotle later conjectured that Thales reached his conclusion from observation and experience.) His importance is that he raised the question of the ultimate reality, and is the first known to have done so. The mythological precursors of Thales only smoothed a path for his philosophy of water as the *arche*. (*Arche*: The first in a series; that from which a thing either is or comes to be; origin, principle, first cause.)

Thales looked at things without taking them for granted and in ever-renewed astonishment. His explanations were not mythological, as explanations were in the past. He observed that all living things are moist, that animal semen is moist, and that deserts occur where there is no water. In his travels he had seen the "rebirth" of the land after the periodic flooding of the Nile. From observations such as these he developed his *hylozoistic* theory of water as the source of life.

Anaximenes in 550 B.C. followed Thales as a philosopher scientist and was the originator of the analogy of the universe as the macrocosm and man as the microcosm. This was the probable consequence of the simple fact that he looked on air as (a) the *arche* and divine and as (b) the "stuff" of the human soul.

Miletus was sacked by the Persians in 494 B.C. and its people were sold into slavery three years after the death of Pythagoras.

Pythagoras was born on the island of Samos in 572 B.C. and probably studied under Thales for a period. He is also said to have studied in Egypt and Babylonia for more than twenty years. Then sometime between 540 and 530 B.C. a small group of Greek scholars led by Pythagoras came to southern Italy near the present town of Crotona. The colony was on a hill above the small harbor. The pleasant climate and healthy atmosphere added greatly to the life of the colony.

Pythagoras, the ascetic leader, was greatly interested in philosophy, astrology, religion, and politics. And it was this interest in politics that later caused him trouble. The Greeks of the time were highly emotional and deeply devoted to Dionysus and his following of satyrs, nymphs, and centaurs with their frenzied dancing and ecstatic sexual visions. Pythagoras and his three hundred followers believed in a doctrine of salvation and ritual.

Their ultimate goal was to free the soul of man from the forces of the heavens at birth. This freed soul then lost all bodily desires and could dwell forever in the spiritual realms. Politics and not spiritual beliefs led to a violent attack by the other colonists. Pythagoras and many others were slain. The rest scattered to the Greek cities. They, the scattered few, influenced all later mankind and modern astrology. Empedocles, Plato, Socrates, and Aristotle studied the Pythagorean doctrine of harmony between heaven and earth—the macrocosm of stars and the microcosm of man.

The legend states that on a beautiful day one spring Pythagoras and his followers looked down from their hilltop. The caressing winds carried the festive sounds of the village to their ears. Revelry filled the air with female voices screaming for more of the red wine. Deep male voices sang a drunken chant as half-nude bodies danced madly in the sunlight. The village was feasting the diabolic Dionysus with a drunken orgy. Pipes and tambourines throbbed out the goat song of the witches' dance.

Pythagoras turned away and smiled. "Behold! The juice of the grape drives them mad. Tomorrow there will be sorrow. Today they are but children, drunk with sensual desires. The flesh has overcome their immortal soul." He went on to say, "You who are the wiser shall share some of the thoughts I have on the structure of the world. As you know, we must ultimately escape the flesh and the wheel of life. The way is hard to spiritual peace."

Pythagoras continued in detail with his explanations of harmony. The soul, to achieve its deepest vision, must be free from the prison of the bestial flesh. The way is by music. The great Orpheus taught that the harmony of spirit was found through the harmony of sound. Just as one purifies the body by medicine, one can purify the soul by music.

The soul achieves a special kind of attunement or harmony by blending opposites. The soul brings about this harmony. Surely music helps to soothe the soul through harmony. Upon what, then, does the harmony of music depend? It depends upon the right combinations of different notes of the instrument that the musician plays. Indeed, when chords are struck upon a lyre, some strings together are discordant, some together are harmonious. Upon what does this depend?

Perhaps the strings of the instrument have something to do with this— perhaps the ratios of their lengths as tuned by a monochord. Pythagoras measured such strings on monochords and found that the chief musical intervals were expressible in simple, whole-number ratios of the first four integers in relation and proportion to the lengths of the strings. Whole numbers and a spiritual harmony are the way to divine truth and being— whole numbers and simple geometrical ratios. Here then may be the key to all reality.

Numbers points, ratios and simple proportions of length, small whole numbers—the key, the key to reality. The harmony of music . . . of the soul . . . harmony and a spiritual balance and symmetry . . . the measure of the soul in its true perfection. Even in the celestial there are points—the stars, and the orbital geometry of the planets, sun, and moon. Heaven too is measurable in simple ratios and proportions. Earth too is geometrical —a perfect sphere. But the earth is not perfect in its bodily substance.

If the stars and planets and sun turn about the heavens in perfect circles, their center cannot be the imperfect substance of the earth. Fire, not earth, is perfect. The center of the heavenly motions must be a thing of "fire." The center of the heavens must be the most precious place in the cosmos. And the most precious place must befittingly be occupied by the most precious thing—fire, the center and hearth of the whole universe. Pythagoras thought that man could not see this central fire; earth from our side must be always turned away from it.

Pythagoras was frowning in thought, deeply puzzled. He drew strange diagrams in the sandy soil with a straight stick. Points and patterns covered the ground in geometrical relationships. The key seemed to be: All things are numbers. He muttered to himself, "People count in tens—decads —and beyond ten, start over again. What is the nature of ten?" He made dots upon the sand in various designs. "If we start with the ultimate unit, then two units, then three, then four—and if we add all these, lo! their sum is ten. The number four, and tetrad, is the secred of ten!" He arranged the dots in triangular form upon the sand, as equivalent to the numbers —one, two, three, and four.

He became even more excited. "The *Tetractys* of the decad—ten based upon four. This indeed must be truth—absolute truth!"

Other problems of this kind engaged his active mind. Triangles laid out as points in equal intervals—the right-angled triangle with its sides of three, four, and five units long. Then, building a square upon each of the triangle's sides, he re-established a fact known to the ancient Egyptians: The square on the hypoteneuse of a right-angled triangle is equal to the sum of the squares on the other two sides.

At high noon, in a grateful state of spirit, Pythagoras went to the temple and sacrificed an ox for these great discoveries. The gods had been good to him. His mind never rested: Back again to the stars and planets and the central fire or "hestia"—the hearth of the universe. What about the distances of each orbit of each planet to the central fire? They must be in simple ratio of small whole numbers like musical chords. Indeed, the harmony of the celestial spheres must yield the cosmic octave! All truth is in number and simple proportions of lengths and distances of the radii.

Geometric forms limit the unlimited of space. The stars, sun, moon, and planets sing in soulful harmony as they move around in the heavens on their perfect spheres. And ten is a perfect number! Heaven must be ten!

But there are only nine heavenly bodies, including the fixed stars and the earth and moon each as one, moving about the invisible central fire. There must be one more orbit. There must be a counter-earth—always opposite to the earth, invisible on the other side of the earth's orbit, also moving around the sacred central fire.

That his idealistic teachings brought large audiences to hear Pythagoras is illustrated by the way people equated numbers and figures with moral qualities. The number one was regarded as the source of all numbers rather than as a number itself—it stood for reason. Two stood for opinion, four for justice, and five for marriage—because it is formed by the union of the first male number three and the first female number two.

In the properties of five lay the secret of color. In the number six lay the secret of cold. In seven was the secret of health, and in eight the secret

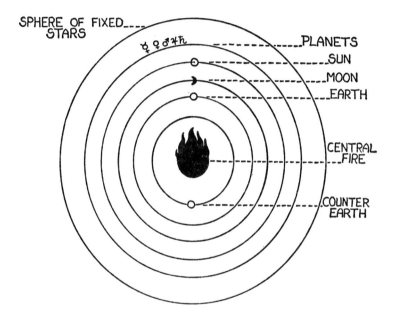

The universe as conceived by Philolaus of Tarentum, a Pythagorean of the fifth century B.C. There is a "central fire" around which the earth, a "counter-earth," the seven planets (including the sun and moon), and the fixed stars revolve, all attached to spheres.

to love was hidden. Three (potency) added to five (marriage) made eight, or love. The six-faced solid held the secret of the earth itself. The pyramid held the secret of fire that was later called *logos spermatikos* by the Stoics—this is the light that lighteth every man.

The twelve-faced solid held the secret of the heavens. The sphere, of course, was the most perfect of all perfect figures. The distances of the stars formed a harmonic number series like the lengths of the wires of the early stringed instruments and hence the "harmony of the spheres."

Numbers were put into classes—of bright and obliging, or dull and discontented male and female classes. There were perfect (absolute) numbers of which all the whole-number factors add up to the number itself. The first of these is 6, of which all the divisors are 1, 2, 3 $(1 + 2 + 3 = 6)$. The second is 28, of which all the factors are 1, 2, 4, 7, and 14 $(1 + 2 + 4 + 7 + 14 = 28)$. Later on the Neo-Pythagorean Nichomachus of Alexandria spent most of his life hunting for the next two such numbers. These are 496 and 8,128. There is not another one until we get to 33,550,336. In a fruitless effort to get so far Nichomachus discovered a great absolute truth: "The good and the beautiful are rare and easily counted, but the ugly and bad are prolific."

There were also amicable numbers, and when Pythagoras was asked what they were he replied: "One who is the other I. Such are 220 and 284." Carefully interpreted, this means that all the divisors of 284 (1, 2, 4, 71, and 142) add up to 220; and all the divisors of 220 (1, 2, 4, 5, 10, 11, 20, 22, 44, 55, and 110) add up to 284. Another class of numbers of good omen was the class of triangular numbers and the magic triangles formed from three, four and five units to a side.

And as time passed, these ideas took hold among the people. Points and numbers became the great key to reality. Other Pythagoreans conceived of points as the basic constituents of all things—veritable atoms or indivisible units arranged in various patterns in the macrocosm. The clue to the ultimate nature of any object, even a human being, was these point-atoms.

Let the outline of a man be drawn around his body as it lies upon the sand. Then fill in that outline with small stones after the man has moved away. The number of stones needed to fill the outline is the number of the man and is significant of his true nature. You have "got his number." Numerology was born from the odd and the even numbers.

After the holy unit, one, comes two—the first feminine number; then three—the first masculine number. Three plus two being five, five is the union of male and female—the number of marriage. Four, the perfect square of two, is the number of justice—to be "four square" is to be just. Verily, a magical universe of numbers.

Observe also some of Pythagoras' other rules: Never step over a cross-bar; do not sit upon a quart measure; do not wear a ring; do not look in a mirror beside a lamp; abstain from beans; touch the earth when it thunders; and do not eat animals.

Also attributed to Pythagoras is the statement, "The world is built upon the power of numbers." In keeping with this theory he and his followers reduced the basic universal numerals to the figures 1 to 9 inclusive. These are the primary numbers from which all others may be formed.

These were listed twenty centuries later by the great Magus, Cornelius Agrippa, in his *Occult Philosophy*, of A.D. 1533 and possess the following significations:

One is the number of purpose, evidenced by aggression, action, and all ambition; the beginning, or "A," the first letter of the alphabet. Straight as an arrow, its aim is always to acquire fame or to rule.

Two is the number of antithesis, with the extremes as day and night. It stands for balance and equality as well as contrast and it maintains its equilibrium through a mixture of positive and negative qualities, or polarities.

Three shows versatility. It is symbolized by the triangle, which represents the past, present, and future. It combines talent with gaiety. It is by far the most adaptable of all the numbers.

Four stands for steadiness and endurance. Its solidarity is represented by the square, the points of the compass, the seasons of the year, and the ancient elements of fire, water, air, and earth. It is the most primitive of all the numbers.

Five symbolizes adventure, attaining its ultimate meaning through travel and experience. Its lack of stability may produce some uncertainty. Yet it is the keystone and though most unpredictable is the luckiest.

Six is the symbol of solid dependability. It is in harmony with nature, representing the six colors of the rainbow. It is the most perfect number, being divisible both by two, an even number, and three, an odd number. Thus it combines the best basic elements of each.

Seven symbolizes occult and other mysteries. Study and knowledge are its ways of exploring the unknown and the unseen. It represents the seven governing planets, the seven days of the week, and the seven notes of the perfect scale. It combines the unity of one with the perfection of six to form a special symmetry of its own, making it the truly psychic occult number.

Eight is the number of material success. It stands for solidity (four) carried to completion (two times four), as represented by a double square. When halved, its parts are equal (four and four). When halved again, its parts are still equal (two, two, two, and two), showing a fourfold perfect harmonious balance.

Nine is the symbol of universal achievement and the greatest of all the primary numbers. It combines the features of the entire group, making it their controlling force when they are developed to the fullest. As three times the number three, the number nine turns versatility into inspiration and success.

Various systems and methods have been devised in the past to reduce large numbers to one of these basic primaries. The simplest, as well as the most accurate of modern numerological methods, is to add the figures of the large number. Then if they total ten or more, to add those figures. This process is continued until a primary number (one to nine) is obtained and the real natural value obtained.

In the "great chain of being" from the macrocosm to man the Pythagorean heritage is clear. Pythagoras described the interrelations of the stars, the elements, the beasts, the plants, and man. Man is pulled in different directions by the higher and lower forces, pulled between the godlike and the bestial.

The stars and planets impel, yet never compel.

The very humors of our earthly bodies correspond to the elements. Melancholy, phlegm, choler, and blood correspond to cold, moist, dry, and hot. Man's four humors are the sublunary elements. Personality is the result of their strife and balance. Sickness results from conflict between the humors and the stars. Health is harmony! Such were the conclusions of one of Pythagoras' controversial students, Empedocles of Agrigentum.

The four elements were thrown into striking relief by Empedocles in his teachings in Sicily about 475 B.C. This is the picturesque hero of Matthew Arnold's poem, who as philosopher, physician, and poet traveled through the Greek cities and who, because of his medical skill, was held by the people to be endowed with the highest supernatural powers. One of his poetic fragments, as rendered by Arnold, shows the unusual reverence in which the Greek physician was held at this time:

> Ye friends, who in the mighty city dwell
> Along the yellow Acragas, hard by
> The Acropolis, ye stewards of good works
> The stranger's refuge venerable and kind.
> All hail, O friends! But unto ye I walk
> As god immortal now, no more as man,
> On all sides honored fittingly and well,
> Crowned both with fellets, and with flowering wreaths
> When with my throngs of men and women I come

To thriving cities I am sought by prayers.
And thousands follow me that they may ask
The path to weal and vantage, craving some
For oracles, whilst others seek to hear
A healing work 'gainst many a foul disease
That all too long hath pierced with grievous pains.

Empedocles introduced into astrology the doctrine of the elements—
Earth, Air, Fire, and Water—as the fourfold root of all things. The human
body is supposed to be made up of these primordial substance, health resulting from their balance, disease from imbalance. He held that nothing
can be created or destroyed, and there is only transformation, which is
the modern theory of conservation of energy. Everything originates from
the attraction of the four elements and is destroyed by their repulsion
and he applies the same idea, under the forms of love and hate, to the
moral world. Development is due to the union of dissimilar elements,
decay to the return of like to like, air to air, fire to fire, earth to earth.

When in 430 B.C. Empedocles went to his death in a blaze of fiery glory,
one of the most honored physicians of early times was caught up in a halo
of myth. Even if the story of his end was more poetic than factual, it was
at least consistent with his theories. Empedocles always seemed more than
a mere man. Surrounded by his many faithful followers, he wore a purple
robe and a girdle made of gold, a Delphic band of golden laurel leaves
about his long hair, and garlands of flowers around his neck. The brass
sandals he wore were recognized by everyone and became his personal
mark of identification. Only Empedocles dared wear such slippers.

Hundreds of legends were told of him. One was that he restored to life
the beautiful Pantheia. She had lain thirty days in a deathlike trance
because of the loss of her love. He whispered into her ear, "Think friendly
thoughts and call on Joy and Aphrodite, the goddess of love."

Another legend was that he saved the town of Selinus from an epidemic
of plague by cleansing the air of the poisonous vapors from the swamp.
He did this by miraculously changing the course of the two tiny streams.
Empedocles also was said to be able to quiet madmen by playing on the
lyre, to bring the dead back to life, and to cure any and all diseases of
man.

These stories illustrate one of his chief contentions—that knowledge
gives power over nature. He also believed that purity is the key to a happy
life and death. For all the legends about him, Empedocles was not a
quack: Science and religion were the pivots of his doctrine.

Empedocles was born about 495 B.C. in Agrigentum, a town of Sicily,
at that time belonging to Greece. His family were statesmen and mer-

chants and sent young Empedocles to school to study under the great philosopher and mathematician Pythagoras. He also studied medicine on the lovely island of Cos, in the temples of the god of medicine, Aesculapius.

After studying medicine for several years, he traveled through the country districts of his native Sicily performing miracles. He was soon surrounded by a host of worshipers of both sexes. Thousands of people acclaimed him and prostrated themselves before him. Later they demanded favorable forecasts for the future; for Empedocles was a fortuneteller of wide renown. They would also demand that he heal them of all disease and infirmity.

His fame in the beginning came from his preventing an epidemic in his native town. Using large stones he sealed a pass in the mountains through which the "poisonous miasma," or wind, entered the city. He was not only a physician and philosopher, but also a poet, mystic, seer, priest, and scientist, who sought to immortalize himself.

Empedocles demonstrated that air was a reality, even though invisible, by experimenting with a water clock in a truly scientific manner. Putting his finger over the air vent, he noticed that the flow of water soon stopped. He compared the effects of air pressure in the water clock to the flow of blood, which he linked to the lungs and breathing by means of an endless number of tubes.

He believed that the four elements—Fire, Air, Water, and Earth—come together to produce life and that when they are separated death occurs. All objects of nature—animal, plant, and mineral—are combinations of these elements. The quality of an object is determined by the varying amounts of each element combining to make the whole. Quality, therefore, depends on the quantity of each element.

All things are formed by the action of the cohesive force of love. Hatred, the opposite force, causes separation of elements and therefore disease. Man is considered to be composed of the four elements, each with its characteristic qualities: Earth—cold and dry; Air—hot and wet; Water—cold and wet; Fire—hot and dry. When one humor gets the upper hand in the human body, the correct medical treatment is to apply its opposite.

Blood is hot and moist (Air); phlegm is cold and moist (Water); yellow bile is hot and dry (Fire); and black bile is cold and dry (Earth). Men are likely to show a balance toward one humor or another without being ill. They are sanguine (blood), phlegmatic (phlegm), choleric (yellow bile), or melancholy (black bile). This doctrine was to influence medicine for nearly two thousand years when modified slightly by Galen.

Empedocles stated: "Beasts are akin to man; he who eats their flesh is not much better than a cannibal."

He was among the first to realize that the human female produces eggs. Yet he accounted for the sex of the child on the basis of the diet of the mother. He felt that twins were due to an abundance of semen on the part of the male.

There is no doubt that he deserves great credit, but his physiology was based largely on speculation and knew little about arteries, veins, nerves, and their functions. He explained sleep, awakening, and death by the amount of blood in the veins. He explained the sterility of mules by assuming that the female's womb did not open and that the male's seed was too fine and cold.

His death was memorialized by Matthew Arnold in his poem *"Empedocles on Etna."* According to legend, a midnight feast was held in his honor. There was much merrymaking, wine drinking, and love for all. Empedocles told the happy crowd the gods had chosen him to become an immortal. He ascended the slopes of Mount Etna and stood alone and unafraid on the brink of the crater. He was going to join himself with the most perfect of his immortal elements—Fire. He threw himself into the fiery crater. It was his hope that no man would find any material trace of him and everyone would suppose he had indeed become one with the flame. His hopes were in vain. Several of his loyal disciples had secretly followed him up the long mountain path. They were too late to see his death, but according to legend his brass sandals were cast up by the fiery volcano and betrayed his secret. However, the people of Sicily have never ceased to honor him, for even today he is revered and loved.

Empedocles did not so much produce a new philosophy as weld together and reconcile the thought of his predecessors. He stated that matter is without beginning and without end, that it is indestructible—although change is a fact that cannot be denied. This he reconciled by the principle that objects as wholes begin to be and cease to be, but that these objects are composed of material particles which in themselves are indestructible.

From the earliest ages in the history of the world, astrology has excited the interest of many men of medicine. This science was never universally accepted, yet it has had countless adherents throughout the history of mankind. One adherent was Hippocrates of ancient Greece. Modern medicine claims him as the "father of medicine" and bases its ethics on the Hippocratic oath. Still, the modern medical man is loath to recognize that Hippocrates firmly believed in astrology.

He believed that the heavenly bodies do have a direct effect on man. The early Greek physicians studied the stars and in the zodiac they read the plans of divine wisdom and the signs foretelling the course of disease in man. But today modern medicine maligns, scorns, and ridicules astrology. It has been branded as mythical, with no foundations in demonstrable truth. We live in a machinistic-materialist age. The machine is reality. What we see, hear, smell, taste, and measure are real. All the rest is superstition. The remote stars and planets have no influence on man—or so say our scientists! In spite of such loose talk, there are more things in heaven and on earth than science can explain.

Medicine in the ancient world developed to its highest point in Greece during the period from 500 B.C. to A.D. 500. However right or wrong their ideas may have been, the Greek physicians showed great clinical skill. Early in this period, practitioners of Greek medicine generally made a decisive turn from supernaturalism to the acceptance of naturalistic and scientific astrological explanations of, and methods of, treatment of disease. The principles established during this period dominated medicine until the sixteenth century; and their influence on present-day medicine is seen in the predominance of Greek words in medical terminology.

The Chaldean number-lore of Pythagoras exerted its most profound influence upon the "Hippocratic doctrine of crises and critical days." This assigned fixed periods for the cure of different diseases. The Greek physicians wanted to predict with scientific power more than anything else and so they turned to astrology. The plastic importance of the number four was combined, with the doctrine of the four elements of Empedocles, as follows:

Corresponding with the four alchemical elements, Fire, Air, Earth, and Water, were the qualities dry, cold, hot, and moist according to this scheme:

$$\text{hot} + \text{dry} = \text{Fire} \qquad \text{cold} + \text{dry} = \text{Earth}$$
$$\text{hot} + \text{moist} = \text{Air} \qquad \text{cold} + \text{moist} = \text{Water}$$

By reversing this scheme the four elements could be resolved into their components. The whole arrangement made up "humoral pathology," which regarded health and disease as the proper balance and adjustment, or imbalance and maladjustment, of the different ingredients. This scheme of things was elaborated on by Galen in Rome and the Arabian physicians. Their remedies and compounds were classified in numerical scales according to the "degree" or relative proportions of their basic qualities. Hippocrates stated that in a state of health the four humors were well balanced. Unbalance in their proportion resulted in disease, and nature made every effort to restore this balance by throwing off the improper matter.

Very little is known about Hippocrates' life, except that he was born about 460 B.C. on the little island of Cos in the Aegean Sea. (Hippocrates was a relatively common name; the great physician's grandfather also bore the name.) He was the second of seven sons of a physician named Heracleides, who professed to be one of the Aesclepiads, a group of physicians claiming Aesclepius as their patron saint. Aesclepius, attended by his daughter the goddess Hygeia and by a serpent, appeared in the patient's dream and he was cured. Temples throughout Greece were built for such sleep healing.

According to tradition, Hippocrates began the study of medicine at the Aesclepieion of Cos, later studying at Cnidus, Thasos, Thessaly, and in Egypt and Lydia, and finally in Scythia. He returned to practice in his home community on the island of Cos, but apparently always traveled widely.

The Hippocratic, or Coan, school of medicine aimed at foretelling the course of an illness by means of a general picture of known disease, with generalized over-all therapy. It centered on the patient and his individual make-up as determined by the stars at his birth. The patient was the reality; the disease was not an entity like the savage's demon but a fluctuating condition of the patient's body, a battle between the morbid humors and the natural self-healing tendency of the body. Treatment centered upon assisting the patient, through his particular nature, to react in his individual way against the disease that was an imbalance of the four humors.

In disease, forces or morbid principles from the heavens brought the humors into a raw condition (*appesia*), with resulting illness. By the natural reactions of the body (*physis*), the apeptic humors were brought into a state of coction (*pepsis*), expressing itself as fever, inflammation, or pus. Recovery resulted from elimination of the wrong humors and morbid material (*crisis*), or by the slower process of increased secretion or excretion (*lysis*). The patient's reaction in each case was just as individual and peculiar to himself as his natal horoscope.

Hippocrates had two sons, Thessalus and Draco, both of whom became physicians of note, and a physician son-in-law, Polybus. They were the founders of a dogmatic school of medicine based on Hippocrates' aphorisms. They carefully preserved the Hippocratic principles, and all their writings bore the name of their illustrious father.

The writings of both Plato and Aristotle follow many of the principles taught by Hippocrates, especially in the concept of the soul. Plato said that the head, the abode of ideas, was spherical in the image of the stars. Unlike the rest of the body, the head was linked to heaven. The neck, a small isthmus between the intelligible and the corporeal, was made in order to separate them neatly.

Plato's world was a magical one, for it was unified and all things were interrelated. The universe was an animal endowed with soul and mind. It had no eyes, for nothing was to be seen beyond it; it had no ears, for there was no place outside of it in which anything could be heard. It had no breath, for the atmosphere was within it. Hands were useless to the world animal, as it had no enemy against whom it could use them. It had no feet, for they were not necessary to revolving movement. The world animal was shaped in the most perfect form: the sphere.

The soul was older than the body and therefore superior to it, said Plato. It was composed of three elements: The indivisible, which partakes of the divine, and the divisible, which partakes of the earthly. Both were related through a third element partaking of each and placed between the two. The three were made one by compression. The compound was cut into strips, which were crossed or interwoven and bent into a spherical shape. Such was the World Soul in which God had placed the corporeal universe, and the human soul was made of the same elements as the World Soul.

The star gods were the children of the creator and they formed man, who would return after death to his star. The World Soul pervaded everything; in man, it circulated in a proper motion that could be perfected by him who observed the motion of the heavenly gods, the planets. Plato believed in the influence of the stars. He is quoted frequently by the astrologers of the sixteenth and seventeenth centuries.

Just as the Persian Zoroaster believed that the good god Ormazd shaped the world with ideas so did Plato attribute a divine character to ideas. Because they dominated the body, the magicians of the West concluded they could induce marvels in the corporeal world through the omnipotence of sovereign ideas. In Plato's world heaven and earth, the elements, the soul and the spirit, the divine and the terrestrial, were all interrelated and partook of one another. Numbers were older than bodies and hence more powerful. The world was formed according to a mathematical scheme and was harmonized according to proportion. Beauty and order were impossible to achieve without numbers. In the size, weight, and intervals of the stars lurked mystic numbers, and around these the creator built the entire cosmos.

In the *Timaeus* there is an extensive and formal exposition of anatomy and physiology, as if Plato were writing a textbook in miniature. This is the only dialogue he wrote that deals with natural science, yet the impact of this single cosmological work was considerable. Although Galen objected to several of the concepts in *Timaeus*, the Platonic doctrines were accepted for at least fifteen centuries, until some conflicting Aristotelian documents were discovered. *Timaeus* was an attempt to amalgamate Empedoclean physiology and pathology with Pythagorean mathematics, cosmology, and theology, and it reveals the grafting of Ionian and Sicilian astrology taking place in Athens at the time. It also contains a cosmogony which sets out to show the primacy of a personal, mathematical mind in the creation of the world.

The world was designed by God's intelligence to be the "best" (most mathematically harmonious) of all possible worlds. Because for Plato God is not omnipotent, the world falls short of its ideal model. In the *Timaeus,* Plato placed the seat of thought and feeling in the brain, and his scheme of the human body tended to trace a parallel between the outer world and man's body. He represented the world itself as a living being and all matter as endowed with life. (This concept is known as hylozoism.)

Plato's famous "myth of the cave" symbolizes the manner in which he saw physical reality: objects seen led only to belief and their shadows led to conjecture. True knowledge came from the mind. He elaborated upon the humoral pathology of the Hippocratics and followed Empedocles in the composition of matter from fire, air, earth, and water.

The best known of Plato's followers and friends was Aristotle, who after the death of Plato became interested in natural history. His down-to-earth mentality had no use for a world of transcendent entities, of a mere visionary duplication of the real world of experience.

Aristotle is the earliest Greek scientist whose writings may be studied in their approximate original form. In general, the Aristotelian writings can be classified under four heads: (a) physical, (b) logical and metaphysical, (c) ethical and political, and (d) biological. The physical treatises are the least satisfactory, when considered in the light of modern science, and the logical and metaphysical ones are mostly criticism of his predecessors. He transformed the Platonic ideal into an instrument for the study of nature in that "ideas," or "forms," do not exist apart from nature but are embodied in it. Growth involves the mixture of fundamental elements and is, according to Aristotle, dependent on the conditions of the seasons. The course of growth is determined by inherent purpose, the action of an essence fixed for each species. There are three basic levels of life: the "vegetable," with the functions of nutrition, growth, and reproduction; the "animal," characterized by sensation, desire and locomotion; and the "human," with the power of choice and theoretical inquiry. He recognized an animating principle in living things, which was designated by the term "soul." Soul and body are closely interrelated in function, but the soul recognizes the unity of the organism and responds to the motion of the stars. Reason is the capacity for grasping the formal aspects of experience.

The activities of man are three: theoretical (seeking of knowledge), practical (regulating conduct), and productive (making things). Human beings also are drawn toward some ideal or a "highest end." Because man has an individual and a social character, the perfection of his nature is happiness. This is attained by reason, and reason counsels moderation in all things—"the golden mean." Man cannot understand life perfectly, so men are responsible beings only to the extent that they can make choices in regulating their lives. The highest goal is friendship and the ideal life, a life of reason and contemplative leisure.

Among the most enduring of all of Aristotle's conceptions are his doctrines of the constitution of matter. In this he followed Empedocles and the Sicilian school, holding that there are four primary and opposite fundamental qualities and four essences: fire, air, water, and earth. Some of Aristotle's statements about the cosmos are:

> For such reasons, then, we believe that the heaven was neither created nor is it corruptible, but that it is one and everlasting, unchanged through infinite time. Hence, we may well persuade ourselves that ancient assertions, especially those of our own ancestors, are true.

> . . . Empedocles asserts, by whirling round faster than its natural motion downwards. Nor is it reasonable to think that it remains unchanged by the compulsion of a soul, untiring and sleepless, unlike the soul of mortal animals, for it would need the fate of some Ixion (bound forever to a fiery wheel) to keep it in motion.

> Further still, since it seems clear and we assume that the universe revolves in a circle, and since beyond the uttermost sky is neither body nor space nor vacuum, once more it follows that the universe is spherical. For, if it were rectilinear, there must be space beyond it: A rectilinear body as it revolves will never occupy the same place; where it formerly was it is not now, and where it is not now it will be again, because the corners project.

> It remains to discuss the earth—where it is situated, whether it is at rest or moves, and what is its form. With regard to its position, all philosophers have not the same opinion. Most of those who assert that the heaven is finite say that the earth lies at the center, while those in Italy who are called Pythagoreans hold the contrary.

> In a similar way there is doubt about the shape of the earth. To some it seems to be spherical, but to others flat, in the form of a drum. To support this opinion they urge that, when the sun rises and sets, he appears to make a straight and not a circular occultation, as it should be if the earth were spherical. These men do not realize the distance of the sun from the earth and the magnitude of the circumference, nor do they consider that, when seen cutting a small circle, a part of the large circle appears at a distance as a straight line. Because of this appearance, therefore, they ought not to deny that the earth is round.

Before we leave the ancient Greeks and their religious observation of the stars we should discuss the influence of Berossus of Babylonia. Both

Plato and Aristotle defended the divinity of the stars, but they did not ask the heavens for predictions of the future. This is true, despite Aristotle's saying: "This world is inescapably linked to the motions of the world above. All power in this world is ruled by these heavenly motions." This attitude nevertheless allowed for popular beliefs in prediction by astrology.

After Alexander's conquest of Babylonia in 331 B.C. the Greeks accepted the astrological views of the conquered people. Berossus, a priest of the Temple of Marduk, moved to Cos where Hippocrates had lived and taught. This Chaldean priest wedded astrology and medicine with a great impact on future Greek thought. The Stoics were enthusiastic disciples and brought astrology to Rome.

The city of Babylon was destroyed by fire in 125 B.C., but the seed of astrology was planted and would mature under Eudoxus, Galen and the Alexandrians. Finally, it would bear fruit under Ptolemy.

FOUR

The Celestial Circles

When the Greeks became aware of the regularity and mystery of the celestial phenomena they began to speculate on their origin, the laws that governed their relationships, and the forces that caused their motions. The most primitive conception of the nature of the earth and its position in the cosmos was found in the writings of Homer. The dome of the sky contained the ether and within it the celestial bodies followed their assigned courses. According to Homer the sun rises in the morning out of the water of Okeanos in the east, travels through the sky, and returns to the hollows of that river's deep in the west for the night, to reappear again next morning.

The early Greek ideas were sophisticated attempts to devise unified generalizations to account for the things seen by the human eye. Clearly the earth was flat and there was a vault above it. That vault was made of solid crystalline material and the stars were attached to it "like nails." The celestial bodies exhaled fiery clouds "ignited by their motions" and were located far away from us somewhere in the infinity of space. It was suggested from early times that the moon shone with the light it reflected from the sun. Leucippus declared that the moon's markings were caused by hills and valleys casting shadows on its surface. The Milky Way, taught Democritus, consisted of myriads of minute stars; while according to Anaximander it marked the former path of the sun. It also was known from the tales of travelers that the southern star Canopus could be seen barely on the horizon from the island of Rhodes and higher in the sky still further south, though that star was never seen in Greece. Empedocles speculated that solar eclipses were caused by the moon's passage between the earth and sun.

It was generally believed that the region around the earth, extending as far as the moon, teemed with evil spirits and exhalations, while the regions beyond the moon were pure. The earth was held in position by the rapid spinning of the rotating heavens "as the water remained in a goblet which is swung quickly around in a circle," explained Aristotle when he presented the views of Empedocles. Initial pressure and compaction gave rise to the air. The North Pole of the heavens was originally directly overhead, but later it was depressed downward to the position it now occupies.

According to Leucippus the axis of the heavens inclined to the horizon because the earth was loaded with ice up north and was thus weighted downward, while the south end was hotter and lighter. Others offered the explanation that the tilting occurred spontaneously with the appearance of life on earth to produce the differences in climate. Some philosophers taught that the sun and moon were nearer to the earth than the planets, while others proclaimed the exact reverse.

It would seem as if throughout Greek history there were premonitions of the notion that the earth was actually round. The concept of the sphericity of the earth has been attributed to several philosophers, though usually the credit falls to Pythagoras. Through an error the rumor was set abroad that Pythagoras was the founder of the theory that the sun was situated at the center of the cosmos with the earth and planets revolving around it. In reality the Pythagorean scheme of the universe was entirely different.

It became clear to the Greek philosophers, most of whom also were shrewd observers and mathematicians, that the stars and planets inscribed circular orbits in the sky and completed their diurnal circles in twenty-four hours. This was not easy to accept. Motion was considered an unsuitable quality for a philosopher, fit rather for a slave. Similarly, motion did not fit ethereal celestial bodies, but rather properly belonged to the crudest of all, the earth.

As far as astrology was concerned, Plato accepted the general Pythagorean concept of a spherical earth stationary at the center of a spherical universe. He also accepted Pythagoras' idea that two circular motions could exist in the universe, but he used them in an intricate way. He assumed that they were created parallel to each other and later split apart, and that then the circular motion along the zodiac was itself divided into seven smaller circles, or whorls. In the first whorl traveled the moon; in the second the sun; and, moving still further out, the planets in the order of Mercury, Venus, Mars, Jupiter, and Saturn. The whole apparent daily rotations of the planets, the sun, the moon, and the stars themselves Plato believed to be due to the rotation of an outer whorl on which the fixed stars were attached.

The exact form of Plato's whorls is difficult to understand. From one description one gets the impression that they are to be considered as shaped like thick, flat disks such as the flywheels used in his day to keep the hand spindles for spinning thread rotating as evenly as possible. Yet a description in another of his books speaks of the stars as embroidered on a fiery sphere that fits closely inside the universe. Later on the idea that the planets were fixed to the inside of perfectly transparent spheres was accepted. There is no doubt that it is from Plato that this belief arose. The transparent (crystalline) spheres formed part of the structure of Plato's universe and the rather involved description of whorls was used as a means of providing a rudimentary theory to account for the motions of the planets. It is no exaggeration to say that Plato himself was far from pleased with his explanation. He certainly exhorted his pupils to work matters out more fully, and this advice quickly bore fruit in the work of Eudoxus.

Plato's conception of the universe was not entirely physical. His mysticism appears time and time again: He supposed that the whole spherical body of the universe was a divine, living soul and that there was an invisible spindle about which the whole conglomeration of spheres and whorls revolved. In his ideas about the distances of the planets we can see this mysticism more clearly, for, following Pythagoras, Plato spoke of a celestial harmony and also worked out a scale of planetary distance to account for it. The scale was arrived at by combining two regular sequences of numbers and applying these to give the distances of the sun, the moon, and the seven planets. Like Pythagoras, he obtained musical intervals, but he did not suppose that an actual harmonious note was sounded. It was sufficient that the essential harmony alone existed. Plato also expressed the belief that colors were associated with the whorls of each planet: Mars was pale red, Jupiter white, while the moon took its color from the seventh whorl that shone on it. Here we have the characteristic mystical approach to the physical fact that the planets are seen to differ in color and that the moon shines by light from the sun or seventh whorl.

Plato's greatest contribution was, without doubt, the logical approach that he trained into his pupils and the enthusiasm for enquiry generated by his teaching.

Plato's pupil Eudoxus was born about 408 B.C. in Cnidus, a city in what is now southwestern Turkey, and here he studied geometry and medicine till the age of twenty-three. He left to sit at the feet of Plato in Athens. Too poor to afford living in Athens, Eudoxus lodged in the seaport town of Piraeus and walked the five miles or so to the Academy every day. He attended for the surprisingly short period of two months before returning to Cnidus and then setting out on travels to Egypt. Gradually Eudoxus grew in reputation and acquired riches, especially after a period of service at the court of Halicarnassus in Turkey. We later find him visiting Plato at the Academy, taking his own pupils with him. Plato was delighted to see him and gave a banquet in his honor. Then the distinguished pupil returned home to help draw up laws for Cnidus and receive the rewards due to a local boy who made good.

Eudoxus is to be remembered for the attempt he made to carry out Plato's instruction to account for the apparent motions of the planets, using the theory of homocentric spheres. There seems no doubt that it was Plato who originated the ideas that Eudoxus put forward. Indeed his theory was really a rationalization of much of Plato's mystical outpourings on the universe. It used a system of closely fitting spheres, which, although much more elaborate, was similar to Plato's description of the whorls that fit closely into one another. The basis of Eudoxus' theory was that each planet was embedded in the middle of a sphere, this sphere rotated on an axis embedded into another sphere that rotated around another axis embedded into yet another sphere, and so on. In other words, his theory was similar to one of those nests of ivory balls that the Chinese were so adept at producing, except that each ball was completely transparent.

An idea of the complexity of this system will be appreciated if you consider the three spheres Eudoxus used in order to account for the moon's motion. Remember that he found four spheres necessary for each of the planets. Three spheres were adequate for the moon's motion because he fixed it to the innermost sphere, to which he gave a west to east motion once every month to account for the moon's monthly orbit of the earth. The two other spheres completed the picture. Of these the outer one spun in an east-west direction every day and dealt with the daily motion of the moon across the sky. The inner sphere of the two performed a similar motion about a slightly different axis once every eighteen years, which took into account the observed shift of the moon's actual orbit.

Complicated though it was, this theory offered an explanation for the motions of the moon and the planets that was far more satisfactory than any previous to it. It did little if anything to basic Platonic doctrines, for by using the perfect shape of the sphere it built up planetary movements from a series of uniform motions. Also, it followed Plato to the extent of proposing the existence of a series of invisible spheres upon equally invisible axes. The theory did not concentrate unduly upon observation, for it failed completely to account for eclipses and was most unsatisfactory in its description of the behavior of Mars.

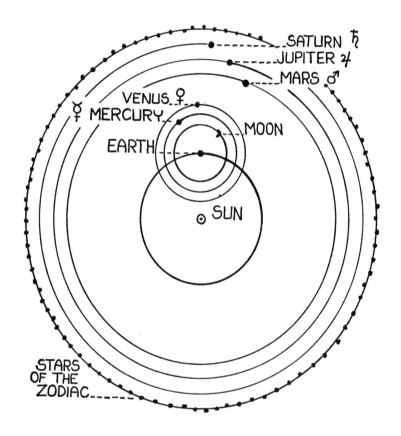

The sun-centered system of Aristarchus of Samos, 280 B.C.

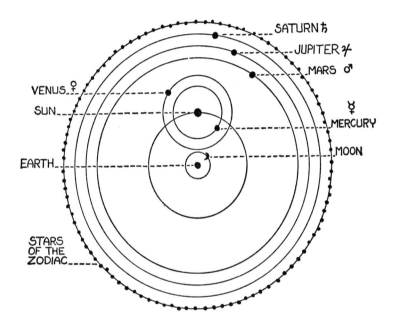

According to Macrobius, an author of the fourth century A.D., there was a theory of planetary motion advanced about 300 B.C. known as the Egyptian theory. The plan supposed the earth to be stationary and the sun to circle around the earth, with Mercury and Venus revolving around the sun. It was a late modification of the theory of Eudoxus.

However, in spite of its many failings, the "theory of homocentric spheres" started the fashion of making detailed attempts to account for planetary movement by regular circular motion, attempts that were to preoccupy astrologer-astronomers for about the next two thousand years.

We find four really great astronomers associated with ancient Alexandria —Aristarchus, Eratosthenes, Hipparchus, and Ptolemy. The first gave us the first true description of the arrangement of the solar system—planets, including the earth, revolving around a central sun—while the last gave us an entirely erroneous description that held the field almost unchallenged until the sixteenth century.

We know but little of the life of Aristarchus. He was sometimes described as "the mathematician," but Bitrubius speaks of him as one of the few great men who possessed an equally profound knowledge of all branches of science—geometry, astrology, and music. He was born in Samos and became a disciple of Strato, who, as one of the earlier peripatetic philosophers, was probably in close touch with Aristotle. Strato tried to explain everything on rationalistic lines, so it is not surprising that Aristarchus should approach the problems of astrology similarly.

He was the first to treat astronomical observations in a truly scientific spirit and to make deductions from them by strict mathematical methods. In a work that is still extant, *On the Sizes and Distances of the Sun and Moon,* he tried to calculate these quantities by deduction from observation.

Aristarchus gave us the true explanation of the phases of the moon. As the sun and moon move about in the sky, that fraction of the moon's surface that is seen at the earth to be lighted by the sun changes continually. At the moment when precisely half is seen illuminated, the angle must be exactly a right angle. If, then, Aristarchus could measure the angle at such a moment he would know the shape of the triangle and so could calculate the relative distances of the sun and moon.

Such was his ingenious and perfectly sound method. But the moment of exact half moon is difficult to estimate. Aristarchus estimated the angle to be only $87°$ at this moment, whereas the true value is $89°51'$. The error was more serious than it appears to be on the surface, because the final result of the calculation turns entirely on the small difference between this angle and $90°$. Aristarchus estimated this at twenty times its true value and concluded that the sun is about nineteen times as distant as the moon. The true figure is just twenty times greater. Nevertheless this calculation was pretty close and it drew attention to the inequality in the distances of the sun and moon. It also showed that the sun and moon must be of very different sizes. They look the same size in the sky, as can be easily verified at an eclipse, so their actual sizes must be proportional to their distances—the ratio that Aristarchus determined.

It remained only to determine the actual sizes of the sun and moon, and these could be ascertained from the size of the shadow the earth casts over the moon at an eclipse; because the sun is so distant the earth's shadow must be almost equal to the earth that casts it. Aristarchus estimated that the diameter of the shadow was about twice that of the moon and concluded that the earth must have about twice the diameter of the moon. The true figure is about four. But his estimates showed that the sun must be many times larger than the earth.

We know nothing of the trend of his thoughts in the face of this great discovery, but we can imagine him pondering on the inherent improbability of the sun revolving around an earth that was so much smaller than itself. Philolaus had already proposed dethroning the earth from its supposed central position and making it revolve with the other planets around a new center; this he called the "central fire" of the universe. Heraclides had taught that the two planets Mercury and Venus revolved around a center that was none other than the sun. Why not, Aristarchus may have thought—combine the two suggestions and suppose that the planets, including the earth, revolve around the sun?

Aristarchus probably saw that if the earth moved in this way, its motion would cause the fixed stars continually to change their directions as seen from the earth. Thus the appearance of the sky ought continually to change. Yet no such change was noticed, and he may have seen that this could only mean that the stars are so remote that the earth's motion around the sun makes no appreciable change in their apparent positions.

In any case, Archimedes wrote a few years later that Aristarchus put forward the hypotheses "that the fixed stars and the sun remain motionless, that the earth revolves about the sun in the circumference of a circle, the sun lying in the middle of the orbit, and that the sphere of the fixed stars, situated about the same center as the sun, is so great that the earth's orbit bears the same proportion to the sphere of the fixed stars as the center of a sphere beats to its surface."

By abandoning the usual Greek methods of speculation and reliance on supposed general principles, Aristarchus attained by observation, almost at one bound, an accurate understanding of the arrangement of the solar system. He gained true ideas as to the relatively minute size of the earth, its apparent unimportance as a mere appendage of a far vaster sun, and the insignificance of both in the vastness of outer space.

In this way astrology was started on the right road. We might expect the rest of the story to be one of rapid progress on highly scientific lines. Actually it was very different. Plutarch tells us that the doctrines of Aristarchus were confidently held, and even violently defended, by Seleucus of Babylon in the second century B.C. But apart from this isolated adherent of these findings, we hear of little support for them until the time of Copernicus and Galileo.

The truth seems to be that such doctrines were simply too far in advance of their time to prove acceptable to the learned men of the day. The solid, sturdy, unimaginative "horse sense" of the average citizen told him it was absurd to imagine that anything as large as the earth could be only a minute fragment. Even still more absurd was to imagine that anything as big and solid could be in motion—and if it were, pray, what could produce the immense forces that, according to the mechanical ideas of the time, would be needed to keep it in constant motion?

We can imagine that the average citizen felt very, very reluctant to surrender his comfortable feeling of importance as an inhabitant of the biggest and most important part of the universe. Man was still a near neighbor of the gods. And so Cleanthes proposed that Aristarchus should be charged with impiety and punished. Anaxagoras had been banished from Athens two centuries earlier for his ideas, and again religious intolerance helped to divert thought from truth. Astrology was brought back essentially to the point at which it had been left by Eudoxus.

Even the great Galileo pointed out that the Aristarchian method of explaining the world often leads, strange though it may seem, to conclusions that do violence to immediate sensible experience. The prime example of this, Galileo said many years later, is the Aristarchian and Copernican astrology, which furnishes the supreme example of the victory of mathematical reason over the senses:

> I cannot sufficiently admire the eminence of those men's wits, that have received and held it to be true, and with the sprightliness of their judgments offered such violence to their own senses, as that they have been able to prefer that which their reason dictated to them, to that which sensible experiments represented most manifestly to the contrary. . . . I cannot find any bounds for my admiration, how that reason was able in Aristarchus and Copernicus, to commit such a rape on their senses, as in despite thereof to make herself mistress of their credulity. Reason even occasionally, by the invention of such instruments as the telescope, gives sense an opportunity to correct her own misjudgments.

Even though not accepted, the novel theories of planetary motion came into their own with the speculations of the two Greek philosophers Heraclides of Pontus and Aristarchus of Samos. According to Simplicius, the famous commentator on Aristotle, Heraclides definitely taught that "the heavens and the stars were immovable and the earth moved around the poles of the equator from the west each day one revolution as near as possible."

Later on he stated that "Heraclides of Pontus assumes the earth to be in the middle and to move in a circle, but the heavens to be at rest." Heraclides also postulated that Venus moved around the sun and around the earth. Similar theories of the earth's rotation were attributed to other Greek philosophers throughout the period and references to them occur in many texts.

At Alexandria with Aristarchus were other great astrologers who recorded the positions of the stars by measurements of their distances from fixed positions in the sky. Thus they defined the positions of the more important stars in the twelve signs of the zodiac, near to which all the planets pass in their orbits. Their observations were used later by Hipparchus in his calculations of star movement.

The philosophy that was the parent of the crude science among the Greeks interested itself in three aspects of the material world: (a) number and form and their relation to each other and to material objects, (b) the form and workings of the universe, and (c) the nature of man. In Alexandria, where science freed itself from philosophy, it was to be expected that there would be systematization of mathematics and astrology. This was accompanied by a similar development in the basic studies with which medicine continued its progressive tradition. Open dissection of the human body was first performed at Alexandria. This procedure was not only against the ancient Greek tradition, but also contrary to the deep-seated feelings of the human race itself. How could such major scientific steps be taken at this time and place?

No complete answer can be given, but at Alexandria about 300 B.C. several significant conditions existed. There was a host of immigrant Greeks, uprooted physically from their homeland and spiritually from their ancient folkways, some of whom possessed a great natural curiosity as to the structure and working of the human body—a curiosity roused by the biological work of Aristotle and his still-living pupil Theophrastus. These immigrant Greeks were in full possession of the works of Plato, wherein contempt for the body as a mere shell for the soul was expressed in terms of moving beauty. These words he ascribed to Socrates in the hours just before his death: "Man, then, was really just a shell controlled and guided by the greater souls in the heavens above."

Since time immemorial people in the Orient have read the prophetic words of the wandering stars. We have neglected this marvelous art much of the time. Reuchlin was the first who called our attention to it, and he was followed by Pico della Mirandola. Talismans, engraved stones, and metal plates are endowed with positive magic power. And how can we explain the fact that people are moved by beautiful paintings and even smile and weep before the artificial work of a painter or sculptor, if there is not a magical sympathy between the depicted scene and nature herself?

The Magi clung to the Chaldean and Egyptian idea that artistic activities were magical operations controlled by the celestial spheres and based upon the principle called the Law of Sympathy. It is possible that the Hebrew legislators of old shared such conceptions with neighboring nations and thus forbade any representation of reality contrary to religion, magic, and the cabala.

Certainly it is true that from earliest recorded history man has been trying to find the meaning of the stars and their effect on human life. The Egyptians consulted astrologers before any major royal act was to be performed. They were respected in Ancient Greece, by the Romans ("Beware the Ides of March"), in the fifteenth and sixteenth centuries (Copernicus, founder of modern astrology, was also a student of medicine because it was accepted that the two were connected inextricably). Nostradamus, the French Magus, wrote his famous prophecies in quatrains. Indian astrologers still prefer to write their predictions in rhyming couplets, indicating their belief that art, science, and more mundane matters are all interrelated—all show man's concern with the power of the stars and are not without dignity.

According to Ptolemy, it was the mathematician Apollonius of Perga who first employed the notion of an epicycle to account for the stationary and retrograde motion of the superior planets. All that was required was to assume that the planet moved upon an epicycle in the same direction as the motion around the earth (or deferent). By properly adjusting the radii of the epicycle and the deferent, the velocities of rotation of the planet, and the center of its epicycle, it is possible to obtain seemingly stationary and retrograde motions. One can even make the proper adjustments for the planet's conjunction and opposition.

The inferior planets Mercury and Venus were also accounted for. The centers of their epicycles lie on a line joining the planets with the sun and earth. This takes care of the consistent proximity of these planets to the sun. Their centers on the deferent must make a complete circle around the earth in the same period as the sun, or one year. However, the planets also move on an epicycle that accounts for their irregularity. Generally speaking, the deferent took care of the inequality of motion in longitude, or the unequal rate of motion along the zodiac. The epicycle also took care of the unequal motion in latitude or vertical deviations from the ecliptic. For the epicycle motion about the sun Mercury requires 88 days and Venus 225. These same epicycles served to represent the motions of the sun and moon, which do not display stationary and retrograde motions but are involved in variable velocities.

The course of a planet was also represented by an eccentric circle. By postulating an epicycle, the Greek astronomers very cleverly accounted for the periodic halts apparent in a planet's eastward motion among the stars (the so-called stations), which are followed by brief retrogressions (the planets' motion westward among the stars and their subsequent resumption of their eastward path). The planet thus describes a loop, a circumstance that thoroughly perplexed the ancients, because it defied the Platonic beauty of a perfect circular orbit. We shall see in the Copernican theory that the cause of the loops is easily explained. The earth's motion is more rapid than that of an outside or superior planet, hence in passing it the line of sight from the earth will yield an illusory picture of the outer planet's motion, first in a forward and then in a backward direction. How skillfully the epicycle accounts for these loops will be seen later when we discuss Ptolemy.

During the Hellenistic period, the "Alexandrian school" of astrology came into being. Two of the earliest of its great astrologers, during the period 296–272 B.C., were Aristyllus and Timocharis. But the first man of this school to do something novel was a geographer. He was Eratosthenes, born about 270 B.C. at Cyrene in Africa and called to Alexandria by Ptolemy Euergetes to become a director of the famous library.

Eratosthenes was the first man to estimate accurately the circumference of the earth. His method was as ingenious as it was simple. To the south of Alexandria was the town of Syene (the modern Aswan), 5000 stadia away, according to the royal messengers. At Syene there was a deep well, and on the longest day of the year the midday sun's rays illuminated the bottom of the well, which meant that the sun was vertically over Syene. But at noon on the same day in Alexandria the sun still cast a shadow. By measuring the length of that shadow, Eratosthenes could calculate that the distance from Alexandria to Syene was 1/50 of the total circumference of the earth. Hence he stated, the circumference was 50 times 5000, or 250,000 stadia. The calculations were full of minor mistakes, yet he came astonishingly close, missing by only 481 miles.

The next great name in the history of astrology is Hipparchus, who worked mainly on the island of Rhodes. Most of what we know of his work was preserved by Ptolemy. In consequence, the system of the cosmos with the earth in its center, which Aristotle advocated, is now spoken of as the Ptolemaic system. This is really the geocentric system, but if any man's name is attached to it, it should be that of Hipparchus, who actually developed the theory; Ptolemy merely perpetuated it.

The three treatises of Hipparchus, mentioned by Ptolemy, were entitled *On the Length of the Year, On Intercalation of Months and Days,* and *On the Change of the Solstices and Equinoxes.* The titles give a good idea of the work in which Hipparchus was engaged—calendar work for the most part. He redetermined the lunary period as 29 days, 12 hours, 44 minutes, and 2.5 seconds (about one second too short). The length of the year, according to Hipparchus, was 365¼ days diminished by nearly 1/300 of a day. He was troubled by the realization that his year and a Babylonian year did not agree and tried to find the explanation.

It turned out to be his greatest discovery.

A year could be either the return to the position of a star, or it could be the return to the equinoctial point. Hipparchus, said Ptolemy, "by careful comparison of observed lunary eclipses of his own time with others which had been observed by Timocharis in earlier times, arrived at the result that in his own time Spica preceded the autumn equinox by 6 degrees and in Timocharis' time by 8 degrees." This was the discovery of what is now known as the precession of the equinoxes. The important point of this great discovery was that Hipparchus recognized it as a continuous process and said so very plainly.

Among other activities of Hipparchus was his utilization of an eclipse (the one in 129 B.C. is the most probable) for determining the distance of the moon and the making of the first known catalog of fixed stars. He spent many long hours on theory as well. Hipparchus had no problems with geometrical demonstrations, but he did not have enough actual observations to establish the proper values. At a later date some of the difficulties of the epicycle theory were removed by assuming that, while the earth was obviously the center of the universe, the center of the main circles (the deferents) did not coincide with the center of the earth. But as we know of Hipparchus mainly through Ptolemy it is not certain that this idea originated with him. There is some reason to think it did, but the question cannot be settled definitely.

There has been a great deal of speculation about the kind of instruments available to Hipparchus. The astrologers of his time sighted along a staff of some kind, but did they have graduated circles? The accuracy achieved strongly suggests their existence; indeed it is impossible to see how astrologers could have done without them. But there is no literary documentation of this.

It was through slaves of Greek origin that astrology first infiltrated Rome. These were mostly charlatans without real knowledge, who would predict anything for anyone. Their first success was confined to the lower classes, and educated citizens looked down on such activities. They were derisively

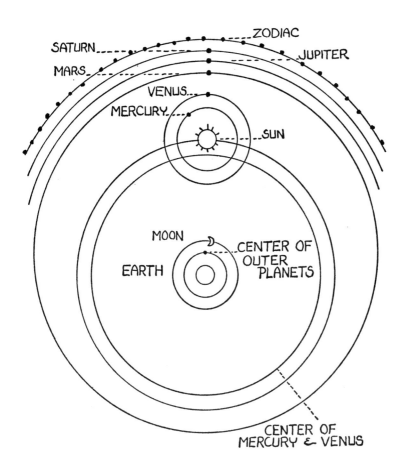

The Eccentric Circle Theory or Theory of Movable Eccentrics of Apollonius (see text for details). By having the center of the outer planets' circle of rotation at one point and the center of the inner planets' circle of rotation at another, the system of movable eccentrics is constructed. Note that the center for Mercury and Venus is the path of the sun itself.

called "astrologers of the circus," because most of their income was from predicting the winners of chariot races.

But the traditional diviners (augurs) of Rome began to feel threatened by the Greek newcomers. They reacted swiftly, and a decree of Cornelius Hispallus expelled from Rome "these Chaldeans who exploit the people under the false pretense of reading the stars." The decree also stated that astrology was an unreliable means of prediction. This decree only helped to strengthen the popularity of astrology.

Under the Roman Republic people were slowly converted to astrology when intellectuals and philosophers began to argue about it. The Stoics, who thought men were toys in the hands of fate, defended astrology. Others, led by the Greek Carneades, opposed it on the grounds that man possessed free will. This idea will come up again in the account of the Christian attack on astrology.

After 139 B.C. Rome entered the troubled period that ended with the fall of the Republic, and this period was favorable to astrology. Marius, Octavius, and later Julius Caesar and Pompey, all had their horoscopes prepared in the greatest detail. There were still a few great men, such as Lucretius and Cicero, who were unrelenting in their opposition to astrology. In his *On Divinations,* Cicero used every valid argument against astrology. Yet when a comet appeared sometime after the death of Julius Caesar, all his objections were brushed aside.

Pliny the Elder in about A.D. 75 devoted but a small fraction of his *Natural History* to the stars and heavens, and had less occasion to speak of astrology than of magic. He recognized, nonetheless, that magic and astrology are intimately related and that "there is no one who is not eager to learn his own future and who does not think that this is shown most truly by the heavens." (The general literature of the time only confirms the widespread prevalence of astrology; allusions of poets imply a technical knowledge of the art on their readers' part; and the very emperors who occasionally banished astrologers from Rome themselves consulted other adepts.) In Pliny's list of prominent men we find the name of Berossus, to whom a statue was erected by the Athenians in honor of his skill in astrological prognostication. In another place where he spoke of the science of the stars, Pliny disputed the theories of Berossus, Nechepso, and Petosiris that the length of human life is ordered by the stars, and also made the trite objection to the doctrine of nativities that masters and slaves, kings and beggars are born at the same moment. He also was inclined to ridicule the enormous figures of 720,000 or 490,000 years set by Epigenes, Berossus, and Critodemus for the duration of astronomical observations recorded by the Babylonians.

But it would not be safe to say that he denied the control of the stars over human destiny. Indeed, in one chapter he declared that the astronomer Hipparchus can never be praised enough because more than any other man he proved the relationship of man with the stars and that men's souls are part of the sky. Pliny disputed the vulgar notion that each man has a star varying in brightness according to his fortune, rising when he is born, and fading or falling when he dies.

Pliny explained thunderbolts as celestial fire vomited forth from the planet Venus and "bearing omens of the future." He also gave instances from Roman history of comets that signaled disaster and he expounded the theory of their signifying the future. What they portend may be determined from the direction in which they move and the heavenly body whose power they receive, and more particularly from the shapes they assume and their position in relation to the signs of the zodiac. He also said that many of the common people still believed that women could produce eclipses by sorceries and herbs.

In the first century we find a favorable attitude toward astrology in those essays by Plutarch that are suspected of being fake or spurious, the *De fato* and *De placitis philosophorum*. The *De fato* repeats the Stoic theory of the *magnus annus* when the heavenly bodies resume their rounds and all history repeats itself. Despite this apparent admission that human life is subject to the movements of the stars, the author of the *De fato* thinks that accident, fortune or chance, the contingent, and what is in us or free will, can all coexist with fate, which he practically identifies with the motion of the heavenly bodies.

One or two bits of astrology may be noted in Plutarch's essays. The man who learned "astrology" among demons in the isle beyond Britain affirmed that in human generation earth supplies the body, the moon furnishes the soul, and the sun provides the intellect. Monstrous animals were produced during the war with the giants because the moon turned from its course then and rose in unaccustomed quarters. Plutarch was, by the way, inclined to distinguish the moon from other heavenly bodies as being passive and imperfect, a sort of celestial earth or terrestrial star.

Galen, the father of experimental physiology and the highest authority on experimental biology and medicine even during the Middle Ages, was the author of a treatise entitled *Prognostication of Disease by Astrology*. This advanced the widespread knowledge of astrological medicine. Galen thought that a physician ought to know and make use of astrology. The moon's stay in each sign of the zodiac and its relation to the other planets had a definite significance for the health and disease of the individual and could serve to predict the nature, causes, and effects of illnesses and afflictions besetting man. In another treatise entitled *Critical*

Days, Galen continued to expound his astrological beliefs not "by reason of dogma, lest sophists befog the plain facts, but solely upon the basis of clear experience."

He also states that the Stoics favored astrology, that the ancients employed the course of the moon in prognostications, and that if Hippocrates had said physicians should know physiognomy, they ought much more to learn astrology, of which physiognomy is but a part. There follows a statement on the influence of the moon in each sign of the zodiac and in its relations to the other planets. On this basis is foretold what diseases a man will have, what medical treatment to apply, whether the patient will die or not, and if so in how many days.

He discusses the moon's phases, holding that they cause great changes in the air, rule conception and birth and "all beginnings of actions." Its relations to the other planets and to the signs of the zodiac are also considered and much astrological technical detail is introduced. But the Pythagorean theory that the numbers of the critical days are themselves the cause of their significance in medicine is ridiculed, as is the doctrine that odd numbers are masculine and even numbers feminine. Later he also ridicules those who talk of seven Pleiades, seven stars in either Bear, and the seven gates of Thebes, or seven mouths of the Nile. Thus he will not admit the doctrine of perfect or magic numbers in his astrological theory. Much of this rather long treatise is devoted to a discussion of the duration of a moon, and it is shown that one of the moon's quarters is not exactly seven days in length and that the fractions affect the incidence of the critical days.

He uses much the same arguments as Ptolemy to assert that the moon governs the earth more than other planets because of its proximity. The phases are, of course, of the greatest potency, producing the changes in the air that govern conception and birth and "all beginnings of action." Galen runs the whole gamut of astrological knowledge in technical detail. To combat superstitions about the number seven he strains his astronomical and astrological knowledge to prove that the periods of the moon's quarters were not quite seven days each. He was an excellent physician, but only a poor-to-average astrologer.

Galen's writings and teachings were marked by brilliant observations and wise treatments as well as by colossal error and, at times, insufferable dogmatism. Yet his books dominated medical thinking and practice for fifteen hundred years, and more than a few of Galen's astute observations are in accord with modern medicine. His errors in medical thought and teaching were not seriously challenged until the stormy Paracelsus, in 1530, the anatomist Vesalius, in 1532, and the physiologist Harvey, in 1628, courageously questioned the infallibility of Galenic authority.

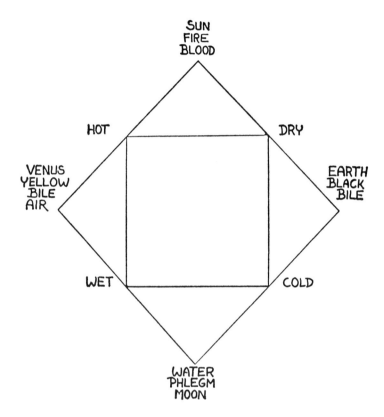

The Galenic concept of the humoral theory of disease in man. This was modified later by Paracelsus in the early sixteenth century.

Galen was born about A.D. 130, in the Greek city of Pergamum in Asia Minor (now Turkey). He was the only child of an engineer and architect, Nicon, a mild, just, and comparatively wealthy man who took a keen interest in the boy's education. His mother, on the contrary, was a shrew, a difficult woman, subject to fits of anger toward servants, and ready to quarrel with her husband. Galen's writings reveal his poor regard for her, but her influence was manifested in his restless, dogmatic temperament.

His father expressed his deepest desires when he named him "Galeno," which means calm or serene. The bright and lively boy's education was supervised by his father on the family farm until he was fourteen. Then he was taken to Pergamum to attend lectures in philosophy and mathematics. To preserve the true spirit of impartiality, his father made him attend courses given by representatives of all four leading philosophic systems of the day. Then, according to Galen's own writings, his father had a dream, influenced by the god Asclepius, which directed that his son should study medicine. Dreams then were taken very seriously and Asclepius was no longer mocked as of old in the days of Hippocrates.

Galen began the study of anatomy in Pergamum at about the age of seventeen, continuing there until his father's death. In fact, he studied until his own health suffered from overwork. After the death of his father, he followed the example of his predecessors and traveled to study at the great centers of learning of the Greek world at Smyrna, Corinth, and Alexandria. He spent a total of nine years adding to his knowledge of medical subjects. About the year 158, Galen, aged twenty-eight, returned to his home town of Pergamum. The head priest of the temple to Asclepius appointed him physician to the gladiators. At each show many gladiators were wounded, and Galen cared for them. This provided him with a great opportunity to study not only practical applications of hygiene and medicine, but living anatomy as revealed by the terrible wounds the contestants suffered during the games.

Galen held the post of gladiatorial physician for four years. Then the restless young doctor departed for Rome, the capital of the known world. There he was a stranger, and the city swarmed with doctors. Some were specialists, charlatans, and competitors, but all seemed to be enemies. Galen sought acquaintances; fortune favored him, and he acquired great fame through spectacular diagnoses and modes of treatment, public lectures, discussions, demonstrations, and writings. His reputation grew to the point where he was called to examine the Roman emperor-philosopher, Marcus Aurelius. Galen's shrewd diagnosis that the emperor was suffering from simple indigestion, as opposed to the complicated illnesses diagnosed by the other physicians on the scene, won him the appointment as court physician.

He made good. Patients of high rank sought his advice. The wife of Flavius Boethus, the consul, was suffering from one of the diseases peculiar to women. Galen promptly cured her, received a fee of four hundred gold pieces, and was appointed physician-in-ordinary to the family. Boethus was greatly interested in medical questions and attended Galen's lectures. Above all he was fascinated by anatomy.

In this field Galen was an expert. A dissecting room was established where Galen demonstrated the anatomy of the lower animals. Boethus was delighted and wanted to have his family doctor's demonstrations put on record. He engaged shorthand writers who took down many verbatim reports. It was in this way that several of Galen's books on anatomy were written.

He had patrons of even greater distinction. One of them was Marcus Civica Barbarus, an uncle of the emperor Lucius Verus; and another was Claudius Severus, son-in-law of Marcus Aurelius. Now that Galen was firmly established as physician to the emperor, his enemies were not able to do anything against him.

Then a strange thing happened in the year 166. Galen the ambitious, now thirty-seven years of age and on the threshold of his greatest triumph, requested his patrons to abstain from mentioning his name to the emperor. Hastily disposing of his household goods, he set out on foot through the Campagna, crossed the peninsula to Brundisium, took a ship for Greece, and then traveled to Pergamum, his native city.

However, Marcus Aurelius soon recalled him from Pergamum to a military camp at Aquileia; then shortly thereafter he was ordered to return to Rome to take over the medical supervision of the emperor's son, Commodus. Galen continued to serve Commodus as a physician when the latter succeeded his father as emperor. About A.D. 192, however, the Roman political climate became so unhealthy for scholars and philosophers that Galen again returned to Pergamum. Presumably he continued to travel and to write until his death eight years later, at the age of seventy.

The medicine Galen practiced, and about which he wrote, was based mainly on the speculative Hippocratic theories of the four humors, on critical days, and on the theories relating to the pulse and urine. These did not give way to more realistic approaches until Paracelsus in the sixteenth century. Despite his mixture of rational science with philosophic speculation, Galen was an excellent observer and shrewd doctor.

The four elements were fire, air, earth, and water. The nine qualities were hot, cold, moist, dry; and the qualities of fire (hot and dry), air (hot and moist), earth (cold and dry), and water (cold and moist)—the ninth quality being the fairly equal distribution of heat, cold, moisture, and dryness in the body of man.

The four humors were blood (hot and moist), phlegm (cold and moist), yellow bile (hot and dry), and black bile (cold and dry). The four members were the fundamental (brain, heart, liver), the subservient (nerves, arteries, veins), the specific (bone, membranes, muscles), and the dependent (stomach, kidneys, intestines). The three faculties were natural, spiritual, and animal. The animal faculties comprised cerebration via imagination (forebrain), cogitation (midbrain), and memory (hindbrain), along with voluntary motion and sensation.

The five operations were the simple: hunger (heat and dryness), digestion (heat and moisture), retention (coldness and dryness), expulsion (coldness and moisture), and the compound (due to appetites and sensations). The three spirits were the natural (from the liver to the body by the veins), the vital (from the heart by the arteries), and the animal (from the brain by the nerves). The ages were youth (hot and moist), manhood (hot and dry), age (cold and dry), and senility (cold and moist). The colors were red, white, yellow, and black according to balance or excess of the humors, and according to external temperature (heat and cold).

The profession of medicine gained a wealth of sound facts and ideas from Galen. Despite conflicting influence on medical schools and philosophic sects, he gave to the world a synthesis of medical thought and astrological medical knowledge solid enough to last nearly fifteen hundred years. His mind was quick and well organized, and he was well informed on many subjects. He continually was open-minded, although he came to be regarded as one of the greatest dogmatists of all time. However, the magnitude of his dogmatism was increased by his followers. During the Middle Ages, when thinking for one's self was not at all fashionable, Galen was accepted as the absolute and infallible master. This was, as George Sarton says, "a creation of the disciples, rather than of the master himself."

But we must leave Galen and pick up the astrological thread again. In the next chapter we shall discuss the greatest astrologer-astronomer of antiquity, Ptolemy. The authenticity of his great work has been questioned—but Franz Boll in 1894 proved that the *Tetrabiblos* was actually written by Claudius Ptolemy and was not spurious.

FIVE

Ptolemy's Cosmology

Because some modern astrologers question the authorship of the *Tetra-biblos, Quadripartitum*, it is well to turn to some solid academic facts at the very beginning of this chapter on Claudius Ptolemaeus. Professor Lynn Thorndike has no doubts about the subject in his classic *A History of Magic and Experimental Science*, and clearly states that it is genuine (Vol. I, p. 110).

The *Tetrabiblos* seems to have been translated into Latin by Plato of Tivoli in the first half of the twelfth century, before *Almagest* or *Geography* appeared in Latin. In the middle of the thirteenth century Egidius de Tebaldis, a Lombard of the city of Parma, translated the commentary of Haly Heban Rodan upon the *Quadripartitum*. In the early Latin editions the text is of medieval translation; in the few editions giving a Greek text there is as well a different Latin translation of this Greek text.

In the *Tetrabiblos* the science of astrology received sanction from perhaps the ablest mathematician and closest scientific observer of the day. From that time on astrology was able to take shelter from any criticism under Ptolemy's authority—not that it lacked other exponents and defenders of great name and ability. Naturally the authenticity of the *Tetrabiblos* has been questioned by modern admirers of Hellenic philosophy. Franz Boll has shown that it is by Ptolemy by comparing it closely with his other works. The astrological *Centiloquium*, or *Kapros*, and other treatises on divination and astrological images ascribed to Ptolemy are probably spurious. German research puts forward Posidonius as the ultimate source of much of the *Tetrabiblos*, but this is not a matter of much consequence.

Some writers have even claimed that Ptolemy only rewrote the *Astronomica* (A.D. 10) of the Roman poet Manilius. This is the oldest known treatise on astrology and was composed during the reign of Augustus. The book is written in verse—with 4,200 verses divided into five books. Because it refers back to the Greek astrologers and their predecessors, it is a compilation of previously known lore and was, most likely, available to Ptolemy. It was in the *Astronomica* that the concept of the Zodiac Man was first clearly mentioned. Each sign was to correspond to a part of the human body. Here is a translation of verses 698 to 706 of Book IV:

The Ram defends the Head, the Neck the Bull, The Arms, bright Twins, are subject to your Rule: I'th' Shoulders Leo, and the Crab's obeyed I'th' Breast, and in the Guts the modest Maid; I'th' Buttocks Libra, Scorpio warms Desires in Secret Parts, and spreads unruly Fires: The Thighs the Centaur, and the Goat commands the Knees, and binds them up with double bands. The parted Legs in moist Aquarius meet, And Pisces gives Protection to the Feet.

But this does not sound remotely like Ptolemy!

Let us now discuss Claudius Ptolemaeus of Alexandria, the greatest astrologer and astronomer of all time. He was born about A.D. 100 at Ptolemaeus in Egypt, but nothing is known about his personal life. He wrote many works, of which two dealing with astronomy have come down to us in the present day—*Almagest* and *Tetrabiblos*. The first is a rich storehouse of all the astronomical antiquity. The second is a mathematical treatment in four parts (or books) dealing with what Ptolemy considered social or applied astronomy.

In Ptolemy's time the two words "astrologia" and "astronomia" meant the same thing; what we now call astrology was called by Ptolemy "prognostication through astronomy." During the period of Persian domination there were many elaborate calculations to explain the movements of the sun, moon, and the complex orbits of the planets. Also, the calendar was undergoing a gradual, steady improvement. Astronomers had observed that the sun moved regularly eastward through the belt of the zodiac. Its path was soon mapped out and four separate points attracted attention. These were the two "equinoxes" and the winter and summer "solstices." The equinoxes were days of equal darkness and light in the spring and fall. The summer solstice was the day the sun at noon was at its highest point in the heavens, and the winter solstice the day the sun at noon was lowest. This concept provided a means of dividing time into years, with each year extending from one spring equinox to the next. The year also could be divided into four seasons, each marked by the sun's distinctive position in the ecliptic of the zodiac.

Astrology first arrived in Greece with the campaigns of Alexander the Great. Chaldean astronomers such as Berossus and Kidenas established schools in Greece after the Alexandrian conquest. They brought with them all the tables, charts, and accumulated knowledge of astrology from Babylonia. Stoic philosophy was ready for this glamorous new arrival from the Orient. The Stoics felt that the universe was a vast "organism" cemented into a coherent unity by forces of sympathy, with fire as the universal principle holding all together. They believed that the bodies were the purest expression of fire in the universe.

Astrology swept across the breadth of the known world and soon became a part of the learning, faith, and folklore of poor and rich alike. Adoration of the sun was its central feature. The sun was given a central position in the universe, long before the Copernican theory was ever hypothesized. The sun was the governor of and reason for the world. The sun god was an abstract image of the active sun; the visible sun was only the material expression of the deity.

Ptolemy agrees, for in the first part of the introduction to the *Tetrabiblos,* he states: "Of the means of prediction through astronomy, O Syrus, two are the most important and valid. One, which is first, both in order and effectiveness, is that whereby we apprehend the aspects of the movements of the sun, moon, and stars [zodiac] in relation to each other and to the earth, as they occur from time to time; the second is that in which by means of the natural character of these aspects themselves we investigate the changes which they bring about in that which they surround." Ptolemy went on to explain that he intended to investigate these changes in a purely philosophical (scientific) way, so that the truth and usefulness of such prognostication might be ascertained.

Ptolemy possessed great insight into the problem of the dichotomy of natural science versus social science: Astronomy was a natural science, while astrology was a social science. The mathematical motion of the heavenly bodies in relation to each other was not useful to man and not nearly as complex as astrology, which *was* useful to man and his daily life.

Astrology dealt with material things that were part of the sublunar (or microcosmos) and that were imperfect and crude, being in the world of man. They did not compare to Plato's perfect form (or macrocosmos), which was surer and purer. Ptolemy was careful to point out how the common man could find it easy to ridicule astrology, but he cautioned that the science should not be abandoned just because it was difficult and hard to understand.

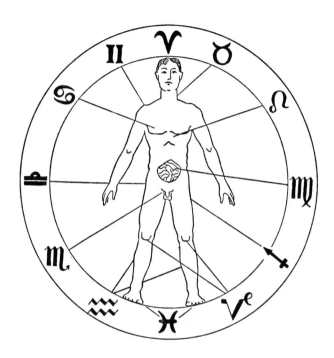

The modern Grand Man of the Zodiac and physical parts of the body ruled by each sign. Aries rules the face, ears, eyes, brain, and all organs above the neck and is in sympathy with the stomach. Taurus rules the neck, throat, eustachian tubes and often creates all kinds of throat troubles. Gemini rules the arms, shoulders, hands, lungs, and bronchial tubes and often produces disease in these parts. Cancer rules the breasts, the stomach and thus its sympathetic action, the lungs and breathing apparatus. Leo rules the heart and is said to govern also the back and spinal column; improper circulation is prominent. Virgo rules the stomach, bowels, and abdomen; reflex symptoms in stomach caused by loss of vital powers. Libra rules the kidneys and bladder, making its subjects susceptible to lower spinal trouble, nervousness. Scorpio rules the sex organs, muscular and excretory system; especially susceptible to sexual disease. Sagittarius rules the hips, legs, liver, and thighs; careful protection should be granted these parts. Capricorn rules the knees; diseases most prevalent are indigestion and melancholy, due to anxiety and worry. Aquarius rules the lower legs, calves, and ankles; subjects its natives to ills affecting the limbs. Pisces rules the feet, and its subjects are susceptible to diseases and excessive perspiration of the feet. You may find it interesting to compare this concept with the Zodiac Man of Manilus (see text).

He made this point very clear: "A very few considerations would make it apparent to all, that a certain power emanating from the eternal ethereal substance is dispersed through and permeates the whole region about the earth which throughout is subject to change." This statement could be compared to the part of the Declaration of Independence that states: "We hold these truths to be self-evident . . ."

One of the main axioms he held self-evident concerned the influence of the sun upon "everything on earth, not only by the changes that accompany the seasons of the year to bring about the generation of animals, the productiveness of plants, the flowing of waters, and the changes of bodies; but also by its daily revolution furnishing heat, moisture, dryness, and cold in regular order and in correspondence with its position relative to the zenith [seasons]."

"The moon," continued Ptolemy, "affects all, for most of them animate and inanimate are sympathetic to the moon. They change in company with her." He explained how the rivers increased and diminished their streams with the strength of the moonlight, how the seas turned their tides with the rising and setting of the moon, and how the plants and animals waxed and waned (fertility cycle) with the moon.

The stars and planets signified hot, windy, and snowy conditions by their positions, and these effects were felt on earth by changes in the weather. As the stars changed so did the seasons. The stars, moon, and planets were in certain variable relationships to each other, while the sun's action was a constant. The changes in the stars and planets modified the constant action of the sun. In this fashion the heavens presented the earth with a variety of effective working forces. All of this was apparent to anyone willing to study the changes in the positions of the sun and stars during the change of the seasons throughout the year.

Ptolemy sought out the weaknesses and shortcomings of astrology and pointed them out for the world to see. These were the actions of the true and honest scientist. He was concerned with facts and deductions, causes and generalizations. All these he examined in the light of reason, being equipped with scientific humility and caution.

It is easy for the modern physical scientist to talk of the superstitious, the supernatural, and the false in evaluating the work of an ancient writer. These moderns feel called upon to classify everything as "good" or "evil", each feature as righteous or sinful. Something within them requires this value judgment! If an ancient viewpoint agrees with their current scientific theory, it is obviously the work of a genius far ahead of his time. If it differs from the modern viewpoint, it is mere superstition and permeated with supernatural rubbish.

Ptolemy was faced with such objections in A.D. 100. He met them head-on in the *Tetrabiblos* and, in so doing, laid the groundwork for the modern science of astrology. A short summary of the four books will show his sound scientific reasoning and pure logical approach. All the possible objections were discussed at length and in detail by Ptolemy in Book I of the *Tetrabiblos*. After acquitting himself of the task of meeting the then current criticisms of astrology, he set out to outline the essence and philosophy of the science of prediction through astronomy.

Book II discussed the procedures for dealing in detail with matters within the limits of accurate prognostication. He pointed out that the predictions were of two kinds—general and specific. The general predictions were swayed by greater and more powerful causes than particular events, which were stronger and more easily foretold (seasons, tides, and floods).

Ptolemy carefully discussed the effect of latitude and longitude on national racial characteristics and the effect of the zodiac belt on the climatic seasons. He concluded Book II with a discussion of the weather and climate for seasons of the year. His discussion of the weather as affected by seasons—thorough and clear cut—was no small task.

Book III dealt with the science of individual and personal prognostications. It was this book that became important in medicine, from the days of Galen to the England of John Locke. Men such as Galen, Avicenna, and even Paracelsus himself followed to a great extent the instructions of Book III of *Tetrabiblos*. They all modified it, but medicine and astrology went hand in glove until the late seventeenth century.

Book IV was concerned with material fortune, riches, honor, and military operations. Ptolemy concluded that general destinies took precedent over special cases and that this principle must be carefully considered when a particular fate was investigated. Cultural, racial, and natural features were not overlooked or confused, for they were essential backdrops for individual prognostication. Ptolemy acquitted himself well in the *Tetrabiblos* and showed logically the scientific basis for prediction by astrology. The sun heats and dries; the moon moistens and putrefies. Mars dries and warms; Jupiter heats and moistens. Venus, between the sun and the moon, warms and humidifies. Mercury vacillates between cold and wet.

Each planet is related to one of the four basic elements: fire, air, earth, and water. Each element has a basic quality: heat, dryness, cold, and wetness. All things are the product of the interaction of these basic qualities. The four regions of the earth and the seasons are products of the four basic qualities. East and autumn are dry, because "when the sun is in that region whatever has been moistened by the night then first begins to be dried." South and summer are hot, and west and spring moist, "because when the sun is therein the things dried out during the day then first become moistened."

North and winter are cold, "because through our inhabited world's inclination it is too far removed from the causes of heat arising from the sun's culmination." Man's temperament is also related to the four basic elements and represents the first medical astrological approach. These complex interrelationships are shown in the illustration.

The zodiacal signs have properties of their own that arise "from their kinship to the sun, moon, and planets." These twelve signs contain six masculine and diurnal signs and six feminine and nocturnal signs in alternated order. Ptolemy was the first to show the great significance of the aspects of signs and planets.

When at an angular distance of 180° the aspects are "Opposition" and the effects are canceling or adverse. When at 120° or "Trine" they are favorable, but at 90° or "Square" they are adverse. Finally, Ptolemy recognizes the "Sextile" position, or 60° apart, as very auspicious. He did not take into account the "Semisextile," or "Quincunx," positions—these were developed later. He did note that signs removed equal distances from the equinoctial points were either "commanding" or "obeying." The signs in which the sun abided in the summer were commanding and those below the equinox were obeying. Signs removed equal distances from the solstices were "equal" and "beheld" each other. Signs that shared none of the relationships were "disjunct" or "alien." Ptolemy's classic descriptions were modified but little by modern astrological science. These classical concepts are too basic to tamper with.

The planets stood in specific relationship to each other and to the various signs of the zodiac. Leo was masculine and assigned to the sun, while Cancer was feminine and assigned to the moon. The planets were beneficent or maleficent and their powers varied according to their positions in relationship to the sun (or their aspects). "Mercury is the ruler of the rational soul, the moon of the animal soul," said Ptolemy. (The concept of the mind and the function of the brain were not known in his day.) The waxing moon at birth produced moisture and a phlegmatic temperament; on her waning she radiated coldness and assisted the earth in producing a melancholy temperament.

"Saturn brings riches through building, or agriculture, or shipping ventures; Jupiter through fiduciary relationships, guardianships, or priesthoods; Mars through military operations and command; Venus through gifts from friends and women; and Mercury through eloquence and grace." Ptolemy went on to state, "Getting rich by inheritance depends on Saturn being in a bicorporeal sign, or in aspect with Jupiter, or holds the application of the moon."

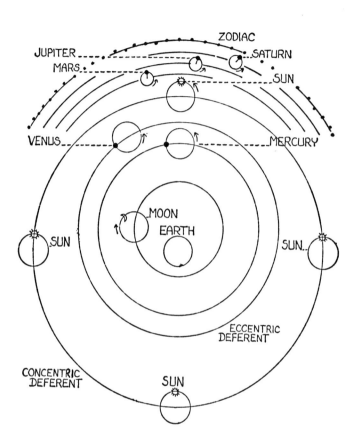

In Ptolemy's system four classes of motion were recognized:

1. The diurnal rotation of the whole heavenly sphere from east to west. In this motion the stars maintain a constant position relative to one another. A heavenly body (moon, star, or planet) west of the sun rises before sunrise. A heavenly body east of the sun sets after sunset.

2. The daily increase of the moon and sun in declination, as they retreat from west to east.

3 & 4. Two independent motions of each planet: one the epicyclic orbit of the planet about an imaginary fixed point; the other, the deferent orbit of this fixed point around the earth. The deferent motion was analogous to the daily increase of the sun's or moon's declination. Planets may have alternate periods in which the R.A. increases daily and slowly diminishes.

The houses as known today were unknown to Ptolemy. Instead, each planet acted directly on the individual by omens. Mercury "makes his subjects scribes, men of business, calculators, teachers, merchants, bankers, soothsayers, astrologers, sacrificers, and, in general, those who perform their functions by means of documents, interpretation, and giving and taking." Saturn "produces a sorry lot of professions, murderers, sneak thieves, burglars, pirates, and villains. Jupiter testifying alone produces men-at-arms, duelists, energetic, clever persons, busybodies, who meddle in others' affairs and thereby gain their living."

Ptolemy developed the theory that "the ages of men are seven in number and ruled by the seven planets." The planets Uranus, Neptune, and Pluto were unknown at that time in Alexandria. Of the seven known planets, the moon and sun were most important for Ptolemy. Their position at the exact moment of birth determined the "very special nature of the body and soul." Finding the fraction of the hour of birth presented great difficulties. Sundials and water clocks were inaccurate; only a horoscopic astrolabe was refined enough. With it, by direct observation of the stars, the sign of the zodiac rising at the moment and the positions of the moon and sun were ascertained. Ptolemy had no emphemeris and no accurate electric clocks to base his horoscopes on. An astrolabe was accurate only to about 2½°, because it had no lenses. Cross hairs and the naked eye were all that was available. Circles were readily divided into arcs of 30°, 15°, 7¼°, and 3¾° by a simple compass alone. Finer measurements were by approximation only.

In comparing a Ptolemaic and a modern horoscope, the changes in the calendar over the years and the shift of the signs of the zodiac by 30° of arc all must be considered. But the major differences are in the accuracy of measurement available today. Degrees and minutes of arc are now commonly used in calculating the planets' positions and the signs of the houses. This practice—coupled with the knowledge of the existence of the planets Uranus, Neptune, and Pluto—produces the greater modern accuracy in interpretation of subtle differences so vital to men's fates. The present-day meanings of houses or "Palaces of the Sky" were developed many years after Ptolemy, yet he was the first to place astrology on a scientific level. His *Tetrabiblos* was the culmination of organized astrological thought in the Graeco-Roman world. It marked the end of the battle against the opposition to astrology.

Ptolemy proved that opposition to the science of astrology on the score of impossibility was undeserved. He stated that many practitioners were poorly trained and made frequent mistakes. This statement of Ptolemy's would apply even today: "Many of its practitioners are in for gain rather than truth or wisdom, and pretend to know more than the facts permit."

Ptolemy also was well aware that honest mistakes were frequently made. Here again he points out a lasting truth: "Science has to be in part conjectural and never absolute." This statement applies not only to the science of astrology, but to all science.

True, astrology did not lead one to riches, fame, and fortune, but neither did philosophy! Some things were performed eternally in accordance with divine unchangeable destiny, while others permitted human interference. Foresight coupled with the study of astrology modified these events and mutated fate. The events Ptolemy regarded as inescapable were those determined by a first cause. The events averted and annulled by human intervention (tempered with knowledge) were those governed by chance and natural sequence.

Even though astrology was his cherished science and though he propounded its lore and logic to the world, Ptolemy very guardedly based all his conclusions on sound scientific and logical reasoning. Ptolemy regarded himself as a practical and conscientious scientist who was merely continuing his task in the field of applied astronomy.

In discussing the causes and nature of lightning he commented: "Lightning portends the future too. Nor do the signs it gives refer only to one or two events. Often a complete series of fate's succeeding decrees is intimated, with proof too plain to demonstration far more distinct than if it were recorded in writing." Again he said: "Anything threatened by unfavorable entrails or inauspicious birds will be canceled by favorable lightning."

"Just in the same way as birds give favorable omens, though they are not moved on their flight for the express purpose of meeting us, God moves them too, it is urged. You imagine He has so little to do that He can attend to trifles of this sort, if you will have Him arrange visions for one, entrails of victims for another." Seneca claims that these signs are directed by divine agency but not with straightforward directness. On the contrary. "Everything which happens is a sign of something that is going to happen. An event which belongs to a series thereby becomes capable of being predicted."

The great influence of the *Tetrabiblos* is shown not only in medieval Arabic commentaries and Latin translations, but more immediately in the astrological writings of the declining Roman Empire. As the culmination of organized astrological thought in the Graeco-Roman world Ptolemy's *Tetrabiblos* marked the end of the battle against the initial opposition to astrology. Men such as Galen had expounded astrological beliefs. Pliny was to make many confusing remarks about astrology in his *Natural History*. He often condemned belief in horoscopes, at times criticized astrological medical practice, and was extremely critical of most of the beliefs and customs of his time. Yet he believed in incantations, magic, omens, and other supernatural ideas. His encyclopedia of natural history shows that he was taken in by many strange phenomena and believed anything strange about the world of animals and plants without question—even the legend of the unicorn.

The Stoic philosopher Seneca (4 B.C.–A.D. 65) ridiculed many of the superstitions of the day. Yet he believed in omens—especially lightning and thunder, for these were two of his favorites. He even said: "The Stars are divine and worthy of worship."

He went on to say: "The Chaldeans confined their observation to the five planets. But do you suppose the influence of so many thousands of other bright stars is nought? The essential error of those who pretend to skill in casting the horoscope lies in limiting our destinies to the influence of a few of the stars, while all that float above us in the heavens claim some share in us. Perchance the lower stars exert their force on us more directly, and the same may be true of the stars that by reason of their more frequent movements turn their view upon man in a different way from that in which it is turned upon other living creatures."

Understand well that Seneca knew science and was not the ordinary old fogy of antiquity. Read his discussions of the rainbow, floods, and clouds to appreciate his greatness and clarity of thought.

Cicero felt that it was good to make predictions on the basis of scientifically obtained knowledge. Then he elaborated and said: "The usual methods of divination are neither reasonable nor scientific." His attack on divination was based on common sense. He asked: "How can the shape of a fat bull's liver have any connection with divine power which ultimately is the cause of all things? Daily experience would speak against such a casual connection." Cicero attacked the science of astrology in exactly the same manner: The influence of the stars on human fate was not real because there was an immense space separating the starry heavens from earth.

These major attacks upon astrology were directed against all magic and science! They were launched by Christianity after the victory over paganism in Rome; yet Christian opposition to science, magic, and astrology was slow in developing. Not until the writings of St. Augustine appeared in the fifth century A.D. did religious opposition become very strong.

Some authors, both modern and ancient, have claimed that Plotinus (204–270) refuted astrology and the casters of horoscopes. But let us see what Plotinus himself says rather than what others have taken to be his meaning. Like Plato, who regarded the stars as happy, divine, and eternal animals, Plotinus believed that the stars have souls and that their intellectual processes are far above the frailties of the human mind and nearer the omniscience of the world soul. Memory, for example, is of no use to them, nor do they hear the prayers that men address to them. Plotinus often called them gods. They are parts of the universe, subordinate to the world soul, although they are able to make other beings better or worse.

In his discussion of the soul Plotinus said: "It is abundantly evident . . . that the motion of the heavens affects things on earth and not only in bodies but also the dispositions of the soul." He also said that each part of the heavens affects terrestrial and inferior objects. He did not, however, think that all this influence could be accounted for "exclusively by heat or cold"—perhaps a dig at Ptolemy's *Tetrabiblos*. He also objected to ascribing the crimes of men to the will of the stars or every human act to a heavenly decision.

For Plotinus, however, the universe is not a mechanical one where only one force prevails. The universe is full of variety and countless different powers, and the whole would not be a living being unless each living thing in it lived its own life. It is true that some powers are more effective than others, that those of the sky are more so than those of the earth, and that many things lie under their power. The constellations in the astrological sense have other powers than those of the bodies that participate in them, just as many plants and stones have marvelous occult powers for which heat and cold will not account. They both exert influence effectively and are signs of the future through their relation to the universal whole. In many things they are both causes and signs, in others they are signs only.

Nor can the gods or stars be said to cause evil on earth, because their influence is affected by other forces. Like the earlier Jewish Platonist, Philo, Plotinus denied that the planets are the cause of evil or change their own natures from good to evil as they enter new signs of the zodiac or take up different positions in relation to one another. He argued that they are not changeable beings, that they would not willingly injure men. To the contention that they are mere bodies and have no wills, he replied that then they can produce only corporeal effects. He then solved the problem of evil by ascribing it to matter, in which reason and the celestial force are received unevenly, as light is broken and refracted in passing through water.

Thus Plotinus arrived at practically the usual Christian position in the Middle Ages regarding the influence of the stars, maintaining the freedom of the human will and yet allowing a large field to astrological prediction. He was more concerned to combat the notion that the stars cause evil or are to be feared as evil powers than he was to combat the belief in their influence and significations. His speaking of the stars both as signs and causes in a way doubles the possibility of prediction from them. If he attacked the language used by astrologers of the planets, and perhaps to a certain extent the technique of their art, he supported astrology by reconciling the existence of evil and of human freedom with a great influence of the stars.

Plotinus reinforced the conception of occult virtue, always one of the chief pillars, if not the chief support, of occult science and magic. On the other hand, men were not likely to reform a language and a technique sanctioned by as great an astronomer as Ptolemy merely because a Neoplatonist questioned their propriety.

In the next chapter we shall see how St. Augustine devoted ten chapters of the Fifth Book of the *City of God* to a refutation of astrology entirely on religious grounds. The views expressed by him marked the height of Christian opposition to astrology. Although Christianity definitely put all science in the wastebasket, astrological folklore dominated the minds of everyone: priest, peasant, and feudal lord.

With man's usual indifference to inconsistency, Ptolemy welcomed a scientific determinism when he wrote *Tetrabiblos; Quadripartitum*, which was a systematic mathematical treatment of astrology. In our own culture of science and technology, one of the fundamental concepts of reality is that fate is dictated by the laws of motion and nature. The great scientists of today are still urged and moved by the emotional needs within them. Now man is again looking upward into the heavens toward the future. Space probes, the question of life on other planets, and the recent trip to the moon of our astronauts have not been considered fantastic or beyond the reach of man.

SIX

The Rejection

The ancient Greeks wove their stories around the stars and constellations in many interesting ways. There were tales of Auriga, the man who invented chariots; Orion; Castor and Pollux, the twins; and Virgo, the maiden who fled from the earth and carried Spica in her sheaf of wheat. And there were tales of many animals too: a whole menagerie of bears, swans, eagles, dogs, bulls—as well as a serpent, a dragon, a rabbit, two fish, a crab, a lion, a scorpion, and many, many others.

All the planets except the earth were named after the gods the ancient Greeks and Romans believed in. Mercury, which travels so swiftly around the sun, was given the name of the messenger of the gods. Venus, which is the brilliant evening star for a part of the time as well as the morning star that shines in the dawn for a part of the time, was named after the goddess of beauty. Mars, which looks reddish from the earth, was given the name of the god of war. Jupiter, the biggest of all the planets, received the name of the chief of all the gods. Saturn was named after the father of Jupiter, and Uranus was given the name of the god of the sky.

The various innovations that the Greeks and the Romans progressively made to astrology would take hundreds of pages to enumerate. Greek mythology describes the Milky Way as being the great road that led to the palaces of the gods clustered about the lofty, cloud-hidden summit of Mount Olympus. In these golden dwellings with their ivory halls and furniture that possessed self-motion dwelt Jupiter, supreme ruler of heaven and earth; Juno, his wife; Mars, the god of War; Venus; Minerva; Mercury; all the other gods and goddesses; and many lesser deities. They drank nectar, poured by Hebe or Ganymede, and ate ambrosia, which gave immortal life. Their statures were immense, for when Jupiter shook the locks of his hair the stars trembled. The gods often disguised themselves as earthly beings and mingled with mankind. At times they issued commands through the voice of an oracle or displayed anger through some exhibition of nature, as when Jupiter threw his mighty thunderbolts.

The names of the five planets then known were Saturn, Jupiter, Mars, Venus, and Mercury, and the custom of naming planets for the gods was also followed when the outer planets Uranus, Neptune, and Pluto were discovered in modern times. These are the Roman names, but the mythology of the Greeks and Romans is so intermingled that the names of their characters often are used interchangeably, although the Roman names seem more popular with astrologers. Many writers on mythology use the Greek names because Roman literature and legends received so much material from Greek poetry.

The planets do not move with the same speed across the sky and they seem to come together, to pass, and overtake one another, assuming different angular positions. We saw in the last chapter how the Greek astrologer-astronomers explained this. They also attached a particular importance to the distances of the bodies in the solar system that happened to be at the apex of simple geometrical figures: the triangle, the square, and the hexagon. Pythagoras' theory of the harmony of spheres was the basis of this new concern. When two celestial bodies are 180° apart at the moment of their appearance on the horizon, this is called an opposition, and it is unfavorable because the influences of the two celestial bodies contradict each other.

The early astrologers divided the heavenly sphere into twelve equal sections, called houses. To give more meaning to the place a planet occupies in the sky, the apparent daily movement of the sun around the earth each twenty-four hours was to the Greek astrologers analogous with the sun's yearly journey. This meant conceiving a special kind of year 365 times shorter than the regular one. By such reasoning they divided the astrological day into twelve parts, in the pattern of the twelve signs of the zodiac. Thus each day the sun passes through the twelve houses 365 times faster·than through the signs of the zodiac; and the planets, which travel through the whole zodiac just as the sun does, cross the twelve astrological houses each day as well.

In his astrological poem *Astronomica*, Manilius described the meanings of these twelve astrological houses, and his descriptions are found without any changes in modern astrological manuals. Because the houses are based on the planetary positions during their daily course, Manilius derived the

Uranus was married to Mother Earth and began in the course of time seriously to consider his numerous and somewhat fearful progeny: the Titans, the one-eyed Cyclopes, and the hundred-handed Hecatoncheires. Foreseeing that his sovereignty might become imperiled, he picked up the Cyclopes and Hecaton-cheires and thrust them out of sight into the Pit of Darkness. Only one was not afraid, a Titan named Saturn who picked up a sharp scythe, wounded his father, and stole the throne.

Saturn made Rhea his queen and ate all the children born to them lest they in turn take the throne. By the time Jupiter, her sixth child, was born, Rhea was aroused to such a point of opposition that she had him hidden on the island of Crete. Here he was fed on honey, milk, and ambrosia while his attendants danced and chattered and kept up a perpetual din to drown the noise of his wailing. This concealment was necessary because his uncles, the Titans, had now become powerful and had decreed that not one of Saturn's heirs but one of them would succeed to the throne. Still, during Saturn's reign there was so much happiness in the world it was called the "Golden Age." Hesiod mentions five ages: the Golden, simple and patriarchal; the Silver, voluptuous and godless; the Brazen, warlike, wild, and violent; the Heroic, an aspiration toward the better; and the Iron, in which justice, piety, and faithfulness vanished from the earth. Ovid omits the Heroic Age. The Golden Age was said to be governed by Saturn; the Silver, by Jupiter; the Brazen, by Neptune; and the Iron, by Pluto. An "Age" was regarded as a division of the great world year, which would be completed when the stars and planets had performed a revolution around the heavens, after which destiny would repeat itself in the same series of events. Thus mythology was brought into astrology.

Jupiter ruled during the Silver Age and was the greatest of the deities, the
king of gods and men; he watched over the state and family; his hand wielded
the lightning and guided the stars. In short, he regulated the whole course
of nature. Because the world soon became far enough advanced to understand
natural phenomena, he was also the last of the Olympian rulers.

Mercury, a son of Jupiter, was a somewhat mischievous but charming young man with wings fixed to his helmet and sandals, and he held in his hand a rod that quieted all disputes. He was messenger, herald, and ambassador for Jupiter. It was discovered by astronomers that the smallest of the planets, named in honor of the god Mercury, not only resembled a drop of "quicksilver," but also possessed the "winged shoe" characteristic of its namesake, for it speeds along at the rate of more miles per second than any other planet.

Venus, the beautiful goddess of Love, has been the inspiration for painters, poets and sculptors in every corner of the world.

> But light as any wind that blows,
> So fleetly did she stir,
> The flower she touched on dipt and rose,
> And turned to look at her.
> —Tennyson.

One of the most famous statues of her is the Venus de' Medici preserved in the Uffizi Gallery at Florence. This statue, which was dug up in several fragments during the seventeenth century, is the work of Cleomenes, an Athenian who flourished about 150 B.C. Venus was called Aphrodite by the Greeks, from *aphros,* meaning foam. Some poets have told how the foam itself suddenly turned iridescent, trembled, and from its center rose the lovely Venus. Others tell how a closed shell tinted like a rose floated to the top of a billow, where it opened and disclosed the pearly daintiness of the goddess.

In Greek mythology Mars was worshiped as a warrior in splendid armor, his name being quite appropriate for the red-tinged planet that shines as a brilliant, fiery star. Discord was envisioned as running before him in tattered garments while Anger and Clamor followed in his train. The names of Deimos and Phobos, children of Venus and Mars, were given to the two satellites (or moons) of his planet, although they were not discovered until modern times.

Neptune ruled during the Brazen Age and was the god of the sea. Around
Neptune's palace waved lawns of seaweed and trees of coral; the currents were
the breezes that fanned and cooled his brow. His scepter was a trident with
which he raised and stilled storms; his chariot was a shell drawn by brazen-
hoofed sea horses. Dolphins, Tritons, and sea monsters made sportive homage
about his watery path, and sea nymphs played among his rocks and grottoes
or sat on the shore in the moonlight drying their long hair. Neptune married
one of these, a lovely dark-eyed nymph named Amphitrite, and made her goddess of the sea. The dolphin that carried him during his courtship was rewarded by being placed on a diamond-shaped group of stars that has ever
since been called Delphinus (the Dolphin).

The kingdom of Pluto, the ruler of the shades, was a level, cloudy country under the ground and was inhabited by pale, fleeting shadows, the spirits of those who had died in the country above. Across the meadows of this dreary land meandered the river of Sighs and the river of Forgetfulness. The flaming river of Phlegethon, with its sulphurous smoke and waves of fire, flowed in an endless circle about the walls of Tartarus, where the wicked groaned and clanked their chains. If a soul was not condemned by the three judges, who weighed the good and evil deeds in their scales, it was led to a place of happiness called the Elysian Fields, which was supposed to be next to Tartarus. The gates to Pluto's regions were guarded by a fiendish dog with three heads, but there were a number of pathways leading to the upper world—for strange vapors drifted out of an unexplored cave in southern Italy and both Hercules and Orpheus went down through caves in Greece to:

> Pluto, the grisly god, who never spares,
> Who feels no mercy, who hears no prayers.
> ——Homer.

meaning of the fourth house from its position directly beneath the earth, at the lowest point of the daily astral round. In Book II he said:

> In the nether part of the sky, at the lower pivot of the world from which the whole circle can be seen above, this house is situated in the middle of the night. Saturn, whose rule over the gods was overthrown, who lost the throne of the universe, exercises his power in those depths. As a father he influences the fate of fathers, and the destiny of the aged is also under his control.

The heritage left by Ptolemy and his successors at Alexandria did not endure. Of the great library and museum there not a stone remains. Enlarged by Augustus and enriched by Hadrian, it suffered grave losses and destruction at the hands of the beautiful but ruthless Syrian queen Zenobia, in A.D. 270. In the next century it was deserted by many of its scholars, who could no longer endure the theological wrangling that split the city; they migrated to Constantinople, where a new library was established. The Alexandrian library continued to function, probably in a depleted state, until Cyril was elected patriarch of Alexandria A.D. 411. As soon as he was appointed this bigoted zealot attacked anything he considered unorthodox or irregular. He evicted one Christian sect from their homes and deprived its bishop of his personal belongings. Jews were driven from their synagogue and his followers were allowed to plunder it. Eventually Cyril turned his attention to the library. In the belief that it was the repository of heathen teachings and pagan ideals, Cyril caused a mob to be incited to such a degree that the library was set on fire and its director, Hypatia, an elegant and scholarly woman mathematician, was brutally murdered. The intellectual tolerance of Greece was gone and forgotten!

This avoidance of anything scientific was not the view of every Christian, and throughout the history of the Church there were those who believed all knowledge was good because it helped to perfect the mind. Clement of Alexandria, born about A.D. 150, advocated such a view which was adhered to by his pupil Origen and later taught by St. Augustine. Although Augustine was converted to Christianity by St. Ambrose, no doubt his earlier education at Carthage led him to support an enquiring outlook and to recommend all men to examine the rational basis of their Christian faith. Yet in spite of such advocacy the bogeyman of pagan philosophy continued to loom large, and the pursuit of knowledge about the natural world was considered of only secondary importance.

The general outlook of the time about every aspect of nature was very different from what it is today and was more foreign to our own way of thinking than the attitude of Aristotle. Throughout the early centuries of western Christendom there was a strong tendency to see in every natural thing a symbolism that reflected some facet or other of the Christian faith, and to use it for an illustration of moral purpose. From the time of Pythagoras, it was the fashion to use animal subjects to underline lessons in human ethics. This became so much a part of everyday thinking that a study of the natural world was expected to provide a new insight into God's moral purpose and the salvation of mankind.

Thus it was more important to realize that the moon was an image of the Church reflecting the light of God than to bother about such details as its path in the sky. It was more significant to consider the life of the phoenix as a symbol of the risen Christ than to enquire as to whether its existence was true or false. Scientific and critical faculties were dulled. Some thinkers even returned to the idea of a flat earth. One of the early Christian opponents of astrology must now be considered, for he influenced religious thought for centuries.

St. Augustine (354-430) in the *Christian Doctrine* stated: "From this genus of pernicious superstition [come] those who are called *genethliaci* from their consideration of natal days and now are also popularly termed *mathematici*." He held that they enslaved human free will by predicting a man's character and life from the stars and that their art was a presumptuous and fallacious human invention. If their predictions came true, this was due either to chance or to demons who wished to confirm mankind in its error.

In his youth, when a follower of the Manichaean sect, St. Augustine was a believer in astrology. Perhaps on this account he felt in his old age the more bound to warn his readers against astrology. In his works he often attacked the casters of horoscopes—especially in the opening chapters of the fifth book of *The City of God*. This fairly elaborate discussion included almost all the arguments he advanced elsewhere. Although he did not originate the arguments, his presentation of them was perhaps the best known of the Middle Ages.

As a matter of fact, St. Augustine's objection to astrology as fatalistic does not set him apart from the astrologers' point of view, for he was the great advocate of divine prescience and predestination. In *The City of God* he held that the world was governed not by chance or by fate—a word that for many men means the force of the stars—but by divine providence. He accused the astrologers of attributing the cause of human sin and evil to the spotless stars or to the God whose orders the stars obediently follow. Then he realized that astrologers would answer that the stars simply signify and in no way cause evil, just as God foresees but does not compel human sinfulness.

Thus diverted from his attempt to show how astrologers enslaved the human will, St. Augustine adopted another line of argument—that from the twins, an old favorite. This he twisted first one way and then another, proposing to the astrologers a new series of dilemmas as he found them likely to escape from the preceding one. He seemed to have been impressed by the thought that persons were born at the same instant, and thus with the same horoscope, whose subsequent lives and characters were different. He used Esau and Jacob as examples and stated that he himself had known of twins of dissimilar sex and life. Moreover, he stated in his *Confessions* that he was finally induced to abandon his study of the books of the astrologers (the arguments of "Vindicianus, a keen old man, and of Nebridius, a youth of remarkable intellect," had failed) by hearing from another youth that his father, a man of wealth and rank, was born at precisely the same moment as a certain wretched slave on the estate.

Both Celsus and Origen, about the second century A.D., had closely associated their thinking with the world of invisible spirits—whether angels, demons, or the visible heavenly bodies. Thus they lead us from magic, which Origen makes so dependent upon demons, to the subject of astrology. Celsus censured the Jews, and by implication the Christians, for worshiping heaven and the angels and even apparitions produced by sorcery and enchantment, while at the same time they neglected what in his opinion formed the holiest and most powerful part of heaven, namely, the fixed stars and the planets. They "prophesy to everyone so distinctly, through whom all productiveness results, the most conspicuous of supernatural heralds, real heavenly angels." This shows that Celsus was much more favorably inclined toward astrology than toward magic and less skeptical about its validity.

Origen represented Celsus—and furthermore the Stoics, Platonists, and Pythagoreans—as believing in the theory of the *magnus annus*. According to this theory, when the celestial bodies all return to their original positions after the lapse of many thousands of years, history will begin to repeat itself and the very same events will occur and the same persons live over again. Origen also complained that Celsus regarded the Chaldeans as a divinely inspired nation, whereas Origen considered them the founders of "deceitful genethlialogy." Celsus identified the Magi with the astrologers, but Origen regarded them rather as the founders of magic.

Origen was opposed both to the art of casting horoscopes and thus determining the entire life of the individual from his nativity and to the theory of the *magnus annus*. He was convinced that to admit their truth was to annihilate free will, but he was far from having freed himself fundamentally from the astrological attitude. Indeed he still showed vestiges of the old pagan tendency to worship the stars as divinities. He was convinced that the celestial bodies were not mere fiery masses, as Anaxagoras had taught, but that the body of a star was both material and ethereal.

In various collections of medieval manuscripts there is to be found a treatise on fifteen stars, fifteen herbs, fifteen stones, and fifteen figures engraved on the stones, which was attributed sometimes to Hermes, presumably Trismegistus, and sometimes to Enoch, the patriarch, who "walked with God and was not." In the prologue to a Hermetic work on astrology in one medieval manuscript we are told that Enoch and the first of the three Hermeses or Mercuries were identical. It is interesting to note that Enoch's reputation as an astrologer, which led the Middle Ages to ascribe this treatise to him, is similarly expressed in "the first notice of a book of Enoch," which stated that Enoch was the founder of astrology. The statement in Genesis that Enoch lived 365 years also led men to associate him with the solar year and stars.

The *Book of Enoch* was the precipitate of a literature, once very active, that revolved around Enoch, and the form that has come down to us is a patchwork from "several originally independent books." The Enoch literature has much to say about angels and implies that they control nature, man, and the future. We are told of Raphael, "who is set over all the diseases and wounds of the children of men," of Gabriel, "who is set over all the powers," and of Phanuel, "who is set over the repentance and hope of those who inherit eternal life." The revolution of the stars is described as "according to the number of the angels." The stars themselves are often personified, and we read of "how they keep faith with each other" and even of "all the stars whose privy members are like those of horses."

The fallen angels in particular are mentioned in the *Book of Enoch*. Two hundred angels lusted after the comely daughters of men and bound themselves by oath to marry them. After having taken unto themselves wives, they instructed the human race in the art of magic and the science of botany—or to be more exact, "charms and enchantments" and "the cutting of roots and of woods."

In another chapter individual angels are named who teach to enchanters and botanists the breaking of charms, astrology, and various aspects of the occult. The revelations include not only magic arts, witchcraft, divination, and astrology, but also natural sciences such as botany and pharmacy— which were apparently regarded as closely akin to magic. The treatise also tells about useful arts such as mining metals, manufacturing armor and weapons, and "writing with ink and paper"—"and thereby many sinned from eternity to eternity and until this day."

Like other great religions the Jewish religion had a belief in spirits of various kinds, some of which were angels. The holy men of the Old Testament engaged in encounters with evil magicians. Moses and Aaron were involved in contests with the magicians of the pharaoh, during which the rod of Aaron turned into a serpent that swallowed those produced by the rival magicians. Under the command of the Lord they placed ten plagues on the Egyptians in a miraculous fashion. Elias (Elijah) fought with the priests of Baal, and was able to set fire to a sacrifice in a supernatural manner. Balaam was a soothsayer; speech was miraculously given to his ass, and he himself prophesied the Messiah, saying a star shall come out of Jacob and a scepter out of Israel. The raising of the spirit of Samuel by the witch of Endor, on being consulted by Saul, was another example of the magic of the Old Testament. The most remarkable feat of all was that of Josue (Joshua), who made the sun stand still—the meaning of which has been variously interpreted by many commentators.

The Jews carefully distinguished between the external, or exoteric, features of their belief and the internal, or occult or esoteric, features. They marked out three grades of knowledge: (1) the law, expounded in the Old Testament and particularly in the first five books, the *Pentateuch,* ascribed to Moses, which was supposed to be learned by all Jews; (2) the *Talmud,* which was studied by all priests and learned rabbis; and (3) the cabala (*Kabalah* or *Kabbalah* [QBLH]), which was the secret knowledge imparted only to highly learned initiates. Even today it is only partly revealed in writing.

However, the cabala is the great repository of all Jewish occult knowledge. In medieval times it had a tremendous influence on theologians and magicians, whether Jewish, Christian, or Moslem. It is still taught and revered in arcane schools surviving to this day. The cabala is a complete system of symbolism, angelology, demonology, and magic. It discusses reincarnation and messianism, which latter has become a bone of bitter contention between Jews and Christians. It was alleged by the Christians that the cabala contained the whole of Christian theology. It also must be noted that some Jewish philosophers rejected the cabala altogether and called into question its fundamental assumptions. Among these were Moses Maimonides (1135–1204), whose *Guide to the Perplexed* was reprinted in recent times, and Heinrich Graetz (1817–1891), the great Jewish historian.

The cabala is an unwritten tradition and should be learned from one who is not only a profound Hebrew scholar, but who also possesses a flair for the occult. This particularly applies to the use of the cabalistic law of correspondences, for the cabalists believe that every word, every letter and every point in the Old Testament script has a meaning and therefore cannot be altered in the slightest. The writer once heard a learned cabalist quote Jesus (from the New Testament) as a learned rabbi: "Till heaven and earth pass, one jot or tittle shall in no wise pass from the law, till all be fulfilled." The cabalists believe that there are many important correspondences between words and sentences, letters and numbers, and letters and other letters.

The Victorian schools of French and English cabalism were inclined to claim that all occult sciences were rooted in the secret tradition of Israel. But it seems more correct to say that the cabala was grafted onto some of them: In this manner we have cabalistic astrology.

It is in ceremonial magic that a cabalistic origin is completely accepted in the western world. The case of astrology is somewhat like that of alchemy. Its history and literature contain little to connect it essentially with early Jewry, apart from the casual traditions and expressed condemnation of the *Zohar*. Astrology is an exact science and this seems to suggest only a few possible analogies with the speculations of a theosophical system such as the cabala.

All western peoples have a double line of ancestors: their own forefathers and the Eastern civilizations. Both sets of ancestors have contributed much to modern methods of astrological prophecy. Indeed, only very few prophetic beliefs are original to any given group of people because most beliefs are mankind's common cultural heritage. Philosophy was transmitted to us along the paths of civilization from the ancient East via Greece and Rome. This is especially true in the case of the most scientific and most common branch of prophecy, astrology.

There are two facts about challenge. First, the Jews were much addicted to astrology; and second, the prophetic science of the stars derived something from the later Hebrews. Against these must be placed two other facts: first, that ancient Israel contributed very little to the science of astronomy (Jewish astrological writings came chiefly from Arabia); second, astrology in Jewry during the cabalistic period was embedded in metaphysical notions and mystical processes.

We are not to deal here with the whole history of Jewish astrology and prophecy. But we know that Josephus traces astrology to Seth and assures us that he himself visited the two famous pillars reported to have survived the deluge and flood—the pillars on which all the rules of astrology were engraved. Josephus may have been deceived easily, or he may have been tempted to claim precedence in astrology for his nation. Seth and the pillars set aside, however, we know that ancient Chaldea was a great center of astrology. We know that astrology flourished among the Babylonians and that it was practiced in Egypt. It is natural to suppose that the Jews acquired some of the knowledge of these peoples.

There may have been even a cabala of astrological procedure. All this speculation, however, is beside the real question.

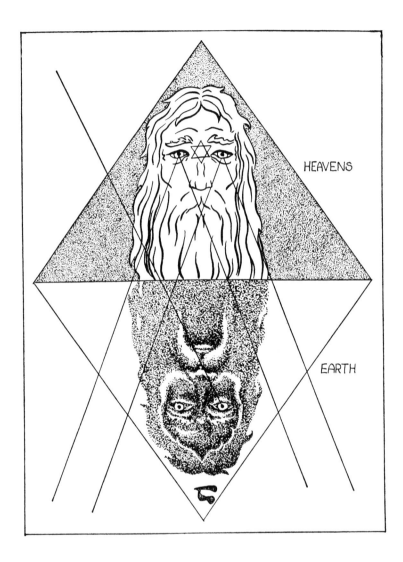

The Magical Head of Zohar: In the book *Zohar* we may read: "Throughout the expansion of the sky which encircles the world, there are figures: Signs by which we may know the secrets and the most profound mysteries. These Signs are formed by the constellations which are to the sage a subject for contemplation."

Astrology works upon scientific knowledge that is very obscure in its origin and history. There are doctrines connected with it that even the "occult student" may find insufficiently grounded in fact. It would be interesting to see whether these doctrines have any cabalistic correspondences, in spite of the veiled condemnation of the *Zohar*.

It was thought that some astrological theorems might have had a connection with cabalistic symbolism. Let us see what was said by early students of the subject.

The attribution of metals to the "Sephiroth" in Mezareph suggests a planetary attribution, and a tabulation was constructed:

1. Kether corresponds to the Empyrean.
2. Chokmah corresponds to the Primum Mobile.
3. Binah corresponds to the Firmament.
4. Chesed corresponds to Saturn.
5. Geburah corresponds to Jupiter.
6. Tiphereth corresponds to Mars.
7. Netzach corresponds to the Sun.
8. Hod corresponds to Venus.
9. Jesod corresponds to Mercury.
10. Malkuth corresponds to the Moon.

It is possible that, as Mezareph affirms, "All systems tend to the one truth." But this scheme is not in accordance with its own attributions. Later students referred Mars to Geburah and Mercury to Hod. When there is no agreement we must not infer that no importance is involved. Attributions and tabulations of this kind have little application to predictive astrology itself.

In modern times, however, all divinatory practices that possess or suggest astrological connections have received some kind of cabalistic attribution. Thus the planetary correspondences of the figures used in geomancy were adjusted to the "Sephiroth." Cabalistic principles were applied to chiromancy. Physiognomy (possibly because it has never been taken up by scientific occultists) is the exception.

What can we say about prophecy and the cabala? Where does it fit into occult science, if not into scientific astrology? It is a doctrine of theosophy that states that the Deity became active and creative to justify all existence. Activity, prophecy, and creativity come through the medium of the ten sephiroth (wisdoms). These are symbolic of man, both primordial and heavenly. Earthly man is but the shadow of the other two. These three form a triad and represent intellectual, moral, and physical qualities.

David and Solomon were the greatest of the students of the cabala. By careful study and revelation they became true prophets, able to use the cabala as a bridge from the known to the unknown. The cabala is thus a mystical doctrine of interpretation and a storehouse of occult knowledge.

The cabala was the hidden secret source for prophecy used by the Magi. It is the key to the explanation of the macrocosm (universe) and the microcosm (man). It is a book that explains the how and why. But astrology is the science of interpretation of the signs and planets. The cabala reveals the reasons for and wisdom behind the harmony of the world above and the earth below. It was the basis for the philosophy of Pythagoras and numerical correspondence.

Space, time, laws, justice, love phenomena—everything in the cabala has its numerical harmony. It is through numbers that the cabala becomes the study of universal harmony and also of man's universal struggle.

The cabala is also the great art of secret relationships. Open a book like the *Formulary of High Magic* by Pierre Piobb, one of the most important and most remarkable books that have ever been compiled, and you will discover that it contains more than one shock for the unprepared reader. You will find a brief sketch of these cabalistic relationships.

For instance, in the Hebrew alphabet there are relationships between the letter, its number, its meaning, its leaf of Tarot, its sign of the zodiac, its sacred name, and its symbol.

In geometry there is a relationship between each figure and its symbol.

In astrology there is a definite relation between the signs of the zodiac, the planets, metals, colors, plants, animals, perfumes, parts of the body controlled, and various magical virtues.

And so in everything else—always the law of analogy is held supreme.

The language of the cabala is symbolical. A whole lexicon might be extracted from the *Zohar*. The technique of the cabala is most complicated, for it is divided into three main groups: Gematrics (relations between different conceptions, based on the equivalent of the value of the letters); Notaries (forming new words with the initials of the word to be interpreted); and Themura (substitution for certain letters of others according to various cabalistic combinations).

The holy cabala thus explains the how and why of "As it is above—it must be below." But it is not astrology—it is theosophy!

The attempt made in 1875 by the foundation of the Theosophical Society to extend and centralize the study of oriental occult philosophy has, in spite of its checkered history, succeeded to a large extent. If we disregard certain claims advanced by the founders and if we regard the society rather as it assumed to regard itself—namely, as an organization designed to promote a neglected branch of knowledge—we have only to survey its literature of the past fifty years to see how large a field it has succeeded in covering. No student should overlook this fact, as the Theosophical Society possesses at least the aspect of importance that it will be useful to see how far the expositions of eastern philosophy connect with the subject of the cabala.

The cosmology and metaphysics of Jewish esoteric tradition were regarded, roughly speaking, by Madame Blavatsky as reflections of derivatives of an older knowledge and a higher teaching that existed from time immemorial in the far East.

As the founder of the Theosophical Foundation and author of *Isis Unveiled* and *The Secret Doctrine*, Madame Blavatsky used an enormous amount of material, but not very wisely. On the one hand, she offered information we are not able to check because we do not know her authorities; on the other hand, she occasionally made statements with which it is difficult to agree.

She distinguished between the ordinary, or Judaistic, and the universal, or Oriental, cabala. If little is known of the one, there is nothing, at least nothing that is definite, known of the other. She implies that its adepts were few, but that the sages who first discovered the starry truths that shone on the great Shemaia of Chaldean lore have solved the absolute and are now resting from their grand labor. Such a statement we cannot check, and for any critical study of the Jewish cabala it has no weight; it may be taken only to indicate a feeling of value or ideals among certain occultists. It may be accepted as evidence because the term cabala signifies an oral reception and has come to be used in connection with almost any unwritten knowledge. Such a course is very inexact and misleading, but the same abuse of words was found in Paracelsus and many other later writers.

The Christians and Jews were not the only ones to reject astrology for magic and other occult arts. In the East a new religion was developing which would have a profound effect on the science of astrology.

The prophet Mohammed was born in 570 and died in 632. He preached a simple monotheistic faith, commanding war against all unbelievers, with the promise of a paradise full of physical pleasure for the faithful. His teachings were taken literally by his followers, who set out to conquer the world for Islam.

The story of the Mohammedan conquests is one of almost incredible speed. In 634 Syria was invaded from Arabia and subdued by 637; then Persia was invaded and conquered within three years; India and Turkey were attacked in rapid order.

The sons of the prophet made a great surge westward, but although they conquered Egypt in 642, it was not until almost 700 that Carthage fell, and not until about ten years later that the greater part of Spain was overcome. Yet in little more than sixty years they had subdued the Middle East. The westward march of Islam was only halted at the battle of Tours in 732.

During this period of Islamic expansion the library and school at Alexandria received their death blow, for Caliph Omar's armies destroyed them completely in 640 when they conquered Egypt. The reason given for destroying the library was that the books it contained were either heretical in that they disagreed with Mohammed's teaching as enshrined in the Koran or that they were superfluous because they were in accord with it. In either case destruction was their proper fate!

Consolidation of this new empire began about 740, and the conquerors settled down to learn and cultivate the arts of peace. The caliphs, the successors of Mohammed, ruled in Baghdad and gathered around them the greatest scholars of every kind and of many religious outlooks. One of the pressing problems to be solved was that of a calendar for civil affairs that could give reckonings based on the moon. Mohammed, like the Jews, had used lunar determinations exclusively for religious purposes.

Thus astronomy and astrology came out of cold storage and slowly began to revive. Observations were made, and the books that had been well enough hidden to escape the two attacks on the Alexandrian library were once again brought into the light of day. Caliph Harun-al-Rashid, who was immortalized in the *Arabian Nights,* provided funds and encouragement for many scholars. Early in the ninth century his son, Caliph Al-Mamun, established a "House of Wisdom," where translations were made of many Greek texts, Ptolemy's *Almagest* and *Tetrabiblos* in particular. The scholars of the House of Wisdom were not, however, allowed to while away their time merely translating and discussing the works of the great Greek authors. Al-Mamun set them to work measuring distances along the meridian, redetermining the size of the earth, and inventing a suitable calendar. Many of the great Greek medical books were translated and the humoral theory was revived.

Avicenna (ibn-Sina, 980–1037) was the most famous moslem authority on medicine and a close follower of Galenic medicine, basing his anatomical writings on Arabic translations of Galen. He also put his faith in astrology and alchemy, as shown by his recommending gilding and silvering pills, not only to mask the bad smell or taste, but also because he believed in blood-purifying effects of these noble metals. In *The Arabian Nights* the slave girl Tawaddud gives an account of Arabian medicine, which well summarizes Avicenna's teaching:

> She replied, "Adam was called Adam, because of his *udmah,* that is, the wheaten colour of his complexion and also (it is said) because he was

created of the *adim* of the earth, that is to say, of the surface-soil. His breast was made of the earth of the *ka'abah*, his head of earth from the East and his legs of earth from the West. There were created for him seven doors in his head, viz., the eyes, the ears, the nostrils and the mouth, and the two passages, before and behind. The eyes were made the seat of the sight-sense, the nostrils the seat of the smell-sense, the ears the seat of the hearing-sense, the mouth the seat of the taste-sense and tongue to utter what is in the heart of man. Now Adam was made of a compound of the four elements, which be water, earth, fire, and air. The yellow bile is the humour of fire, being hot-dry; the black bile that of the earth, being cold-dry; phlegm that of water, being cold-moist. There were made in men three hundred and sixty veins, two hundred and forty-nine bones, and three souls or spirits, the animal, the rational and the natural, to each of which is allotted its proper functions.

Avicenna discussed the four elements and their relation to each other in the *Visionary Recital*. A contemporary Persian commentary on this treatise states:

He constituted these four elements in such wise that they change into one another: earth becomes water, and water becomes earth. Water becomes air, and air becomes water. Air becomes fire, and fire becomes air. Because of this divine solicitude, and through the nature of these four elements, an edge of the water became earth and then rose, while an edge of the earth became water and then sank. And this is the second mixture of the elements one with another. When the mountains were formed, mines of all kinds were also formed in them: gold, silver, jacinth, iron lead . . .

Know lastly that the more the mixture of these things one with another progresses, the further they depart from their simple and elemental nature that opposes them to one another, and the more they tend to find their harmony and equilibrium in the human being. When the mixture became better, animals of all kinds made their appearance: some that are engendered, others that hatch.

Avicenna was a man of the world, a statesman and physician by day, but ready at night to forsake philosophizing for feasts, old wines, fresh maidens, and the guitar. He did this more ardently, perhaps, than was good for his health. His career was a series of ups and downs—at one time in princely favor and at another in prison. He died at the age of fifty-eight, his bodily powers exhausted. However, he left behind a great number of works and his fame was greater than any of the other scholars of his day. He was himself an Aristotelian, and was regarded by posterity as the second Aristotle.

The Arabian legacy to our civilization is vast: fireworks, gardens and

palaces, geology, algebra, ceramics, botany, and medical chemistry. The
Arabs discovered various acids, silver nitrate, benzoin, saffron, camphor,
and laudanum. They developed alchemical techniques such as crystalliza-
tion, distillation, and sublimation. Their high rate of blindness from
trachoma led them to make a thorough study of human vision and optics.
Avicenna proposed a wave theory of light based on his studies of the rainbow, and his idea of the workings of the human eye was later accepted
by Roger Bacon (1214–1294). Dante's attitude in the *Divine Comedy*
was to put Mohammed in hell, but he placed Avicenna in Limbo, for
Dante was not a Thomist pure and simple and he owed too much to the
Arabic philosopher-physician.

Throughout the twelfth century may be traced the transit to north-
western Europe of learning from the Arabic world, and more particularly
from the Spanish peninsula. Three points may be made concerning this
transmission: It involved Latin translation from the Arabic; the matter
translated was largely mathematical, or more especially astronomical and
astrological in character; and it was often experimental.

The real attack upon astrology, directed also against magic or science
in general, was launched by Christianity after its victory over paganism
in Rome. The reasons are quite understandable. Christianity brought with
it new concepts: social justice, the nobility of love of man, kindness, self-
effacement, love of God, the insignificance of earthly life, and the imminent return of Christ. Science, or rather, awareness and knowledge of
the material world, lost the attraction it had held for the Greeks and Romans and sank into oblivion.

Only a few things mattered—love of God and man, the millennium,
the kingdom of heaven! Why worry about the puny things of this vale of
tears when there was glory and eternity in the offing after death—or fire,
brimstone, and eternal hell? Life tomorrow—in the hereafter—that was
what was important.

Even the Jews lost interest in astrology. Moses Maimonides (1135–
1204) was well acquainted with the art of astrology, for he asserted that
he had read every book in Arabic on the subject. Maimonides not only
believed that the stars were living, animated beings and that there were
as many pure intelligences as there were spheres, but he stated in the
Guide for the Perplexed that all philosophers agreed that this inferior
world of generation and corruption was ruled by the virtues and influences
of the celestial spheres. While their influence was diffused through all
things, each star or planet also had a particular species especially under
its influence.

He held that the movement of the celestial sphere starts every motion
in the universe and that every soul has its origin in the soul of the celes-

tial sphere. In his letter on astrology to the Jews of Marseilles he repeated what all the philosophers and Hebrew masters held, that whatever was in this inferior world the blessed God had brought about by the virtue that arises from the spheres and stars. As God performs signs and miracles by angels, so natural processes and operations are animated and endowed with knowledge and science by the spheres and stars. Even so, Maimonides was more interested in magic and the cabala.

It was probably Albertus Magnus (1193–1280) who kept astrology alive in the West. He accepted the Aristotelian description of the sky and heavenly bodies as formed of a fifth element distinct from the four elements of earthly objects. He subdivided the heavenly substance into three elements composing respectively the sun, moon, and stars—and the sky apart from the celestial bodies. The stars were nobler than any inferior bodies, "less involved in the shadows and privations of matter," and closer to the first cause of the universe. Their motion was eternal, unchangeable, incorruptible. Some called them animals, but Albert held they were not animals in the sense that we apply that word to inferior living creatures.

Like Aristotle, Albert regarded the heavens and stars as instruments of the first mover or prime intelligence, just as the and is the instrument of the human intellect in making a great work of art. They were mediums between the first cause and matter. Albert believed in a number of heavens "existing from the first heaven to the sphere of the moon." The first mover moved the first heaven and through it the other spheres included within it.

Albert had a good deal to say about the effects produced by the conjunctions of the planets, and attributed to them power over great mortality and depopulation, or "great accidents and great prodigies and a general change of the state of the elements and of the world." To a conjunction of Jupiter and Mars with other planets aiding in the sign of Gemini he attributed the pestilential winds and corruption of the air that resulted in a great plague.

Albert also discussed comets, and why they signify wars and the death of kings and potentates rather than the death of some poor man. Their close connection with wars was explained by the astrologer Albumazar as due to their association with the planet Mars. As for kings, owing to their greater fame and power, the relation of the celestial phenomena to their destinies was observed more carefully than the fate of the poor. The horoscopes of kings had more planetary dignity, so it was customary to give greater importance to them.

But the idea of free will no more restrained Albert than it did Ptolemy from acceptance of the art of genethlialogy or the casting of nativities.

He stated that the astrologer who understands the virtues of the signs of the zodiac and of the stars in them at the moment of a birth can prognosticate the entire life of that person. But free will restrained others from casting horoscopes.

In the next two chapters we shall see how astrology became secondary to magic, witchcraft, and satanism during the dark ages of Europe. The people were much too downtrodden to worry about their future on earth. Life was drab, dull, and cheap, and worshiping the devil had certain physical pleasures attached to it that appealed to the masses.

SEVEN

The World of Dante

Dante calls across the space of seven centuries like a father calling to his lost children. And we respond with deep nostalgia and longing for the world that was his home but is no longer ours. Lost and lonely, we may look back across the abyss of the irreversible years and see the world vision of Dante as a dream. We have wandered far from that universe where love was the prime and pervasive power moving from God, through the shining stars, to microcosmic man. You may ask, what has Dante to do with us or we with Dante?

The dramatic contrast between Dante's world and our modern cosmology lies in the complete reversal of the order of the basic qualities defining the world. Since the days of Galileo, Kepler, and Descartes, modern man has transformed the categories of reality into primary qualities (space, time, mass, motion, figure, number, measure, and so on), while secondary qualities (sensations, colors, sounds, odors, taste, and so on) and tertiary qualities (emotions, values, wishes, images, ideas, thoughts, and so on) are all coldly explained by the primary qualities. We speak of newspaper headlines as being electrifying; we say that we "shift our gears," or even that we "strip our gears," or "blow our cool"; and we talk about "social friction."

In other words, we take the modern primary qualities as the basis of all qualities and seek to explain everything in objective terms. We even reduce man to a collection of conditioned or inherited reflexed and electrical circuits in our bodies.

Dante used what we call tertiary qualities as his primary qualities. The prime moving force for both God and man was love. The celestial heavens of stars and planets turned under the radiating influence of love. All other values were thought of in terms of more or less love, or as for or against love. The cardinal sins of man according to Dante were Pride, Envy, and Anger (distorted love); Sloth was a deficiency of love; Avarice, Gluttony, and Sensuality were excessive love. In Dante's world the physical was explained in terms of the spiritual, so now let us look at his world and times.

There is no better place to start than with Roger Bacon, who was credited with numerous discoveries and inventions. He was supposed to have been persecuted because he advocated experimental methods, but Thorndike points out that this assertion has not a shred of evidence behind it. In a masterly chapter he concludes that Bacon was a typical product of medieval thought. Bacon continued the Christian attitude of noble literature, and his books were written by a clergyman for clergymen. There is no denying that he was a herald of modern science and that he frequently was very scholastic and metaphysical. Yet he was critical in many respects and insisted on practical utility as the standard by which science and philosophy must be judged.

There was in the Middle Ages no book quite like the *Opus Majus,* nor has there been one quite like it since. It was true to its age and is still readable today. It will always remain one of the most remarkable books of the remarkable thirteenth century and the world of Dante.

Bacon, though a man of impassioned enthusiasm, possessed common sense about the practical and experimental. He wrote:

> Machines for navigation can be made without rowers so that the largest ships on rivers and seas will be moved by a single man in charge with greater velocity than if they were full of men. Also cars can be made so that without animals they will move with unbelievable rapidity; such we opine were the scythe-bearing chariots with which the men of old fought. Also flying machines can be constructed so that a man sits in the midst of the machine revolving some engine by which artificial wings are made to beat the air like a flying bird. Also a machine small in size for raising or lowering enormous weights, than which nothing is more useful in emergencies.

Roger Bacon was born in 1214 near Ilchester in Somerset, England, and his boyhood was one of remarkable precocity. He entered the order of St. Francis and studied mathematics and medicine at Oxford and Paris. Returning to England, he devoted his attention to philosophy and wrote Latin, Greek, and Hebrew grammars. He was a pioneer of astronomy and was acquainted with the properties of lenses to a degree that he may have foreshadowed the telescope. We are indebted to Bacon for important discoveries in the science of chemistry. His name is associated with the making of gunpowder.

His study of alchemical subjects led him to believe in the "philosopher's stone" by which gold might be purified to a degree impossible by any other means, and also to believe in the elixir of life by which the human body might be fortified against death itself. Bacon was looked on with a suspicion that grew into open persecution. The brethren of his order practically cast him out, and he was forced to retire to Paris. He was forbidden to write, and it was not until 1266 that Guy de Foulques asked him to break his enforced silence. Bacon took the opportunity and in spite of hardship and poverty finished his *Opus Majus, Opus Minus* and *Opus Tertium.*

Bacon returned to Oxford to continue his scientific studies and scientific works. He wrote a compendium of philosophy, but its subject matter was displeasing to the Church and Bacon's misfortunes began again. His books were burned and he was thrown into prison, where he remained for fourteen years. He was freed about 1292 and died in 1294.

Bacon's works were numerous, and although many still remain in manuscript, about a dozen were printed at various times. The *Opus Majus* was divided into six parts treating of the causes of error, the relation between philosophy and theology, the utility of grammar, mathematics, perspective and experimental science.

On the matter of astrology Bacon's attitude was entirely in conformity with the new spirit, for he said, "It is manifest to everybody that the celestial bodies are the causes of generation and corruption in all inferior things." He held that the stars were regulated by angelic intelligences. The nature or "complexion" (character) of an individual was determined by the sky at conception and at birth. The functions of the body in health and disease were under the influence of the stars; hence medical treatment should hinge upon astronomical configurations. The wise physician should be aware of the fact that hour by hour the bodily states vary with the changing positions of the planets. For these purposes the zodiac and the moon were given proper care and caution.

Evil and good conduct, as well as the possibility of resurrection, in men was accounted for by the stars. Different regions of the earth were inhabited by different races and nations because the latter were under the influence of different constellations. Planetary conjunctions were of particular note in religion. Christianity was associated with Mercury—most impelling when in Virgo—while Venus denoted sensuality and represented Mohammedanism.

Bacon made a series of prognostications concerning the fates of historical figures, nations, and religions that were of ominous import. Even the birth of Christ was brought under the rule of the stars. Elections, horoscope images, favorable hours, and the entire astrological arsenal was elaborately and devoutly expounded. He declared, "The astronomer can form words in elect times which will possess unspeakable power over matter and over men."

He was especially attracted to the doctrine of Albumazar concerning the conjunctions of the planets and he derived his evidence of the superiority of the Christian faith from the astrological explanation of its origin according to the successive conjunctions of the other planets with Jupiter.

Bacon believed that not only could the future be foretold, by means of astrology but also that marvelous operations and great changes could be effected by it throughout the whole world, especially by the arts of elections and of images. As the babe at birth receives from the stars the fundamental physical constitution which lasts through life, so any new-made object is permanently affected by the disposition of the constellations at the moment of its making.

In Bacon's philosophy astrology was important and represented an exact science. Others felt differently about the art; not all agreed that the four elements and the qualities were subject to the signs and planets along with the animal and vegetable kingdoms. But even Bacon and Thomas Aquinas felt that man's free will and rational soul were exempt from stellar influences.

Thomas Aquinas, like his master Albertus Magnus, ascribed an important place in natural science to astrological theory. He refused to explain magic by the stars but he accounted for the occult works of nature and for natural divination by astral influence. Aquinas believed in the incorruptibility of the heavenly bodies, but he (although aware that Plato and Aristotle attributed souls and intelligences to them) insisted they were material substances. He regarded the stars as media between "the separate intelligences" and our material world, and was inclined to answer yes to a question which was put to him, namely: Do the angels move the stars?

Aquinas affirmed that God rules the inferior through superior creatures and earthly bodies by the stars. No wise man doubted that all natural motions of inferior bodies were caused by the movement of the celestial bodies. Reason and experience, saints and philosophers, have proved it over and over again. Indeed, throughout his arguments for astrology Aquinas made the church fathers—famed for their attacks on astrologers—seem to favor the limited rule of the stars over all nature. Aquinas further said, "By some other more occult observations of the stars to employ judicial astrology concerning corporeal effect."

During Aquinas' lifetime many spurious writings were ascribed to Hermes and the first and main one was entitled *Poimanderes.* This and other treatises attributed to Hermes Trismegistus followed a general out-

line including the names and powers of the twelve signs, astrological medicine addressed to Ammon the Egyptian, thunder and lightning, and some
hexameters on the relation of earthquakes to the signs of the zodiac. There
were various allusions to and versions of tracts about the relations of herbs
to the planets or signs of the zodiac or thirty-six decans. These treatises
attributed magic virtues to plants and included a prayer to be repeated
when plucking each herb.

However, the most important astrological work produced in the thirteenth century was the *Liber Astronomicus* of Guido Bonatti, a volumi-
nous work written about 1277 and divided into a dozen treatises. In the
preface Bonatti stated that he wrote the book particularly for the use of
his nephew: the work was "long and prolix" and on this account he did
not include "disputations nor many proofs." Bonatti expounded the doctrine of astrology so clearly in this book that it was said, "It seemed as if
he wished to teach women astrology." Bonatti used the classical authorities
of Ptolemy and Hermes, and Dante's consignment of Bonatti's soul to hell
does not seem to have kept people from reading his book.

Some idea of Bonatti's method and content may be seen in the following
translation of his account of the properties, significations, and effects of
the planet Jupiter:

> But if Jupiter shall be unfavorable, Ptolemy is witness that the child
> will be ignorant of well-doing, versed in diabolical practices, that he will
> intrigue under a hypocritical exterior, will linger in places of prayer, will
> gladly live in crypts and caverns and caves, and there will predict the fu-
> ture. He will love no one, though he may have a few friends; he will abhor
> his children, will shun human conversation, will seek no honors from any-
> one, will be untrustworthy, and no one can depend on him. In fine, he
> will be bad, weak, stupid, weary and heavy-laden, of evil election.

One of the stories told of Bonatti concerns an astrological image. Sorry
for a poor chemist with whom he played chess, Bonatti gave him a wax
image of a ship and told him that if he kept it hidden in a secret place he
would grow rich, but that if he removed it he would become poor again.
The man became wealthy, but he was afraid that the image was the work
of witchcraft. Having made his fortune, he decided that he should save
his soul in confession. He told a priest about the image, and the priest
advised him to destroy it. But then, as Bonatti predicted, he lost his entire
fortune. He begged Bonatti to make him another image, but Bonatti
cursed him and told him that the image was no magic one, but derived
its virtue from a starry constellation which would not recur for another
fifty years.

It was into such a world that Dante Alighieri was born at Florence, Italy, in May of 1265. He became deeply involved in the political and military activities of Florence and in the struggles of the Roman church to maintain its powers. Dante, author of the *Divine Comedy,* was not a scholarly recluse, though he was well versed in the intellectual heritage of his culture. His biography is familiar; and his devotion to Beatrice after her death was the greatest symbolic compliment ever paid to ideal womanhood.

Dante himself was the father of one daughter (Beatrice) and several sons by his wife Gemma. His fifty-six years of life on earth were rich, violent, and varied—with exile, travel, political struggles, university studies, and writings all thrown together. His was a time of great turmoil and change. Within Dante's own lifespan St. Thomas Aquinas died and Giovanni Boccaccio was born. It was the end of an old order and the beginning of a new. Such a person as Dante may well speak for his tumultuous times and for a significant vision of the universe and of man's place in it. And in the *Divine Comedy,* the greatest work of his age, he spoke memorably, poetically, and passionately of such a vision.

Dante always exhibited a marked interest in astrology—the influence of the heavenly bodies upon our mortal and moral lives. But it should be emphasized that his astrological interests were essentially reflections of his cosmic world view in which the power, wisdom, and love of the Almighty were transmitted through the stars and planets to man upon earth. The stars incline, but do not compel man's decision. And the cause of true corruption is not only in Saturn, but in man as well. The Southern Cross caused a number of heated astrological discussions because of a passage in Dante's *Divine Comedy.*

> At right, in the direction of the southern pole,
> I saw the lights of a quadruple star
> Which Eve and Adam only were to see.
> The heavens glorified in its radiation.
> O you poor widowed barren North,
> You never see the marvel of this constellation!
> ——*Purgatori* (lines 22–27)

Amerigo Vespucci, who called the Southern Cross the "rhombus," was the first to identify Dante's *quattro stelle* with his "rhombus." But not until much later did somebody realize that the *Purgatorio* was written about 1318. This was long before any Western navigator pushed south far enough to see the constellation as a whole. By then it could also be shown that the constellation had been visible in Mesopotamia a few thousand years before Dante. At least some of the stars of the Southern Cross appear under the name of "chambers of the south" in the *Book of Job*. Dante's statement that "the first people," (Adam and Eve) saw it was factually correct. It seems almost incredible that an Italian poet of his time could have had the factual knowledge of the existence of this constellation or have been acquainted with such an astrological detail as its former visibility from Mesopotamia. Was this all an incredible coincidence, or did a great poet have true "mystic vision"?

Even when men completely rejected the concept of "mystic vision," the problem was interesting enough to entice Alexander von Humboldt to devote a special study to it.

Dante's source for the existence of the four stars was no doubt Arabic, though we do not know which of the actual sources he used. One possibility is a globe of the sky showing the Southern Cross, which was made in Egypt by Caissar ben Abucassan just about a century before Dante wrote his famous lines. Another such globe was made in 1279, when Dante was a young man.

While there is no way of proving that either of these globes was taken to Italy, just the fact there were two of them indicates that there probably were even more. Dante might have even seen them or at least been told about them.

When Emperor Friedrich II of Hohenstaufen, the son of Friedrich Barbarossa, returned to Italy in 1229 from the Fifth Crusade, he brought with him a very unusual Arabic tent. It is described as having a cupola-shaped roof showing the constellations and a hidden clockwork that made the stars move. Two centuries ago the story of this "astronomical tent" was disbelieved by all astrologers; but now that we know of the Antikythera machine, and it appears that the Arabs made such tents.

Dante, therefore, could have known of the existence of the constellation, which, since his sources were often not Christian, was not called a cross. A few lines later he states that "the Wain [Big Dipper] had disappeared," which is not surprising either. Northerners have always complained when they have gone south to places where they cannot see this most reliable of all favorite constellations.

The soldiers of Alexander the Great were perturbed by this, and Pliny the Elder consistently made a point of mentioning that the Dipper could not be seen from this or that place. The fact that the North Star was not visible from Sumatra is the only astrological reference in all of Marco Polo's writings. The only remaining mystery is the reference to the former visibility of the Southern Cross from Mesopotamia.

In all probability Dante's vision was truly mystical and exactly right. The concept of Dante that all the sky could be seen from Paradise (while it was on earth) is not hard to understand, because Dante's main moving force was always love. It is also well to recall that in Dante's *De Monarchia*, which was reworked into the political passages of his *Paradise*, he insists that the only form of government for earth was ordained by love and must be a direct reflection of the authority of the heavens.

This points up the basic symbolism of Dante's cosmology: Divine heavenly values permeated the universe and entered intimately into the practical affairs of man upon earth. The power of love, as the ultimate source of all values, took precedence over the Holy Roman Church and even over the redemptive first coming of Christ. For Dante, truly virtuous pagans born and dead before the Christian era were susceptible of being rewarded in Paradise. Ordinarily, good pagans such as Aristotle and Plato were found in the meadow of limbo in the first circle of Inferno. But by a special dispensation from the Heavens some pagans were brought there.

Astrologically, the cosmos of Dante was earth centered. Dante's geocentric view was based on Ptolemy, Aristotle, Plato, and others. The moon, sun, planets, and fixed stars revolved on celestial spheres about the earth. The ultimate sphere, or Primum Mobile (prime mover), moves all the other celestial spheres within it. Dante placed love in the infinite realm of the tenth heaven—Empyrean—beyond all the celestial spheres.

Below the moon lay our earth, composed of the four elements: fire (hot, dry), water (cold, moist), earth (cold, dry), and air (hot, moist). Each element had its proper place with respect to the center of this universe: fire and air naturally were located UP (above the earth's surface) while water and earth had their natural location DOWN (toward the earth's center). Dante goes on in his *Comedy* to explain things in more detail.

When Lucifer, now Satan, fell from the heavens, he struck the earth in such a manner and with such force that he tore a conical pit to its very center—and by the impact the Isle of Purgatory was formed on the opposite side, thrust up from the ocean floor of the southern hemisphere.

The departing dead reached the Isle of Purgatory from the Tiber River in Rome, by means of an angelic vessel sailing to the southern hemisphere. After long penance in Purgatory these souls attained salvation in the heavens, passing through the shadow of the earth. The heavenly shadow was not simply the astronomical shadow cast by the earth in the light of the sun, but indeed it was highly symbolic—for the first three heavenly spheres over which the shadow of the earth was supposed to move as a cone had its apex ending at the orb of Venus. These souls that achieved their final destiny in any of these spheres were still "within the shadow of the earth"—no man who had given his love to man on earth could give quite as much of his love to the Almighty. For most people the shadow of earthly love remains. Likewise, the shadows or spots on the moon, visi-

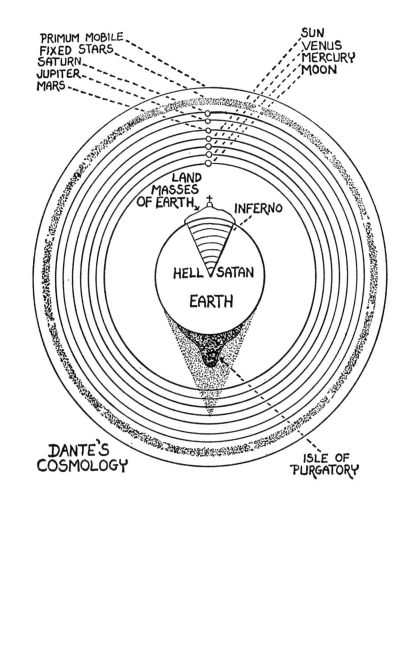

PRIMUM MOBILE
FIXED STARS
SATURN
JUPITER
MARS

SUN
VENUS
MERCURY
MOON

LAND
MASSES
OF EARTH
INFERNO

HELL   SATAN

EARTH

DANTE'S
COSMOLOGY

ISLE OF
PURGATORY

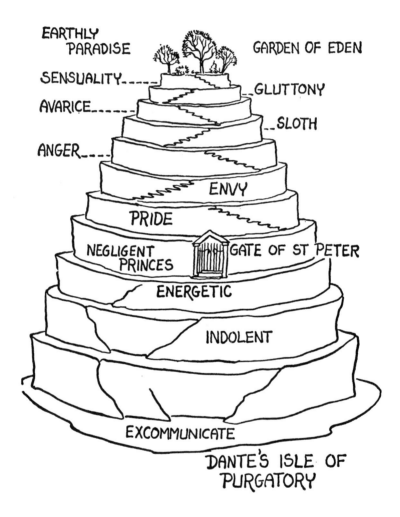

EARTHLY PARADISE

GARDEN OF EDEN

SENSUALITY----

GLUTTONY

AVARICE----

SLOTH

ANGER----

ENVY

PRIDE

NEGLIGENT PRINCES

GATE OF ST PETER

ENERGETIC

INDOLENT

EXCOMMUNICATE

DANTE'S ISLE OF PURGATORY

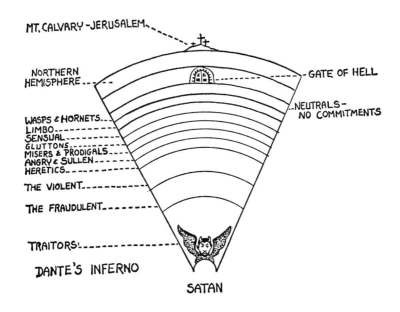

MT. CALVARY -JERUSALEM.

NORTHERN HEMISPHERE

GATE OF HELL

NEUTRALS - NO COMMITMENTS

WASPS & HORNETS
LIMBO
SENSUAL
GLUTTONS
MISERS & PRODIGALS
ANGRY & SULLEN
HERETICS

THE VIOLENT

THE FRAUDULENT

TRAITORS.

DANTE'S INFERNO

SATAN

ble to the naked eye, were not for Dante anything other than signs of the spiritual imperfections of those human souls who dwell on this lowest heaven.

The prime moving power of love was transmitted through the heavenly spheres by the different orders of angels—the highest of which were the Seraphim. The various angelic orders were originally described by a Neoplatonist of the fifth century, Dionysius the Areopagite. His views were well known to Aquinas and Dante. The essential point was that in the cosmological notion moving forces of the universe resided as values.

Also worth noting is Dante's concern with numerology. There were three "trinities" in the angelic hierarchy distributed in the first nine heavens. The highest trinity consisted of the Seraphim, the Cherubim, and the Thrones. The second trinity included the Dominations, Virtues, and Powers. And in the lowest trinity were the Principalities, Archangels, and Angels. The angels were the working messengers from the heavens to man. The titles of the heavenly orders more or less describe the functions. The nine orders are numerically a perfect square of three, reflecting in triplicate (three threes) the ultimate trinity. We see in all this how numbers and degrees and forces are explained as being entirely under the overriding notion of values and persons.

The question as to whether Dante belongs to the Middle Ages or to the Renaissance is a difficult one to answer. This Janus-faced poet at times seems to be from both of these epochs. In many ways he had nothing to do with the Renaissance: he summed up the Middle Ages rather than announced the dawn of a new age of man. His *Divine Comedy* was a thoroughly Christian epic that is often called one of the last great Gothic masterpieces.

As for his place in his own time, instead of being far ahead of it, he was in reality far behind. He dreamed of vanished utopias, whose visions and hopes became increasingly old-fashioned as time passed on. Yet the more modern poets of the Renaissance were reluctant to concern themselves in the least with this austere ascetic with his frightful visions of hell fire and damnation. Dante succeeded in clothing his mystical astral visions of the Beyond in a strictly symmetrical, poetical, and Pythagorean pattern.

We may summarize the cosmic world view of Dante by saying that it is not only geocentric but, in the spiritual sense, anthropocentric. The world below and the world above are both devoted to man's spiritual life: The "vectors" of spiritual concern point toward man from heaven above and from hell below. And man thereby finds his spiritual home in the cosmos. To create such a universe Dante must have had visions and knowledge of the astral world.

But many secrets of nature still remained undiscovered, and so it is not surprising that the idea of some occult virtue in nature—of occult influence exerted by animals, herbs, and gems or by stars and spirits—prevailed among men of the highest scientific attainments then possible. That this conception was a strong one is shown by the continued use of amulets, ligatures, and suspensions; by the general belief in fascination, physiognomy, number mysticism, and divination from dreams. Some believed in the occult forces of words, figures, characters, and images—or in this or that rite, ceremonial, and form. Especially surprising was the prevalence of lot casting under the pseudoscientific form of geomancy. But others doubted the efficacy of some or most of these things. Animism had pretty much had its day, and necromancy received relatively little attention. The Church encouraged them by insisting upon the existence and power of evil spirits.

In the writings of Duns Scotus we find the conception of occult virtue accepted and even given a greater extension than most people would then accept. Duns Scotus regarded astrology and alchemy as reputable sciences. In any case we see Duns Scotus fully as favorable to astrology as Aquinas. The science had at least the qualified approval of both the Thomist and Scotish schools of philosophy and of many members of the Franciscan and Dominican orders.

But before we leave this long-lost world of Dante with love as its prime moving force we must look at another man—one who became a legend in his own time, one who was not a great author or churchman, but a working astrologer. Nicholas Flamel was born in the fourteenth century at Pontoise, France, of a poor but respectable family. He received a good education and his natural abilities allowed him to make good use of it. At an early age he went to Paris and obtained employment as a public scrivener (similar to our present day Notary Public). Sitting at the corner of the Rue de Marivaux, copying or writing letters and other documents, he soon built a prosperous business.

His reputation grew and his business prospered, so in a fairly short time he owned many bookstands for the sale of copies of famous manuscripts. At the same time he conducted classes in cultural enlightenment for the Parisian nobility. He married a widow who was learned, educated, and energetic, and who brought with her a handsome dowry. Together they built up a business in cultural articles from which they grew richer year by year. Flamel's quick wit suggested to him that he could make more money in the pursuit of astrology. He began casting horoscopes and telling fortunes. He was right, for he made even more money. Those who study the magic art for profit or amusement generally finish by addicting themselves to it with a blindly passionate love. So it was with Flamel.

Then Flamel had a remarkable dream. An angel appeared to him, holding a most impressive old and antique book in his right hand and saying to him: "Nicholas Flamel, behold this great volume. You understand nothing thereof, nor do many others to whom it will remain unintelligible, but one day you shall discern in its pages what none but yourself will see."

Flamel reached out for the book, but it suddenly vanished together with the angel. He retained a good picture of it in his mind and thought of it continuously with a great longing and regret. As a result of this vision, Flamel and his wife Pernella became interested in the hermetic arts and practiced alchemy in a laboratory they built in their home. In spite of his extensive business Flamel found time to pursue the philosopher's stone and the grand elixir. His bookstores, offices, and home were gathering places for occultists and adepts in the great art and were veritable scientific forums and academies. Flamel devoted himself day and night to his fascinating pursuits and soon acquired a thorough knowledge of all that had been written previously about the "elixir vitae," the universal Akahest, and the philosopher's stone.

Day in, day out, Flamel hoped for the return of the angel or some other harbinger of the grand secret. He almost abandoned hope, until one day he happened to buy an ancient volume from a traveling scholar in need of ready cash. He casually put it aside after admiring its mysterious and curious appearance; a few hours later he was suddenly struck by its resemblance to the book seen in his mystical dream. Rushing back to the book he was amazed to find it the very book the angel once held in his hand. It was a most unusual book, made of tree bark covered with Greek texts inscribed with a steel instrument and containing three times seven leaves. The printing was marvelous, but the Latin was cryptical. Each seventh leaf was free of words, but was emblazoned with beautiful drawings.

The first drawing showed a serpent swallowing rods, the second drawing showed a cross with a serpent crucified, and the third showed fountains playing in an arid desert surrounded with serpents trailing their slimy folds from side to side. Upon the first of the printed leaves, written in capital letters of gold was: "Abraham the Jew, Priest, Prince, Levite, Astrologer, and Philosopher, dedicates this volume to the nation of the Jews dispersed by the wrath of God in France and wisheth them health." The wrath of God was invoked upon anyone "that should look in to unfold it, except he were either Priest or Scribe." The text consoled the Jews and advised them to wait patiently for their coming Messiah. It then described the process and explained the use of every apparatus. Abraham said that this was to the end that the adept might help and assist his dispersed people to pay their tribute to the Roman Emperors. The text even pointed out the proper seasons for each experiment.

In fact, the book would have been perfect but for one thing: It was addressed not to the student but to an adept. It took for granted that the adept was already in possession of the philosopher's stone. This was a terrible obstacle to the inquiring Flamel. The more he studied the book the less he understood it.

He studied the text and he studied the illustrations. He invited the wise men of France to come and study them as well. But no light was thrown upon the mystical darkness. Flamel was worried about whether he was worthy enough to dare continue to read the book. He was very impressed with its scholarly exposition of metal transmutation. The procedure, the vessels, and experimental technique were clearly described. However, there was not one word about the philosopher's stone, except an insinuation that it was painted and described symbolically somewhere in the book.

The text was interspersed with numerous diagrams: such as Mercury attacked by Saturn; colorful and strange flowers swaying in the wind on a tall mountain amidst leaves of purest gold; fantastic trees growing in streams of milk; a king directing his soldiers to kill infants, collect their blood and pour it into a bathtub in which the sun and moon were bathing. Many pages of the book were covered with strange hieroglyphics, and other pages were filled with some ancient oriental script.

There was much in the Latin text Flamel did not understand. The figures and signs he copied on the walls of his chamber. Many of his friends mocked him, but Anselm, a scholar in physics and alchemy, took a strong interest in the mysterious volume. Anselm discussed many sections and processes with Flamel, even though Flamel never let him see the book. Flamel followed Anselm's suggestions, devoting twenty-one years of his life to the suggested experiments. But all was in vain!

The incomprehensible text almost proved to be an insurmountable obstacle. But his good wife Pernella finally advised him to find a learned rabbi to help him. It was the consensus of various experts that, although it contained much Latin, it was an old Hebrew book kept in the temple of Solomon and taken from there at the time the Emperor Titus destroyed Jerusalem.

There were no rabbis in Paris in Flamel's time, because the Jews had been banished from France some time earlier by Philip Augustus. Flamel, therefore, bade good-bye to his wife and friends. As the chiefs of the Jews were mainly located in Spain, to Spain went Flamel. There he remained for two long years. Finally he met a converted Jew, a most learned physician and alchemist named Canches, who was the right man to help him. No sooner did Canches grasp the idea of the book than he was beside himself with joy. He abandoned all he held dear in Spain and set out with Flamel for Paris to study the ancient work and its great occult mysteries.

"Our voyage was prosperous and happy," wrote Flamel. "He most truly interpreted unto me the greatest part of my figures, in which even to the points and pricks, he could decipher great mysteries, which were admirable to me." Their friendship was unfortunately cut short by fate. When they reached Orleans the Jewish savant suddenly died of an unknown illness and in great mental agony. Canches passed his last days without ever having cast eyes upon the greatest and most sacred book of all in alchemy.

Alone and depressed, Flamel continued his homeward journey; though when he reached Pernella he was considerably wiser than when he left her. Clinging desperately to each word be remembered his Spanish-Jewish friend had spoken, he resumed his study. After unceasing efforts at experimentation, he finally succeeded in making a projection on Mercury and obtained pure virgin silver on January 17, 1382. A few months later he converted a large quantity of Mercury into pure shining gold. At last he owned the secret of the philosopher's stone and had won the battle of transmutation. The "grand elixir" was his. He was master over longevity, disease, corruption and all imperfection.

This enabled him to prolong his life to a venerable age and to accumulate gold. He administered the life-giving potion to his wife, who reached nearly as great an age as himself. With all his pursuits of learning, of practical alchemy, and the mysteries of Abraham's ancient text, Flamel grew fabulously wealthy and was called the richest man in France. Many people thought that his great wealth came from his alchemical experimentation. In reality, one cannot indulge freely in alchemy unless one is rich. Like a true adept, however, Flamel lived a simple life—humble in dress and home and without luxury.

Long before Flamel and Pernella reached old age they spent a large part of their fortune on charity. He endowed a famous church near his home and seven others in France. He built fourteen hospitals and three chapels and contributed funds to many worthy institutions in Paris. He had beautiful paintings placed on numerous monuments. He published many small treatises on alchemy, such as *The Philosophic Summary* and *Le Desir Sire*, which achieved great popularity.

His alchemical studies were but the disguises of his crooked practices, to account for the immense wealth he acquired by money-lending to the young French nobles and by transacting business between the Jews of France and Spain. Flamel enjoyed great fame in his later years. The most celebrated doctors of Europe came to his humble dwelling to pay him homage. King Charles VI of France sent a special representative to greet

him. He is believed to have died in 1418, and his fame and honor left a
deep imprint on alchemy. Fables of his vast learning and his nobility of
character persisted so long that in 1816 a house in Paris thought to have
been lived in by Flamel was bought by a nineteenth-century gold seeker.
This man then ransacked every wall in his quest for the hidden gold presumably left by the alchemist.

Astrology, Flamel claimed, was a science that made extremely high
demands upon its disciples. They had to possess a "thorough acquaintance
with all the infinite detail of Nature and the powers of mind and body.
It is a wonderful science even though it is plagued by many impostors
and deceivers." In its pure state it "speaks the truth in most cases and very
rarely fails of correct prognostication except in certain particulars." Flamel
met honestly all the diverse objections that were advanced against astrology and cited the opinions of all the established authorities in science,
philosophy, and religion. He harped upon the fact that though the science
is difficult and complex, it is honorable and noble. He stated bluntly,
"Those who attack it in the name of religion are hypocrites."

Precious stones and herbs cannot owe their marvelous virtues to the
elements that constitute them, but must derive them from the stars. Only
experience can tell us what these virtues are, since they can in no way be
deduced by reasoning. As a medical authority he advised: "Those who
pursue medicine as they should and who industriously study the writings
of their predecessors, must grant that this science of astrology is not only
useful, but absolutely essential to medicine."

Astrology can also foretell changes in weather relevant to the cure of
the patient. The medical practitioner should look up the patient's horoscope for proper and complete diagnosis. No surgery should be performed
when the stars or planets are unfavorable. The eighth sphere of the stars
was of special importance in determination of past historic events, though
planetary conjunctions, of greatest significance in individual fates, would
justify history as well. All these hypotheses were applied by Flamel to
biblical events. Believing that knowledge was power, Flamel explained
that by further study of the sky and the occult virtues of the heavenly
bodies, the astrologer would ultimately find himself in a position even to
influence future events and transform threatening misfortune into something desirable.

The fascination of astrology emerges most convincingly from the private
lives of the astrologers—lives devoted to a noble cause in a spirit of rare
altruism and loyalty. In an age when religious fervor made thousands of
men and women abandon all earthly pleasures for devotional meditation,
scientific pursuits matched that faith by producing an equally impassioned love of learning and research. Nothing can better describe such

an age than the lives of these knights in quest of something loftier than the Holy Grail, namely, the philosopher's stone, the great elixir, the universal panacea, and the gift of prophecy.

Just as astrology and alchemy were a congeries of empirical and speculative values in chemistry, philosophy, religion, and science, so were the records of the lives of the disciples a mixture of fact and fancy, of history and romance. But exact historical accuracy is relevant only to the academic biographer. From our point of view it matters little whether a person like Alfarabi actually was a great musician, or whether Flamel left Spain in March or August. What does matter is the setting that writers of the period assigned to these heroes and in what colors the thinking and reading public wished to see them painted. The lives of these Magi constituted the intellectual folklore of the time, enjoyed by the ignorant and learned alike. Similarly, Horatio Alger stories injected the values of a specific period in our United States into a literary mold. Each period of each culture invades its art and literature in a basically similar fashion.

The world of Dante, like our own, created its own heroes and idols and fashioned romances around them, just as we do today with our television and popular magazines. Now let us turn to the darker side of this world, the side inhabited by witches, demons, and even Satan himself. Dante told the people where to find the devil; folklore told them when and how to seek his satanic advice and aid.

EIGHT

Witchcraft and Satanism

We may get an idea of the popular superstitions and observances of the fourteenth century, often of primitive or pagan origin, which survived in different localities of western Europe into the fifteenth century, if we note some examples. All sorts of signs of the future were important. Whoever of the bridal pair rose first from kneeling at the marriage would dominate the other. If a screech owl, white barn owl, or magpie perched on the ridge-pole of a house, it portended the death of someone inside. It was a very bad sign to meet a pregnant woman on leaving one's house in the morning. The only way to escape ill consequences was to insult her and run back indoors immediately. It was considered unlucky to be born during the hour before midnight or on Good Friday.

There were many signs which told the sex of the coming child. To predict the weather for the ensuing year, one put salt on twelve split onions representing the months of the year and went to midnight mass. On returning the rainfall of each month was estimated by the state of the salt on each onion. If one's head cast no shadow on the wall at the Feast of Epiphany, one would die before the end of the year. It was the custom to take a handful of straw from the mattress of a dead person and burn it at the cross-roads. If there were a foot-print in the ashes, there would soon be a death in the house towards which the foot-print pointed. When there were no tracks, the death would be in that house towards which the smoke from the burning straw blew.

Protective measures against sorcery were common, and included such everyday measures as putting a little water in the milk, or breaking the shells of eggs which were eaten. The bridal pair entered the church encircled by a chain of silver or of copper with silver-plating. To get even with sorcerers who bewitched away the cows' milk, the milk was heated and a knife plunged in it.

Some traced the figure of King Solomon's ring on the foot of their beds to keep away nocturnal spirits. Others recited a passage from the Gospel according to St. John to guard against fairies and sorcery. Surviving place names show how widespread was the belief in fairies. The peasants said the medicinal virtues of certain springs were due to them, and the best the church could do was to change the claim to say it was the influence of its saints. Ghosts were feared, and in preparing a corpse for burial care was taken to tightly stitch up the shroud.

Charms were employed as preservatives from lightning or disease. Eating an egg laid on Good Friday was thought to ward off all fever for a year. Putting a coal from the Christmas fire in one's bed kept off thunderbolts. Hen's eggs, if perfectly round, were smashed immediately since they were laid by cocks and would hatch out into serpents. On the midnight of January first the peasants sprinkled themselves and their domestic animals with water to ensure good health. A bouquet of flowers was deposited at the village fountain by the first-comer, or if none could be procured, a handful of straw was burned. A cricket in a house brought good luck, and the head of a stag-beetle was a charm against lightning.

A white hen was carried before a wedding procession on the end of a pole, as a symbol of the bride's chastity. More likely it was the intent to ensure her chastity or for some other magical purpose. To ensure a quick delivery, women wore their husbands' clothing. Peasants, to make the carrots grow large, touched the thigh while planting them and said, "Long as my thigh, big as my head."

It was considered dangerous to plant anything during the full moon, and the crops would be poor if one came home from midnight mass by the light of the full moon. Marriages contracted during the waxing of the moon were believed to turn out best. And one must not sow hemp or make dye during Rogation week. To insure the success of an undertaking, one should place an eyelash in his shoes.

Cats played a large part in the popular superstitions. A girl who wished to rid herself of an unwelcome suitor would send him a cat, or lay a broom before her door. When the villagers danced about the bonfires on the Eve of St. John the Baptist or jumped over them and drove their domestic animals through them as protection from disease, it was customary to hang one or two cats above the flames. Black cats were suspected of attending witches' sabbats, and their tails were cut off to prevent this. If the house cat died a natural death, someone of the household was believed likely to follow it soon. It was a bad omen to meet a cat when starting on a long journey.

The virtue of herbs was associated with sorcery, since witches were believed to scour the woods for herbs to use in their concoctions on St. John's Eve. They plucked them with the right hand and threw them into their basket without looking at them, lest they lose their magic virtues. The time factor was also important here, since the herbs must be plucked while the clock was striking noon. Some villages rang the bell only two or three times instead of twelve in order to stop the sorcerers' botanizing.

Witchcraft is older than civilization. It was probably, as its proponents maintain, the first religion. Prehistoric cave paintings and carvings indicate its basic concept was a nature god incarnate in human or animal form. The Egyptian cult of the dead, the orgiastic Greek Mysteries, Druidism with its sun worship and magic-stone circles, all suggest the same rites.

Throughout Europe witchcraft persisted openly alongside Christianity. Its followers considered themselves the true traditionalists, the orthodox religionists. Then, as the Christian Church grew powerful, they were driven underground. Medieval prelates denounced the incarnate nature god as Satan, and condemned the witches as devil worshipers guilty of every conceivable offense against humanity. The Church condemned thousands of suspected witches to the gallows, the headsman's block and the stake, though many of the victims were innocent. In the hands of the Inquisition the label became a weapon to use against anybody considered an enemy of the Church, whether heretic, atheist or Jew.

The witches' status did not improve during the eighteenth century; only the rationale behind the suppression changed. The British Witchcraft Act of 1735 held that since no such thing as witchcraft existed, the pretense of magical powers became simply a fraud meriting severe punishment. Spiritualist mediums were prosecuted under that same act until parliament finally repealed it in 1951.

How easy it is to dismiss the world views of Dante and Thomas Aquinas as merely the intellectual babble of scholars and monks. How easy to suggest that monastic and university life really had little to do with the common people of the Middle Ages. What did these people have to do with the high-flown scholasticism or the literary symbolism of priests or poets? Surely the serfs and peasants knew little about cosmology and only vaguely understood the celestial and infernal geography. The academic world of that time had not entered into the culture of the laborer plowing in the field of a serfdom.

In a sense, this is all probably true enough. Serfs were certainly poorly educated in their day. All this, however, overlooks two essential questions: How did the common medieval man function in terms he believed to be the values and goals of his own life? Did these values reflect in any way the world picture of Dante and Aquinas? The answer to the second is a complicated "Yes," and in explaining it we will answer the first question.

In his verses Dante imprisoned some contemporaries in hell—Michael Scot (1170–1232) and Guido Bonatti (died about 1300).

Scot was condemned for his crimes of magic, a magic doubly criminal since (according to Dante) it was a fraud. Little is known of the Scotsman's life. He died early in the thirteenth century, and wandered in the eighth circle of the Inferno, looking back over his shoulder, because there those who attempted to predict the future were not allowed to look forward. Scot was astrologer to Emperor Frederick II, the extraordinary ruler who invited to his court many seers and magi of the East and of the West. At Frederick's request, Scot wrote his extensive works dealing with the occult. The book, *Introductions, Particularis,* and one on physiognomy (the study of man's face, where the planets have marked the events of each individual's life) were his most famous. Scot also translated Avicenna's work.

Among his contemporaries, Scot was considered a great scholar. Bacon believed—erroneously—that Scot introduced Aristotle to the West. But Albertus, the saintly man, was more cautious, for he censured his writings severely, saying Scot had failed to understand Aristotle. Yet Albertus used Scot's translation of Aristotle's *History of Animals* extensively in his writings. What crimes did Scot commit which caused his eternal banishment to hell? Although he labeled as experiments many of his magical operations and actually condemned magic, especially necromancy, he spoke too much and in too detailed a way about these practices. The full description and publication of such forbidden arts was condemned throughout the centuries in the fear the people might become inspired by them.

Whatever magic arts existed were described in detail by Scot. Conjurors mixed blood with their ritual water, because the demons were attracted by blood. They sacrificed human flesh and bit off their own flesh or that of corpses. They cut off doves' heads, and used their bleeding hearts to draw magic circles. They made use of Biblical verses in their diabolical incantations.

In his book on astrology, Scot told of the spirits of the air and of the planets, of images, prayers and conjurations for each hour of the day and night, things which we encounter frequently in the black books of the Renaissance and of our recent times. His treatise on physiognomy contained all the traditional elements of the subject. The stars influence the generation of man and imprint their seals upon the face of man. Therefore we can read in man's features what the heavenly bodies decided about him. Scot interpreted dreams and believed like everyone in his time that stones, herbs, and plants were endowed with marvelous virtues.

He accepted alchemy and divination. In short, he was a great expert of magic, concerned solely, except for his astrological medical practice, with the occult arts. No theological treatise counterbalanced this prodigious amount of suspect learning for Dante; thus the condemnation to eternal hell's eighth circle.

Primitive people in various parts of the world, when subjected to sorcery or black magic, may become seriously ill or die. Voodoo (voudou) has been reported among Negroes in Africa and Haiti and among the aborigines of Australia. In 1972 some educated and civilized persons find it difficult to believe that areas still exist where sorcery is actually practiced.

In ancient Hawaii the treatment of the sick was based on the belief that poor health was caused by malevolent spirits or disease-producing demons. Illness was considered the result of sorcery, or in some cases some ramifications of a taboo. Among the Hawaiians there existed a group, the kahunas or "those who were keepers of the secret," whose wisdom was gained by divine guidance. Kahunas were grouped into various categories, some good others bad. Sorcery was practiced by a group known as the kahuna anaana.

The practicing kahuna anaana was feared and considered an assassin. He was clever and skilled in many crafts, including the art of poisoning. With his occult power, known as mana, his success was assured. The essence of the kahuna anaana's power lay in his ability to scare his victims to death; he was an accomplished psychologist and used potent weapons of maleficence. The device frequently used was to inform the victim the sorcerer had singled him out. In his terror, the victim would refuse food and drink, and his strength would wane. In a few days he would die.

Dr. Walter Cannon has suggested that voodoo death is similar to kahuna, and is the result of a shock produced by a sudden release of adrenalin. Kahuna victims would breathe rapidly, have a fast pulse, and lose fluids from the blood to the tissues. The heart beating at a very fast rate would lead to death.

The power of the kahuna in Hawaii is still strong today, and witchcraft is still practiced in many civilized parts of the world. So, believe it or not, there are men and women today who will willingly accept death, not seeking medical aid, if they believe that a witch is praying them to death. Books on Black Magic are available in many book stores, and even some of the very ancient volumes are being reprinted.

One not readily available is the work of Antonius de Monte Ulmi entitled *Of Things Occult and Manifest* or *The Book of Intelligences,* written about 1385. It was an exposition of astrological necromancy and the performance of magic by invoking spirits, which went to surprising extremes for a doctor of medicine. In the first chapter Antony treated of the constellations in which the intelligences or spirits lived and under which they operated. There were four chief orders of intelligences for the four points of the compass, and their power over inferiors depended in part upon their astrological position. They also specialized in certain sins and temptations, some to luxury, others to guile, and so on. In the third chapter Antony noted that there were twelve altitudes of angels for the twelve signs and that they had relations to one another corresponding to the sextile, quadrile, and triune aspects of the planets in the signs.

When a child was born, the chief intelligence of the sign of the zodiac then in the ascendent appointed one of his subordinates having greater or less virtue in operating, according to whether the child was of high or low estate. Antony professed that this assertion was supported by the Christian faith which said every person from birth had his opposing angel. In the fifth chapter he related the spirits to the planets and explained he did not mean the intelligences appropriated to the orbs of the planets, i.e., the Aristotelian movers of the spheres, but "intelligences deprived of divine grace"—the fallen angels. In the same chapter he even suggested, although pretending he found it incredible, that good angels also operated under celestial influence and were divided into twelve altitudes like the signs of the zodiac.

Meanwhile in the second chapter he stated that magicians especially observe the sun and spirits of the east, that the first hour of the night was reputed the most favorable for necromancy, and that Christians ought to pray to God at that hour to protect them from the plottings of such evil intelligences. Other astrological rules were given, but he warned the word horoscope had a different significance in astrology, chiromancy, and magic. While for the astrologers Aries was the initial sign, Cancer takes its place in magic. Astrological times must be observed in magic, since Aristotle was so informed by a demon whom he consulted.

Various questions were answered by Antony as to the apparition of spirits. They often appeared tumultuously and in a fury because they came from opposing parts of the sky or were angry at being exorcized. Those of the oriental signs were of a nobler grade and more placable and appeared more quickly and with less fury and in a more beautiful form and were more readily controlled. Antony abstained from revealing the exact hours at which it was best to summon them, because he had already stated them elsewhere and to do so now would be in the nature of a digression. Only certain persons were able to perceive the presence of these spirits, while others heard and saw nothing, since the greater scientific attainments of the intelligences enabled them to feign objective appearances. These met the senses of one person and not of another or were near one person's eyes and not visible to those of a bystander.

The intelligences appeared most often to persons in a virgin state because they themselves were incapable of sexual intercourse. They manifested themselves more in water and highly polished surfaces than elsewhere because they produced their feigned appearance by reflection better in water or mirrors than in air. Nor could they achieve their colors and figures as well when wind and rain disturbed the air as when it was clear and bright. Antony found by experience that they made apparitions even in rainy weather but not with any degree of facility.

The difference in the suffumigations which were employed in invoking spirits—fetid substances being burned for some and odiferous ones for others—were explained by the planets and constellations with which the intelligences were associated. When spirits of the south were imprisoned in bottles or crystals, these were kept in fetid places like dunghills. When the intelligences were impelled to a good work they required odiferous suffumigations, while fetid suffumigations were in order for a bad end. They enraged the demons and made them the readier to commit evil, especially since it meant in the end a severer penalty for the exorcist or conjurer.

Antonius employed the term exorcist for anyone invoking spirits and not merely for an ecclesiast who drives out evil spirits. The reason why the spirits were influenced by suffumigations, although they have no sense of smell or other sense organs, was partly astrological and partly because they wished to seduce men in sacrificing to them and offending their Creator.

Beware of diabolical possession, exhorted the priests. Withdraw ye then from the things of this earth! Be ye immaculate and pure of spirit, even as the Virgin Mary, who was worshiped and adored. Enter ye into celibacy, into the monastery. Slaughter the lustful flesh, overcome the demons which are everywhere around and within you. Preserve your soul for the Judgment. Abstinence and virginity are Christian virtues—pray to the Holy Virgin—exhalt Her. And confess: your womanhood is unclean with the sin of Eve! Better to die undefiled like Dante's Beatrice.

The priest and nun withdrew from this world—and from the people of the soil. The Church called to her flock—in Latin. They came as Christians, but could not comprehend. The "great divorce" began. The priests on the side of the Feudal Lords of the Serfdom, the serfs at the mercy of those in the castle whose gloomy towers cast down their threatening shadows upon the poor plowman.

No hope from Church or Feudal Lord—your peasant bride was not yours even on that first night, but theirs, in the castle. To whom to turn? God? Oh no, He was with the Church, and the Church is with them. The serfs were alone—helpless.

They turned, in despair, to the olden spirits of the soil upon which they labored, to the ancient pagan roots fertilizing the earth—the elfs and little demons of the hearth and home, their humble hut where a wife labored alone. Here was their little kingdom. "Be kind to the wee small sprites and here at least they may be kind to you." Wife knew those invisible creatures who relieved her during the chores, the boring drudgery of her lonely anxious day while her man was in the fields. She often spoke to them of her fear and sorrows.

Always hungry, half-starved and weak, she seemed to feel the presence of tiny creatures who touched her tattered skirts and whispered in her nervous ears . . . voices, hints, small quick fingers in warm hidden places —lonely and responsive, secret dreams fulfilled, embarrassed moments of sudden pleasures. And lo! One day her dull housework was done for her— she could not recall having done it herself. The little gods were kind for the secret satisfactions they have shared. She told about these things— why not? No real harm—they were so tiny, and at least someone was on her side in this terrifying world where priest and baron offered no hope or consolation, and were an ever-present threat.

You ask if they were pagans, and the answer is: "Yes!" I have no doubt some people will say "Pagan! Surely this means 'heathen, unenlightened.'" This was the meaning given in the dictionary, but the word was derived from the Latin *Pagus*—meaning a country district. So pagan simply means "of the countryside."

The word "witch" was derived from the Anglo-Saxon word "wicca," meaning "wise one" or "sorcerer." The wiccan were the priesthood of the old religion which worshiped the Sun-god and Moon-goddess. Inseparably connected with the Moon-goddess was the cat, the symbol of the feminine aspects of the divine.

Wherever the witch cult existed, its followers met four times a year to celebrate the mysteries of their faith. These were the four great Sabbats —Candlemas, May Eve, Lammas and Halloween (or Samhain, it was called then, meaning "summer ends"). This division of the year emphasized the breeding seasons for some wild and domestic animals.

In the old days the "coven" of witches had their weekly meetings known as Sabbats. They were partly business meetings and partly religious. The witches were the advisers to the ordinary people, the serfs.

They were healers, skilled in the use of herbs and the distilling of potions. At the great Sabbats, when everyone got together, a feast was held to celebrate the gifts of the gods.

It was believed witches rode to these meetings on flying broomsticks, although I think that the only flying through the air done by witches was in their imaginations. There are many recipes for "flying ointments" which have come down through the ages, and quite obviously the contents of some of these, such as aconite and belladonna, when rubbed into the skin, induce trance-like states, hallucinations and a feeling of flying. Broomsticks were used in fertility rites, and witches danced round astride their broomsticks, leaping high from time to time. If they leaped very high, the crops would grow high. It is generally known that the witches were naked in their rites. This gave rise to disapproval, although it seems obvious people were just as immoral with their clothes on as with them off. Female witches always wore a necklace, the symbol of rebirth, and the high priestess wore a wide silver bracelet with her witch name engraved upon it.

Familiar in the streets of any medieval town was the ancient crone with bent back, muttering between her toothless gums; people gave her a wide berth, as few doubted her malevolent powers to bring down hailstones on crops, sickness to the herds, disease and misfortune on an honest townsman and his household. Yet in the dark of the moon, the men and women furtively sought out the old woman, to coax from her a love potion, a poison cup or a cure for impotence or the itch. Her medicines were not all fraud and fantasy: mingled in her cauldron with eye of the newt and toe of the frog were powerful ingredients.

A 1603 description of a typical witch follows: "An old weather-beaten crone, having her chin and knees meeting for age, walking like a bow, leaning on a staff, hollow-eyed, untoothed, having her limbs trembling with palsy, going mumbling in the streets; one that hath forgotten her paternoster, yet hath a shrewd tongue to call a drab a drab."

A witch was not always evil; many "white" witches practiced a form of folk medicine compounded of magic and herbal lore. The Renaissance physician Paracelsus declared that he learned all his medicine from the "good women" (white witches), also from shepherds and hangmen. Kings and nobles could employ household physicians; the poor had recourse only to monks or witches. Why witches were more often female than male was explained by King James I:

For as that sex is frailer than man is, so is it easier to be entrapped in these grosse snares of the Divell, as was over well proved to be true by the serpent's deceiving Eve in the beginning, which makes him the homlier with that sexe sensine.

The white witch practiced only healing arts: she removed warts, cured fits, counteracted spells laid on cattle by bad or "black" witches. The "grey" witch might deal in either good or evil according to her client's need. The black witch was completely malevolent; she derived her power from Satan in return for selling him her soul. The witch was well versed in astrology, necrology and the doctrine of signatures, and these principles guided her methods of gathering and preparation of herbs. Each plant operated under specific planetary influences; those governed by the moon had certain particular virtues, thus the witches in *Macbeth* set great store by "slips of yew silver'd in the moon's eclipse."

Associated with death and corruption were the leaves of funereal trees such as yew and poplar, strands of hangman's rope and torture instruments, corpses whole or in part. Based on the doctrine of signatures was the choice of plants with lurid flowers of strange shapes; most potent of these was the mandrake. The resemblance of its forked root to human form identified it as an evil spirit in vegetable guise. The mandrake's most favorable habitat was supposed to be under a gibbet (gallows) where it thrived on the drippings from decomposing corpses, and when pulled out of the ground it emitted human shrieks which brought madness or death to its gatherer. The approved method of gathering it was to tie a hungry dog to the root and lure the animal from a distance with proffered meat.

The full moon was the witches' best time to gather plants, preferably done in bare feet and with hair unbound. A naked maiden and an unclouded moon were needed to pick the highly prized selago or club moss (Lycopodium); this herb sacred to the Druids permitted one to understand the speech of beasts and birds. The time and order of mixing were governed by strict rules, and accompanying the preparation were a circle dance and suitable incantation: Hecate in Middleton's (1615) *The Witch* chanted over a poison cup she concocted for a duchess:

> Black spirits and white, red spirits and gray,
> Mingle, mingle, mingle, you that mingle may!
> Round, around, around about, about!
> All ill come running in, all good keep out!

The use of psychic drugs like LSD to escape reality is not a new experience for man. Thousands of years ago a cave man chewed on what he thought was a harmless mushroom and found himself in a world of bewildering sensations and brilliantly colored dreams. He told the local medicine man and the long weird history of psychic hallucinogens started. Since the dawn of civilization and even much earlier, man has fed on berries, fruits, seeds, roots and leaves. His selection of vegetables for food came by trial and error—he continued to eat the plants which agreed with him and shunned those that made him ill.

Through the ages since the cave men, men sought out drugs to dull their physical aches and pains or to alleviate their mental ones. More treasured still have been the substances used to bring mortal flesh into the presence of the divine. Such was the mysterious "soma" mentioned in a Sanskrit chronicle and the "Nepenthe" of Homer. Nomads on the Kamchatka Peninsula lofted themselves into the dazzling world of the gods with the mushroom *Amanita muscaria,* and discovered that the visions of one eater could be passed to as many as five others if each drank the urine of the man before him. In South America, before Columbus, witch doctors took "cohoba" snuff to converse with gods and the dead.

When we look at a medical and astrological text of the seventeenth century, such as *Culpeper's Complete Herbal,* there is an amazing profusion of herbs, shrubs, and trees with their roots, barks, woods, flowers, fruits, and seeds, all reputed to be of great medicinal value. Certain plants were used because of some striking quality. They were used in magical or religious rituals, and so were later credited with medicinal properties. Through the centuries there was a rough general law at work in the use of vegetable drugs. If the substance was rare, palatable, and caused no deleterious effects on the body, it was usually sold as a drug for a time. Later, if it was easily cultivated near the market place and then became plentiful, it decreased in value. It must then prove its worth as a medicine or be discarded. If it amused, nourished, or pleased, it became a food or spice. Today's supermarkets contain scores of foods and condiments which were once used as medicines or by witches.

The toxic magic plants of ancient folklore excited wonder in those days. Their deadly effects on the mind, when taken internally, were wondrous to behold. In Greek mythology, the herbs were the property of the divine witches, Hecate and her two daughters Circe and Medea. With their various love potions they turned men into swine and dignified persons into debased beings. The mandrake, the deadly and common nightshade, wolfbane, and others were consecrated to the infernal deity of Satan. The witches of the Middle Ages used them freely in their magic and witchcraft.

During the years from 1400 to 1500, anytime early in the summer on a sultry evening somewhere along the Mediterranean one might see an old stone house with a large chimney pouring out smoke. A full red moon loomed over the eastern horizon. Upstairs, an alchemist worked among his crucibles, muttering amidst the varied colors of flames, smokes, and sharp stenches. Peering at scrolls and books in the fitful light, the old man dreamed and puttered.

Downstairs, an elderly woman and her young niece listened to the sounds above and smiled at each other. The evening star, Venus, dropped quickly in the western sky. The moon swept upward; a silver glow fringed the shadows of silent buildings in the sleeping city and the witching hour approached.

The old hag, shaking with palsy, her eyes shining, carefully closed and barred the doors and windows. The glowing red coals in the giant fireplace were extinguished with a large kettle of water. The girl looked on eagerly, removed her scant clothing, and brought out a stone bowl filled with a grey-blue grease; human fat with aconite, belladonna, henbane, poppy, night-shade, hemlock, and mandragora. Trembling, the grinning old hag rubbed in the ointment vigorously. It penetrated their sweating pores. Their bodies turned to fire! They crawled naked and drunken into their wooden troughs—each astride a broom. Vertigo, lightness, and visions assisted them. The brooms carried them up the chimney to the "Black Mass" or "Witches Sabbat."

As they climbed into the night, they greeted a host of flying figures on brooms, in wash tubs, and on pigs or goats, men, women, defrocked priests, necromancers, magicians, lovely young girls, and old crones. All were headed into the rushing winds.

All were off to the godless gathering to fornicate and fear not. To meet the great *He-Goat*, the giant Priapus.

Fair is foul—foul is fair. The Devil protects you. Lucifer be with you and come to the Sabbat. Join in the orgiastic union!

We know about the drugs and induced hallucinations, but they did not. Their faith was in the "power of Satan," and not in drugs. Yet, it was the drugs and herbs which created their witchcraft and magic.

Charms and love potions also had their uses, even among the feudal lords and ladies, where "courtly love" was romance with adultery. The diabolical two-horned headdress of the feudal dame symbolized the sophisticated dictum of those days: "No love possible betwixt married folks." Marriages were made (contractually) in heaven, but romances between a feudal dame and her young squires and pages were fostered by philters bought from Satan's Chosen Bride—the witch. "Please—just something in her wine—just something so my courtly mistress will deign to look upon me, her lowly squire, with love." For a price, the witch obliged. And what satisfaction for the peasant-witch-sorceress so to gain control over the lordly lady—what Satanic triumph!

Necromancy, black magic, and above all, the quest for the philosopher's stone—alchemy—to transmute base metal to gold, the legend of Hermes

Trismegistus, the new Prometheus—ancestor of the future Paracelsus. What lures, what powers over earthly things could come from the Prince of Nature—Satan. Even the priest fell to these temptations. He practiced his profession in the day, the Holy Mass, but at night, his soul was devoted to the Black Mass. He was no hypocrite, for he was professionally ordained, yet personally fallen from grace. He believed in God, but he knew his own soul was in Satan's possession.

The Black Mass of the Witches' Sabbath! The worship of Satan! The marriage to the great He-Goat: "I believe in God the Father, Lucifer, Who created Heaven and Earth, and in his Son, Beelzebub."

Witchcraft and demonology was played to the hilt in its time. And, as the Faust legend, the underlying ideology lingered on into the following centuries, long, long after witch-trials ceased. Old myths die slowly, for their roots are the roots of life. Only another myth of greater vitality can supplant an older myth. It was the transition from the world of the dark ages to the world of the Renaissance—and its struggle of two cosmologies— that things slowly began to change.

Raphael of Pronasio wrote *De communi et proprio,* which was printed at Venice in 1508. He explained early in this treatise on the magic art that he previously had dealt with the same subject more briefly in a letter to Christopher of Reggio, a noted physician, and he now intended to discuss the matter more fully and deeply. The opening chapters dealt with the meaning of the word magic, the antiquity of the magic art, its origin and effective cause, and the natural proof of the existence of demons. Raphael used the usual theological position that magic was worked by the aid of demons, and the chief feature of his work was to determine how great were the powers of the demons in this regard. He believed they sometimes rendered themselves perceptible to the human senses, that they could move material objects, transport human beings from one place to another, and form worms in the body and bowels.

To the explanation that incubi and succubi, though themselves without generative organs or functions, affect generation by transporting semen from male to female over a great distance instantaneously, Raphael added the possibility of their effecting a sort of spontaneous generation: "From which things may be gathered that it is not wholly false or impossible which is reported today, forsooth, that certain women have sexual intercourse with demons under diverse forms."

At the same time Raphael granted many of the operations of magic and of the demons were illusory and fantastic. From the heading of his tenth chapter, "In which it is shown how one body can be in two places," one might think he believed this possible, but the text demonstrated the contrary. In fact, no one seems to have even thought of the possibility of a material body being in two places at once. One opinion was that the soul would leave the body, but Raphael claimed that even demons cannot do this and that death would result. A second opinion was that every human body had two spirits, one good and one evil, and the good spirit never left the body, but the bad spirit occasionally went off with the devil to perpetrate evil deeds. Raphael felt the body really remains in one place but that angels or demons by fantastic appearances make it seem to be elsewhere. Many persons dream they are far away while they are actually asleep in bed all the time.

It is highly questionable that the Black or Satanic Mass was actually practiced prior to the very late seventeenth century, and for the most part was probably a mere literary creation such as the one described in the Marquis de Sade's *Justine* (around 1790), or forced as a confession under torture, from "witches," after 1600. But such notions were certainly implied in the diabolical service included in earlier ideas of witches' sabbaths. The seeds of the Black Mass may have been planted by the nocturnal assemblies of men and women (and children) which occurred from about 1100. The relics of paganism certainly survived among the serfs through the centuries, along with the worship of the moon, which exerted influences over the soil, and the burning of candles to Diana-Luna-Hecate.

Perhaps the Druid festival, October 31, Allhallows Eve; or the eve of May 1, Walpurgis Night, added to the tales. Or again, perhaps it is the Spring festival, or the Eve of St. John the Baptist, when the He-goat of Priapus-Bacchus-Sabazius was slaughtered ritually. Only at night was the serf free to indulge in such carnivals and roam the countryside. Then he was a true nocturnal animal, becoming really alive only after dark. Sometime beyond 1400, the picture of the Witches' Sabbath or Sabbat took a firm hold in Europe. Of course, the notion of a witch is itself biblical: "Thou shalt not suffer a witch to live" (Exodus XXII, 18).

Let us now look at men such as Paracelsus, Agrippa, Nostradamus and Cardan. This was a time when the occult, alchemy, and astrology were blended into a single mystical study.

NINE

The Cynical Rebel

Pressure from the Church against witchcraft increased with the spreading of occult beliefs that the Church was unable to erase. From the East, imported by the crusaders, the dualistic heresy filtered through for many years; and from the eleventh century on witches paraded their knowledge openly in Italy.

In 1080 Pope Gregory VII still recommended moderation to worldly leaders in prosecuting witches. But numerous sects grew with disquieting speed: the Paulicians, Bogomiles, Beghards, the Pauvres of Lyons. In 1209 Pope Innocent III ordered a crusade against the Albigenses and the Kathari. Crusaders ransacked Beziers and Carcassonne, and though protected by the Count of Toulouse the Albigenses were defeated at Muret and at Toulouse. This terrible war, in which the king of France participated, finally came to an end in 1229.

Only a few years after the peace treaty a papal bull referred to the Luciferians, who worshiped the principle of evil. The struggle between the orthodox Church and the Dualists (worshipers of both God and the Devil) continued throughout the thirteenth century. In 1233 Gregory IX established the Inquisition, a special tribunal of Dominicans who were to combat all heresies. The Inquisition tortured and condemned culprits to the stake on the grounds of heresy. However, the Dualists were not mere heretics but actually members of a faith independent of Christianity. In 1274 the earliest example of an inquisitorial condemnation of a witch occurred. She was burned in Toulouse, the center of the Katharan movement.

Then, in the years 1318, 1320, 1331, and 1337, additional papal edicts against witchcraft and heresy were published. The example set by the Church was followed by the civil authorities, but mass persecution of witches was most drastic during the sixteenth and seventeenth centuries. Then the burning of witches was an economic gain as the event drew large carnival-like crowds to the town. It was during these eventful years that Agrippa practiced his trade as alchemist and astrologer.

Henry Cornelius Agrippa of Nettesheim was not reckoned of much weight in intellectual history nor is his book on occult philosophy so important a work in the history of magic as one might think at first sight. He was not a person of solid learning, regular academic standing, and fixed position, but rather one of those wayward geniuses and intellectual vagabonds so common in the later fifteenth and early sixteenth centuries.

This German soldier-physician was very adept in alchemy and magic, as well as being an astrologer. He was born at Cologne on the 14th of September 1486. He was educated at the University of Cologne and while still a youth he served under Maximilian I of Germany. In 1509 he lectured at the University of Dole, but a charge of heresy was brought against him by a monk named Catilinet. This forced him to leave Dole and he resumed his former occupation of soldier. In the following year he was sent on a diplomatic mission to England and on his return he followed Maximilian to Italy. There he spent seven years, now serving one noble patron, now another.

He held a post at Metz, returned to Cologne, practiced medicine at Geneva, and was appointed physician to Louise of Savoy, mother of Francis I. When he was given a task he found irksome, he left the service of his patroness and denounced her bitterly. He accepted a post offered him by Margaret, Duchess of Savoy, Regent of the Netherlands. On her death in 1530 he retired to Cologne and then to France, where he was arrested for some slighting remark about the Queen Mother, Louise of Savoy. He was soon released, however, and died at Grenoble in 1535.

Agrippa was a man of great talent and varied attainments. He was acquainted with eight languages and was a physician of no mean ability, as well as a good soldier and a philosopher. He had many noble patrons, yet he never seemed to be free from misfortune, persecution, and financial difficulties. These dogged his footsteps, and in Brussels he was imprisoned for debt. He himself was in a large measure responsible for his troubles. He was, in fact, very adept in the art of making enemies. He also enjoyed the persecution of the monks with whom he frequently came into a conflict that was bitter and increasing. His principal written work was a defense of magic, entitled *De occulta philosophia*. It was not published until 1531, though it was written some twenty years earlier.

His interest in alchemy and magic started at an early period of his life and gave rise to many tales of his great occult powers. It was said that he was always accompanied by a familiar in the shape of a large black dog. It was in Germany that all the strains of the occult were gathered together by Paracelsus and his followers into a conception of Nature directed toward a practical medical art. And it was there that Agrippa, drawing upon Reuchlin's Neoplatonic mysticism and magic and initiated by Abbot Trithemius into the occult sciences, wrote *De occulta philosophia*. It was in sharp opposition to the academic Aristotelian physics of the day and to mathematics as well. Within a Neoplatonic and Cabalistic framework of three worlds (intelligible, celestial, and elemental) Agrippa emphasized the unity of nature. In all worlds, man participates as the microcosm and, therefore, all worlds are accessible to knowledge.

> For it would be absurd if the heavens, the stars, and the elements, the source of life and animation for all things, should themselves lack them: if each plant and tree took part in a nobler determination than the stars and the elements which are their natural begetters. . . . There is therefore a World Soul, a single life filling and coursing through all things, holding together and binding all things within itself, so that the machine of the whole world is rendered a unity. . . . Just as in the human body the movement of one member calls forth that of another, and as in a lute when one string is touched all the others vibrate it, so each movement of the part of the world is reflected and imitated in all the others.

In such an interconnected and unified universe, it was easy for man to discover the forces hidden in things and by the proper manipulations of magic and astrology to bend the higher powers to his service. In Agrippa's revealing treatise we find instructions for the magician and the worker of miracles. He recommended purity and "dignification." The faculty of the soul was the only producer of wonders, "which when it is overwhelmed by too much commerce with the flesh and occupied with the sensible soul of the body is not worthy to command the divine substances." Our Renaissance Magus had in common with the wise men of old the belief that magical forces dwell in the visible and the invisible world, forces that are controlled for good as well as for evil.

Such ambivalence made it impossible to define the western Magus clearly. Faust, the black wizard, made use of the same force that enlightened Paracelsus, the white magician. The distinction is now but slight between the charlatan and the scholar. However, even the worst of the Magi exerted, in some way, good influences. Their enchantment awakened interest in nature's mysteries and challenged the critical attitude of the skeptic. They leveled social differences, showing the value of the individual who could unassisted accomplish great things by the power of his intelligence and knowledge. This was especially true in the case of mathematics. Numbers were used in magical diagrams. Knowledge of mathematics was necessary for musical harmony, which was a reflection of the harmony of the universe.

In the third book of his work, Agrippa asserted the necessity of religion in every magical venture. "Religion is the most mysterious thing," he said, "and one about which one should keep silent, for Trismegistus says that it would be an offense to religion to confide it to the profane multitude." "Religion was the accomplishment and key of magic, a discipline leading to the dignification of a man," he added.

Agrippa's conception of religion was far from being orthodox; it was rather a mixture of Christianity, Neoplatonism, and the Cabala. He spoke of planetarian spirits, of demons good and bad, of conjurations and sacred pentacles, and of the ten sacred names of God. He knew the language of the angels and their names as well as those of the star spirits, those of the elements, and those of the four corners of the world. He exposed the secret of sacred Cabalistic hieroglyphs with the intention of instructing the Magus in the manner of conjuring the supernatural. He believed this: "Though man is not an immortal animal, like the universe, he is nonetheless reasonable, and with his intelligence, his imagination, and his soul, he can act upon and transform the whole world."

The precious fragments of the ancient lore were collected and incorporated into the mosaic of the new world image. During the Renaissance the influence of ancient magic gained new strength. Profane learning, though led by religion, ventured into the most hidden compartments of human thought. Many inquired eagerly into wisdom formerly forbidden. More than ever the Orient fascinated people. The Crusades brought the East closer to the West; its mysteries now seemed less impenetrable, for an expanding trade reached across the Mediterranean. Also, with the discovery of America, the equilibrium of Europe was greatly disturbed.

Magic soon was a distinct branch of learning. The Magus, though despoiled of his antique splendor, made his official entry into Christian society. But simultaneously arose the critics who railed at those who believed in magical wonders. Skepticism found its expression in the praise of folly. "All is vanity; men are sinners, but still more, they are fools." Those who bought magical books and could not understand them laughed at themselves.

Magic also carried men of the clergy into the occult whirlpool. Trithemius (1462–1516), a Benedictine, encouraged Agrippa to write on magic, after having himself written on the names of angels and their government, on Cabalistic cryptic alphabets, and the like. Agrippa, the

Magus and Neoplatonist, found himself lost in confusion and reached the radical decision that all human enterprise was folly. He who was alchemy's champion now proclaimed its madness, exposing the tragicomic character of the adepts. His prejudice blinded him, and he failed to see that these men who devoted themselves so ardently to the quest of the unknown might deserve interest and compassion rather than ridicule.

There is no greater madness than to believe in the fixed volatile or that the fixed volatile can be made—so that the smells of coal, sulphur, dung, poison, and puss are to them a greater pleasure than the taste of honey— till their farms, goods, and patrimonies are wasted, and converted into ashes and smoke; when they expect the rewards of their labors, births of gold, youth, and immortality, after all their time and expenses; at length old, ragged, famished, and with the use of quicksilver, paralytic; only rich in misery.

On his death bed, Agrippa renounced his magical works and addressed his familiar thus: "Begone, wretched animal, the entire cause of my destruction!" The animal fled from the room and straightway perished.

At the inns where he stayed, Agrippa paid his bills with money that appeared genuine enough at the time, but which afterward turned out to be worthless bone or shell. It was like the fairy money that turned to earth after sunset. He was said to have summoned Tully from the dead to pronounce his oration for Roscius, in the presence of John George, Erasmus, and other eminent people. Tully duly appeared, delivered his famous oration, and left his audience deeply moved.

Agrippa owned a magic glass, wherein it was possible to see objects distant in time or place. On one occasion John George saw his mistress, the beautiful Geraldine, lamenting the absence of her noble lover. One other story concerning the magician is worthy of record. Once when about to leave home for a short time, he entrusted to his wife the key of his museum, warning her on no account to permit anyone to enter. But the curiosity of a boarder prompted him to beg for the key. Finally the harassed hostess gave it to him. The first thing that caught the boarder's attention was a book of spells, from which he began to read.

A knock sounded on the door. The boarder took no notice, but went on reading, and the knock was repeated. A moment later a demon entered, demanding to know why he had been summoned. The boarder was too terrified to answer, so the angry demon seized him by the throat and strangled him. At the same moment Agrippa entered the room, having returned unexpectedly from his journey. Fearing he would be charged with the murder of the youth he persuaded the demon to restore him to life at least for a little while, and walk him up and down the market place. The demon consented! The townspeople saw the young man apparently alive and in good health.

Then the demon allowed the semblance of life to leave the body and it was thought the young man died a natural death. However, later examination clearly showed he had been strangled. The true state of affairs leaked out, and Agrippa was forced to flee for his life.

These fabrications of the popular imagination were encouraged rather than suppressed by Agrippa, who loved to surround his pursuits of alchemy and astrology with an air of mystery calculated to inspire awe and terror. It is known that he wrote to all parts of the world, and from the replies to these letters he gleaned the knowledge that was popularly believed to come from his familiar—the black dog.

The most renowned and controversial figure in the world of astrology at the time of Agrippa was Paracelsus, who may have been the true Dr. Faustus.

A new access to truth and its dispersion by means of the printing press reinforced the smoldering revolt against the adherence to the Arabic shibboleths. Paracelsus, one of the most amazing characters of his time, fanned the flames of this revolt. He publicly burned the "Canon" of Avicenna in front of the University of Basel. He often appeared as a mountebank, his language was unbridled and abusive, and his habits were as bad as his morals; but he was equal to the task thrust upon him by the age in which he lived. He has been variously described by some as a drunken quack of an alchemist, and by others as a prophet and genius. This cynic and rebel stirred with impatience and rigor the weed-grown pool of the rigid authority of the schools, and advocated, in strident tones, personal opinion and independent judgment.

Paracelsus believed that most men are neither truly pious nor truly scientific: "Were Christ to descend from Heaven, he would find no one with whom he could converse; were Jupiter to come down from his planet, he would encounter here below no inquirers but only schools of men who repeat the wisdom gathered by their forefathers from the Stars. These schools of old are dead and their followers remain blind to the mortal light."

He complained how few raise their eyes to the starry heavens, from which flows a constant enlightenment guiding mankind to new sciences and arts. Music, for instance, is offered by the planet Venus. "If any musicians were open to receive her light, they would create a music more beautiful, more celestial, than the tunes of the past which are still repeated mechanically."

Such poetic images uttered by a physician were too much for his colleagues, who based all their knowledge upon the herb medicine of Galen. Their recipes were complicated and expensive. Their Philistine minds abhorred the ways of Paracelsus, his negligence about clothes, his rude language, his writing in German rather than in Latin. These good bourgeois detected the vagabond in him. They considered his magic signs and talismans as objects of heresy. In vain Paracelsus explained that in this physical world all things were related, and that the sign of a specific planet engraved upon a talisman was endowed with astral forces. When used for magic, the medal was related to the planet that thus enforced the power of the talisman. These signs were the marks imprinted by the stars like signatures upon earthly bodies.

While no belief was as popular in his day as astrology, whether among the masses or among the intellectuals, Paracelsus did not wholly and completely believe in it. Even though he would not give an enema, bleed a patient, or prescribe a charm without consultation of the zodiac, his criticism of astrology was very outspoken. In his *Volumen Paramirum* Paracelsus stated:

> The stars determine nothing, incline nothing, suggest nothing; we are as free from them as they are from us.
> The stars and all the firmament cannot affect our body, nor our color, beauty and gestures, not our virtues and vices. . . . The course of Saturnus can neither prolong nor shorten a man's life.

The Paracelsian concept of the world is centered around his basic concern with man's relation to God: "Man as the beginning and center of all creation. In man all life culminates. He is the center of the world; everything is seen in terms of man."

In man, God and nature meet and because man is the image of God, he holds the highest rank in the cosmos. In his *Coelum Philosophorum* he stated:

> The art is this; after you have made heaven, or the sphere of Saturn, with its life to run over the earth, place it on all the planets, or such, one or more, as you wish, so that the portion of Luna may be the smallest. Let all run, until heaven, or Saturn, has entirely disappeared. Then all those planets will remain dead with their old corruptible bodies, having meanwhile obtained another new, perfect and incorruptible body.
> That body is the spirit of heaven. From it these planets again receive a body and life, and live as before. Take this body from the life and the earth. Keep it. It is Sol and Luna. Here you have the Art altogether, clear

and entire. If you do not yet understand it, or are not practised therein, it is well. It is better that it should be concealed, and not made public.

This cynical rebel was born not far from the monastery of Our Lady at Einsiedeln in Switzerland. His father's name was Wilhelm Bombast von Hohenheim and he was a man of Swabian lineage who married a Swiss girl. Past his house ran the pilgrim's way, which after crossing the St. Gothard, led northward through Schwyz to the famous Benedictine Monastery. Year after year thousands of the faithful came to worship at the shrine of the Black Mother of God in Einsiedeln, and many of them found it necessary to consult the doctor after the hardships of the journey. Two years after Hohenheim's marriage, a son was born to him in the year 1493. Columbus was just returned from his first voyage to the New World. The boy was christened Philippe.Theophrastus, or to give him his full Latinized appellation, Philippus Aureolus Theophrastus Bombastus von Hohenheim.

When the boy was ten years old, his father moved from Switzerland to Carinthia to practice at Villach. His mother was dead and father and son were alone in the world. There were mines in the neighborhood and there was a school of mining in which Wilhelm von Hohenheim taught. Here also were Count Fuger's smelting works, which opened a new world and a new side of nature to young Theophrastus. He had occasion to learn the practical arts of mining and smelting. He saw how the elements attracted and repelled one another, combining to form new substances. He learned the fundamentals of chemical analysis and came to recognize its eminent practical importance.

The years ran their course and the time came for the young Hohenheim to go to a university where he could systematically study for the medical profession. He went to Italy, where the new science was in its prime, and reached Ferrara. Here his master was a gray-haired humanist who translated the aphorisms of Hippocrates into elegant Latin and who was one of the first to read the classical authors with a critical mind. He also had been one of the first to describe the new "love-pestilence"—or syphilis—decades before Fracastora. Young Hohenheim studied after the manner of other students of his day, took his doctor's degree, and following the current fashion, Latinized his name to Paracelsus (meaning "greater than Celsus").

Away he quickly went from the stuffy atmosphere of the classroom into the free air and back to nature. That was where true art was to be found. It would not seek anyone out, but must be eagerly and diligently pursued. He took a pilgrim's staff, fully realizing no one could become a geographical discoverer who remained seated by the fire. He stated:

If a man wishes to become acquainted with many diseases, he must set forth on his travels. If he travels far, he will gather much experience, and will win much knowledge.

On his travels he learned not only about illnesses, but also about remedies. Peasants, old wives, handicraftsmen, barbers, and barber-surgeons —such people often had knowledge well worth acquiring although the professors at the universities knew nothing of such matters.

Paracelsus set forth on this voyage of discovery through the world, which, with a few interruptions, was to last until his death, leading him through all the lands of western Europe. He visited the mining districts, studied the healing springs, and made a long series of chemical experiments. He continued always to practice as a physician, helping and healing wherever he could. He had thrown away his doctorial biretta and wore an ordinary slouch hat. Disciples joined their fortunes with his; many of these persons were of low degree. It was a motley company that moved from place to place. As he traveled, it became more and more evident to him that the traditional art of healing was on a false path. Its theories were false and its therapeutic methods were false. He began to keep a record of his own observations and ideas. He wrote, as he thought, in German—his mother tongue.

By the time he was thirty Paracelsus was a mature man, and he saw and learned much. He paid a visit to his father at Villach, went thence to Salzburg, where he lived for a time. Perhaps his wanderings might have ended if the Peasant's War had not broken out. In such times there could be no question of a tranquil practice, so Paracelsus set forth once more—to the Black Forest, to Freiburg, to Strasburg. He was weary of journeying and longed for some fixed establishment where he could continue his studies and elaborate his experiences and write. He enrolled as a citizen of Strasburg in December of 1526.

At Basel, less than a hundred miles up the Rhine, the famous bookprinter Frobenius was seriously ill. Because of an accident five years before he had horrible pains in the right foot, and the doctors of the town, dreading gangrene, advised amputation. But the fame of the wandering physician had reached Basel. Frobenius, before deciding to undergo this formidable operation, wished to get Paracelsus's opinion. Paracelsus came to Basel, took over the treatment, and was able to cure the patient without the use of the knife. Frobenius was soon well enough to ride all the way to Frankfort. The office of town physician fell vacant at this time and it was natural that the municipal council should offer Paracelsus the appointment, which carried with it the right to give lectures at the university.

In the spring of 1527 he transferred to Basel and immediately sketched

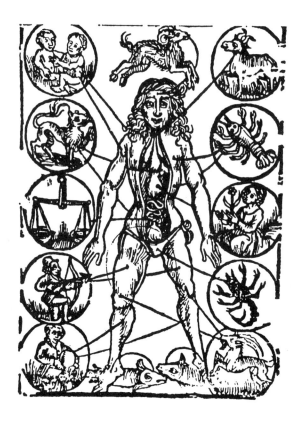

Paracelsus stated that the significations of the signs of the Zodiac are as follows:

Aries rules the head, ears, eyes, and brain.
Taurus rules the neck and throat and the diseases of them such as squiancy, hoarseness, and such.
Gemini rules the arms, shoulders, and hands.
Cancer rules the breast, paps, and upper belly.
Leo rules the heart and blood.
Virgo rules the guts and entrails.
Libra rules the kidneys and bladder.
Scorpio rules the privy parts and causes French pox (syphilis).
Sagittarius rules the thighs and hot fevers.
Capricorn rules the knees and causes melancholy.
Aquarius rules the legs, black jaundice, lameness of the joints, and swellings.
Pisces rules the feet and gout of those parts.

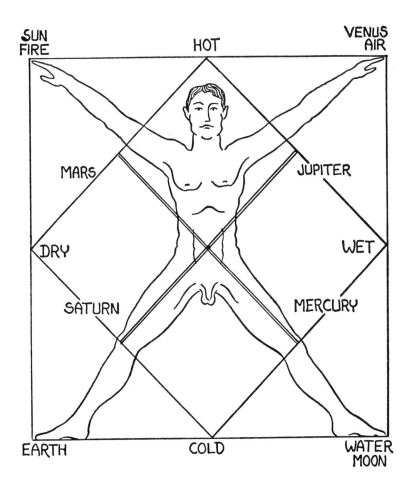

The planets have the following signification with regard to the body, according to Paracelsus:

The Sun is dry, hot, and sanguine and acts chiefly on the heart.
The Moon is wet, cold, and phlegmatic and acts chiefly on the stomach.
Venus is wet, hot, and choleric and acts chiefly on the bladder and kidneys.
Mars is dry and hot and acts chiefly on the head and brain.
Saturn is dry and cold and acts chiefly on the legs to cause dropsy and gall.
Jupiter is wet and hot and acts chiefly on the shoulders and lungs.
Mercury is wet and cold and acts chiefly on the shoulders and lungs.

a program of reform, printed it as a pamphlet, and distributed it. It proclaimed what was wrong with the medical profession and ended by saying, "Farewell, and come with a good will to study our attempt to reform medicine." This the faculty considered a declaration of war, along with the fact that he did not go through the usual formalities connected with obtaining such a position. The faculty forbade Paracelsus to use the lecture theater and wanted even to forbid his practicing in the town. A battle began. Paracelsus applied to the town council, which summoned him to Basel, and insisted upon his right to use the lecture theater. With no regard for the storm of opposition he was arousing, he began his teaching activities, including giving surgical lectures in German rather than Latin and publicly burning the works of Galen and Avicenna in a students' bonfire on St. John's Day. With increasing wrath the faculty watched the behavior of this innovator who was disregarding the forms sanctified by use, who was teaching unprecedented doctrines, and who regarded his colleagues as little better than idiots.

They would have to fight him tooth and nail if they wished to maintain their own positions. His stay in Basel lasted only ten months; in February 1528 he left the city to renew a migratory existence. His brief career as a university teacher was a momentous one, for he never lost the sense of injury and disillusionment in his future writings. For thirteen years he wandered, wrote, and was driven by poverty, never spending a full year in any one place.

Medicine was still a pseudo-science based on the teachings of Hippocrates of Cos, Avicenna, and the Persian Prince of Physicians, and Galen of Pergamum, gilder of pills and dissector of swine and apes. Superstition, mysticism, and false theories were the cornerstones of medicine's structure in the days of Paracelsus. In his own system of medicine he placed the magnet above all other remedies on his lists of infallible cures. He called it "A Monarch of Secrets. . . . The Magnet contains mysterious healing virtues; it is impossible to dispense with it in the treatment of disease." He went on to say that although its physical properties had been known for a long time, he was the first to employ it medicinally. "The magnet, like the stars and other bodies of the universe is endowed with a subtle emanation, 'fluidium', which has a favorable influence on the health and life of man. It assures cure for discharging sinuses of the limbs, for fistulae of the various parts of the body, for fluxes of the eye, ear, and nose, and for jaundice and dropsy."

Since the main interest of Paracelsus lay in medicine and since he rejected the ancient authorities on both the theory and practice of medicine, it does not seem out of place to discuss his theories on the subject. He made great effort to harmonize this with his philosophy of nature and the results of his experience and observation. To the question as to the causes of disease, Paracelsus distinguished five causes or five principles. They might be called powers or realms. They were:

1. *Ens Astri* (the influence of the stars; astrology).
2. *Ens Venei* (the influence of poisons).
3. *Ens Naturale* (the influence that exists in the nature of the individual, the microcosm).
4. *Ens Spirituale* (the influences acting not directly upon the body but through the spirit).
5. *Ens Dei* (the influence of the will of God acting directly to produce illness by way of warning or punishment).

With respect to the first power or realm, Paracelsus recognized the influence of the planets and zodiac without admitting their complete control on the destinies of men. One of the fundamental concepts of this philosophy was the interrelation of all activity of the universe, in that every phenomenon has an influence on every other. As the earth was thought to be the center of the material universe, so man was considered the center of the external universe—man being the microcosm (little universe) with the external universe the macrocosm (large universe).

The opposite was also thought to be true—that man through knowledge and wisdom would be able to exert an influence on the powers of nature in marvelous occult ways.

The created world has been given over to man in order that he may fulfill it. More than that: man's original and specific mission is to lead it to perfection; he has been placed in the world solely for this purpose.

The medieval hermetic alchemy of the transmutation of metals was not only a chemical process, but in addition a spiritual and psychic process symbolic of the pattern that was followed by everything in creation.

Certainly Paracelsus' thinking in regard to man's place in Nature was in part formed by the austere world view which Dante supplied in his *Divine Comedy*. Proof of Paracelsus' belief in Free Will and transcendence is shown in the following quotation:

Just as the firmament with all its constellations forms a whole in itself, likewise man in himself is a free and mighty firmament. And just as the firmament rests in itself and is not ruled by any creature, the firmament of man is not ruled by other creatures, but stands for itself and is free of all bonds. For there are two kinds of created things: heaven and earth are of one kind, man is of the other.

He goes further in this discussion of man transcending the stars when he states in *Volumen Paramirum:*

The course of Saturn disturbs no man in his life, neither lengthens nor shortens it. For if Saturn had never been in the heavens nor in the firmament, people would be born just so, and though no moon had been created still would people have just such natures. You must not believe that because Mars is cruel, therefore Nero was his child. Although they had the same nature neither obtained it from the other. Man's wisdom is in no way subjugated, and is no one's slave; it has not renounced or surrendered its freedom. Therefore the stars must obey man and be subject to him, and not he to the stars. Even if he is a child of Saturn and Saturn has overshadowed his birth, he can still escape Saturn's influence, he can master Saturn and become a child of the sun.

Paracelsus died on September 24, 1541 at the age of forty-nine. Legend has supplied many causes for his death. His friends said he was murdered by an assassin and his enemies said he died in a drunken brawl. However, modern research has shown both of these are probably false, since he suffered from childhood from rickets and three days before his death he dictated to a notary-public his last will and testament. The lengthy epitaph he composed for his gravestone reads:

Here lies buried
Philip Theophrastus
the famous doctor of medicine
who cured wounds, leprosy, gout, dropsy
and other incurable diseases of the body
with wonderful knowledge
and who gave his goods to be divided and distributed
among the poor.
In the year 1541 on the 24th day of September
he exchanged life for death.
To the living peace, to the entombed eternal rest.

Paracelsus was a true child of the Reformation. He illustrated its independence, its self-confidence, its boldness of thought, as well as its confusion of old and new ideas and its struggle to free itself from the bondage of tradition. During the last four centuries the name and fame of Paracelsus have been identified with the man who was Faust in legend and poetry. He was surrounded with a legendary haze and believed to be inspired by God or by the devil! Many regard him as the most profound mind in German culture, while others dismiss him as a charlatan.

Paracelsus, with his humanistic outlook on man, felt that man was capable of transcending the astrological influence of the stars by wisdom. This wisdom was acquired by the direct study of nature, wherever and whenever possible. Above all, he did not study nature in the classroom or by consulting the ancient lore, but rather by going to nature itself.

Paracelsus was a Utopian. He overestimated the possibilities of his science. He strove to discover truths for which the science of his age had neither definition nor method of verification. He tried to grasp the whole before knowing the details. His concepts are poorly defined, and his language shows a struggle with words.

The legend of Dr. Faustus or Faust was enlarged by details drawn from the life of Paracelsus. Goethe in particular drew heavily from his study of Paracelsus in developing the main character of his master drama. The earlier work of Christopher Marlowe, *The Tragedy of Doctor Faustus*, also describes a central figure much like Paracelsus.

During the Renaissance and Reformation there sprang up in Europe a tale of a magician and charlatan who was ready to forego salvation and risk damnation to gain understanding and power over nature. Dr. Faustus had traveled extensively and studied all forms of books, but found inadequate the learning of his age. Desiring to know the mysteries heretofore concealed from human eyes, he bargained with the Devil. He was given power over space and matter and created the homunculus (little man). A black poodle, really a devil, was at his side constantly. When Dr. Faustus died, the dog ran away with his soul.

In *Index sanitatis*, Philip Begardi places Faust with Paracelsus—"wicked, cheating, useless, and unlearned doctors." In *Ignatius*, John Donne places Paracelsus among four pretenders to the "principal place right next to Lucifer's own throne," beside Copernicus and Machiavelli.

Goethe introduced a new thought to the Faust tale. Unable to believe that knowledge leads to damnation, he absolved the hero. When the Devil appears to take Faust to Hell, the angels are there too and say:

> Him who unwearied still strives on
> We have the power to save.

Goethe's *Faust* departs widely from the older versions of the legend. Faust does not repent but simply emerges by the inborn force of his character into a higher state:

> Man errs so long as he is striving,
> A good man through the obscurest aspiration
> Is ever conscious of the one true way.

This idea inspired a similar theme revealed by Robert Browning in *Paracelsus*.

Rumors of his day held that Paracelsus may have been the damnable Doctor Faustus; however, there were others who were credited with being Faustus. Paracelsus himself became a legend, and as recently as a hundred years ago, during an epidemic of cholera, people made a pilgrimage to his grave in Salzburg, searching for magic healing.

Before we close this chapter we should consider one other mystic who was treated quite shabbily by history. Yet he was a true follower and contemporary of Paracelsus. Jerome Cardan was a great mathematician physician, and astrologer who was born at Pavia on the 24th of September, 1501. He was the illegitimate son of Facio Cardano, a learned judge of Milan and distinguished by a taste for complicated mathematics. Jerome was educated at the University of Pavia and later Padua, where he graduated with honors in medicine. He was, however, excluded from the College of Physicians at Milan on account of his illegitimate birth, and it was not surprising that his first book was a colorful exposure of the fallacies of the learned faculty.

A fortunate and timely cure of the child of the Milanese senator, Sfonfrato, brought him into public notice. The interest of this patron procured him admission into the medical society without trouble. About 1539 he obtained additional fame and notoriety by the publication of his *Practica Arithmeticae Generalis*, a work of great merit and scholarship. He became engaged in correspondence with Niccolo Tartaglia, who discovered the solution of cubic equations so vital to progressive astrology. This discovery Tartaglia kept to himself, but he was ultimately talked into teaching Cardan the method under a solemn promise it should never be divulged to the vulgar public or to skeptics. Cardan, however, published it in his comprehensive treatise on higher algebra, which appeared at Nuremberg in 1545.

Two years previously he had published a work on astrology even more highly regarded. As a student in astrology Cardan was on a level with the best minds of his age. The greatest distinction consisted in the comparatively cautious spirit of his inquiries and his disposition to confirm his assertions by an appeal to solid hard facts. A very considerable part of this great treatise was based upon observation carefully collected by Cardan, personally. These were well calculated to support his theories of astrology as far as they extended. Numerous instances of his belief in dreams and omens collected from his writings show he especially valued himself as being one of the five or six celebrated figures to whom (as to the great Socrates) was vouchsafed the assistance of a guardian "Astral Spirit."

In 1547 he was appointed professor of medicine at Pavia. The publication of his works on algebra and astrology at this time gained for him a widespread European renown. It also procured flattering offers of employment from Pope Paul III and the King of Denmark, both of whom he declined. In 1551 his reputation was furthered even more by the publication of his greatest work, De Subtilitate Rerum, which embodied the soundest physical learning of the time. It simultaneously represented the most advanced spirit of speculation on astrology.

It was followed some years later by a similar treatise, De Rerum Varietate; the two made, in effect, but one book. A great portion of these are attempts and endeavors, commonly futile, to explain ordinary natural phenomena. But their chief interest for us now consists in the hints and glimpses they afford into principles beyond the full comprehension of Cardan himself. Yet the world was then by no means ready to entertain such great ideas. The inorganic realm of Nature he asserted to be animated no less than the organic.

Thus he was the first to study and write about the astral planes of being, and show that all creation was a progressive development. All animals were originally worms. The inferior metals were regarded as "conatus naturae" toward the production of astral gold. The indefinite variability of species was implied in the remark that Nature was seldom content with a single variation from a customary single type. The oviparous habits of birds were explained by their tendency to favor the perpetuation of the species, precisely in the manner of our modern naturalists. Animals were not created for the use of man, but exist for their own sake. The origin of life depends upon astral cosmic laws, which Cardan naturally connected with his sincere study of astrology.

The physical divergencies of mankind came from the effects of climate and the variety of human circumstances in general. Cardan's views on the dissimilarity of languages were much more philosophical than was usual during his time. His treatise altogether, though weak in particular details, was strong in its pervading sense of the unity and the omnipotence of Natural Law. This rendered it in some degree a prophecy of the course of science after Cardan's day. It was attacked by Professor J. C. Scaliger, whom Cardan refuted without any difficulty.

The notoriety that Cardan acquired led in the year 1551 to a journey to Scotland as the medical advisor to the Archbishop Hamilton of St. Andrews. The Archbishop was supposed to be suffering from consumption, a complaint that Cardan, under a false impression, represented himself as competent to cure. He was still of great service to the Archbishop, however, whose complaint proved to be asthma and not tuberculosis. But the principal interest attached to his expedition was derived from his account of the disputes of the medical faculty at Paris and the court of Edward VI of England. The French doctors were disturbed by the findings of Vesalius, who introduced anatomical study from the human subject.

Cardan's wisdom and lack of temper led him to sympathize with Vesalius. His account of Edward VI's disposition and understanding was also extremely favorable. He was a competent observer without bias toward either side of the religious question stirred up by Vesalius. He cast the king's nativity and made a number of predictions that were most effectually proved by the royal youth's death the following year.

Cardan now attained the summit of his financial prosperity, and for the rest of his life a series of disasters continually faced him. His principal misfortune arose from the crimes and failures of his sons. One was an utter reprobate and child of Satan, while the tragic fate of Battista, the other overwhelmed the father with deepest anguish. This son, Giovanni also a physician, contracted an imprudent marriage with a girl of lowest character. She subsequently proved unfaithful to him and the injured husband sought revenge with poison. The foul deed was detected, and the exceptionally harsh severity of the punishment justified Cardan in attributing it to the rancor of his own medical rivals. These men never at any time were on good terms with Cardan. The blow all but crushed him!

Cardan's reputation and practice waned; he soon became addicted to gaming, a vice to which he was always prone. His great mind became unhinged and filled with distempered imaginations and dreams. He was ultimately banished from Milan on a false accusation; and although the decree of banishment was ultimately rescinded, he found it advisable to accept a professorship at Bologna in 1562. While residing there in moderate financial comfort, and mainly occupied with writing supplements to his works, Cardan was suddenly arrested on a false charge that was not stated. But in all probability this charge was heresy leveled by the Inquisition.

Though he was always careful to keep on friendly terms with the Church, the bent of his mind was openly toward free thought and the astral. The circumstances that probably attracted the attention of Pope Pius V, who then ruled the Church, were Cardan's humanistic naturalism and belief in cosmic law. Through the intercession of some influential cardinals, Cardan was finally released; but he was deprived of his professorship and prohibited from teaching and publishing more books. Later on he was sent to Rome, where he spent the remaining years of his life in receipt of a meager pension from the Pope. It seems that everyone felt, which was in his favor, that his intellect was severely and permanently disturbed by grief for the loss of his son. Cardan frequently dreamed of and had visions of this lost son of Satan, visions that lent some countenance to the idea that Cardan was insane. The existence of any serious derangement of mind was completely disproved by the lucidity and coherence of his last writings.

He spent his time at Rome in the writing of his commentaries—*De Vita Propria* and a companion treatise, *De Libris Propriis*—which are our principal authorities for his biography. Though he burned much he left behind more than a hundred manuscripts. Only twenty of these were ever printed. He died at Rome on the 21st of September, 1576.

Intellectually and morally, Cardan was one of the most interesting personages connected with the revival of astrological science in Europe. He had no special bent toward any scientific pursuit, but he appears now as a man of versatile ability who delighted in research for its own sake. He possessed the true scientific spirit of perfection and curiosity, yet he claimed, among the king of France's treasures which appeared to him as worthy of admiration, a certain piece which he mistakenly took for the horn of the unicorn. It was very injurious to his later fame to have labored partly in fields of research where no important discovery was attainable, and partly in those where his discoveries could only serve as the stepping stones for others.

His medical career serves as an illustration of the former and his mathematical studies of the latter. His medical knowledge was wholly empirical. He was restrained by the authority of Galen and debarred from the practice of anatomy by the Church. Nothing more should be expected than that he stumbled on some fortunate and healing nostrums. As a mathematician, on the other hand, he brought about important advances in science. But these merely paved the way for even greater discoveries that obscured his own. From his astrology, positive results could be expected. But even here, the scientific character of his mind was displayed in his common sense and scientific treatment of what usually passed for a mystical and occult study.

His prognostications were as strictly empirical as his prescriptions and they rested upon the observations that he himself made in his practice. As frequently is the case with men incapable of rightly ordering their own lives, he was full of wisdom and sound advice for others. His ethical precepts and practical rules were always excellent, and just to complete the catalog of his accomplishments, he was an excellent poet.

The work of Cardan's, however, that holds most interest for this modern generation is his autobiography, *De Vita Propria* (or *Memoirs*). In its clearness and frankness of self-revelation this book stands alone among such records. It may well be compared with the autobiography of another celebrated Italian of the sixteenth century, Benvenuto Cellini. But it is much more free from vanity and self-consciousness, unless the extreme candor with which Cardan reveals his own errors is to be regarded as vanity in a most subtle form. The general impression the *Memoirs* leaves with the reader is highly favorable to the writer. Cardan's impetuosity and fits of reckless dissipation appear as mere exaggerations of the warmth of heart that imparted such strength to his various affections. In the region of science the book shows a passionate devotion to research that could alone enable him to persevere so resolutely and effect such marked advances in such multifarious fields of inquiry.

All in all, Cardan was treated shabbily by history. Many biographers pass over him by calling him a "so-called magician," who lived about the end of the fifteenth or the beginning of the sixteenth century. Still, he left in his *Memoirs* a frank and detailed analysis of a curiously complicated and abnormal intellectuality, sensitive, intense, and altogether free from the taint of insanity. He declared himself subject to strange fits of abstraction and exaltation. The intensity of these fits became, at length, so intolerable that he was forced to inflict on himself severe bodily pain as a means of banishing them. He would, he tells us in his *Memoirs,* talk habitually of those things which were most likely to be distasteful to the few friends he made. He would argue on any side of a question, quite irrespective of whether he believed it right or wrong, and he had an extraordinary passion for all forms of gambling.

Cardan tells us of three personal peculiarities, in which we may trace the workings of a rampant imagination. In the third of these, at least, we see a supernormal delicacy of perception that characterized him so well. The first was the faculty of projecting his Spirit outside his body into the Astral, this to the accompaniment of strange physical sensations. The second was the ability to perceive sensibly anything he desired to perceive even at great distances. As a child, he explained, he saw these images involuntarily and without the power of selection, but when he reached manhood he could control them to suit his choice of the moment. The third of his wonderful peculiar qualities was that before every event of great moment in his life, he had a vivid dream that warned him of the forthcoming event.

Indeed, he himself wrote a commentary of considerable length on Synesius' treatise on dreams, in which he advanced the theory that any virtuous person can acquire the faculty of interpreting dreams. In fact, anyone can draw up for himself a code of dream interpretations by merely studying carefully his own dreams. We cannot today put much faith in Cardan's wonderful dreams. His was not the type of mind to which we would go for an accurate statement concerning mental psychic phenomena. But such significant dreams as he had were probably, as already suggested, the result of his supernormal subconscious perceptiveness. In one instance, his prediction was not entirely successful. He foretold the date of his own death, and at the age of seventy-five. But he was obliged to abstain from all food in order to die at the time he predicted.

Astrology and modern science owe much to this great man. He paved the way for others to follow. Many of these mere followers are credited with discoveries made possible by Cardan, the mystic. In the next chapter we shall see how the idea of "free will" entered into astrology and how the Church and the astrologers arrived at some slight agreement on whether man was compelled by the stars or only guided by them.

TEN

Free Will and the Rational Soul

The entire history of man and his relation to astrology is a history of trying to gain control. First, in the primitive state, we see man laboring under
the necessity to control the animals, to control his amount of exposure
to the elements, and to find some means of providing for himself. In the
Book of James it was said man learned to control almost anything but
his own tongue. Even against the fiercely raging natural elements, man
learned to establish some shelter for himself.

Early in the fifteenth century science declared that all matter was subject to natural law. Man could not escape, because he was composed of
matter. Philosophy and religion brought in many arguments against
such a view. Even the poets insisted that thunder occurred by natural law,
and it was only various forms of matter acting and reacting. It was so
because God established this law. Nothing could be simply the natural
result of the interaction of material forces without any reason or cause.
If such were so, then all things were accidental!—accidents that could at
any time take the form of utter destruction, since there was no divine
reason or law to hold nature to a rational pattern.

The predominant belief was that man, who tried to live by rational
thought, was a part of a universe of vast cosmic infinitude that had divine
reasoning to direct its course. If this were not true, man reasoned, then
all his efforts were counter to reality and he was indeed struggling against,
and seeking to keep his foothold in, something completely chaotic.

Shakespeare wrote: "There is a destiny that shapes our ends, rough
hew them how we may." He also wrote: "The fault . . . is not our stars
but in ourselves that we are underlings." These statements point out the

fact that both the stars and we are totally involved, as was first explained by Paracelsus. By the middle of the fifteenth century astrologers were familiar with the finer details of the Ptolemaic system now taken directly from the Greek, not from some corrupt Arabic translation. Books were written setting out the Greek ideas and making them more widely accessible. And so it was by the close of the fifteenth century that the original Greek ideas were largely completely recovered. Ptolemy was now well understood by the better astrologers of the day.

In Vienna George Purbach, who took his name from his Austrian birthplace, taught at the university after having traveled widely in Germany and Italy. He was the first in Western Europe to expound Ptolemy's epicycle theory in a book called *New Theory of the Planets*. He inserted it into Aristotle's world system by separating the region of each planet from its neighbor by solid spherical shells.

Regarded as more crucial in the path of modern astrological science is the pupil and collaborator of Purbach, Johann Muller, or Regiomontanus. He was equally outstanding and influential in the fields of mathematics and astrology. Like his master, he lectured as a young prodigy at Venice, Rome, Ferrara, and Padua and later accepted an invitation from the king of Hungary to arrange and evaluate his precious collection of recently acquired Greek manuscripts.

The king's sponsorship terminated and Regiomontanus moved to Nurnberg, the most cultured city in Germany at the time, a city famous for its printing presses and scientific interests. He was enthusiastically received there by the citizenry and struck up a fruitful friendship with one of its richest and most learned merchants, Bernhard Walther. Walther supported him for many years, collaborated with him in his labors, and established for him a printing enterprise in which Regiomontanus published not only the works of his master Purbach, but many other valuable scientific treatises.

Regiomontanus (1436–1476) was born at Konigsberg in Franconia on the 16th of June, the son of a miller, and his name originally was Johann Muller. But he called himself after the name of his birthplace, Jon. de Montergio, an appellation which became gradually modified into Regiomontanus. At Vienna, in 1452, he was the pupil and later the associate of George Purbach. They jointly undertook a reform of astrology rendered necessary by the errors they detected in the Alphonsine Ephemerides.

During the years 1456–61 Purbach and he made many observations of eclipses, comets, and solar altitudes; in the course of these studies they found that the Alphonsine Tables were several degrees in error. Their desire to obtain better manuscripts of Ptolemy was stimulated by a diplomatic visit to Vienna by Cardinal Bessarion, who held a high rank in the Byzantine Church. Their plan to join him on his return to Italy was frustrated by Purbach's early death. Regiomontanus alone accompanied the Cardinal to Italy. He collected and copied Greek manuscripts and attended lectures on astronomy. He rapidly mastered Greek while in Rome and Ferrara, gave lectures on Alfraganus at Padua, and completed (1463) Purbach's *Epitome in Cl. Ptolemaci magnam compositionem* (printed at Venice in 1496).

After a short visit to Hungary, where King Matthias Crovinus had acquired Greek manuscripts during his wars against the Turks, Regiomontanus finally settled in the town of Nurnberg in 1471. Here in this center of middle European trade and flourishing commerce and handicrafts were offered the most favorable opportunities for the construction of astronomical instruments as well as for the printing of books.

Indeed, the newly invented art of printing opened up many new possibilities for astrological science. The printing of books, with careful corrections of the text, put an end to the annoying evil of the numerous copying errors of the early handwritten manuscripts. The new process, it was true, did not yet include the printing of tables and figures. Regiomontanus had, therefore, to found a printing office himself and to instruct the compositors in this art.

Still preserved is a circular letter written by him in which he enumerated the titles of the books he intended to print and publish. This list of twenty-two items, all in Latin and mostly editions of ancient astronomers and mathematicians, included Ptolemy's *Geography* and *Astronomy*, the works of Archimedes, Euclid, Theon, Procius, Appollonius, and others. These would be followed by his own works, yearly almanacs and other writings.

He began the venture by publishing the planetary theory of his teacher Purbach and the astronomical poem of Manilius. Then he printed carefully computed almanacs in Latin and in German. He won great fame with his *Ephemirides*, in which the positions of the sun, the moon, and the planets were computed for the thirty-two years from 1475 to 1506.

His own *De Triangulis* (Nurnberg, 1533) was the earliest work treating trigonometry as a substantive science, and was published posthumously. A quarrel with George of Trebizond about his blunders in the translation of Ptolemy's *Almagest* obliged him to leave Rome precipitately back in 1468. He went to Vienna and was summoned to Buda by Matthias Corvinus, king of Hungary, for the purpose of collating the Greek manuscripts at a handsome salary. He also finished his *Tabulae Directionum* (Nurnberg, 1475), essentially an astrological work, but also containing a valuable table of tangents.

The outbreak of war meanwhile diverted the king's attention from astrological learning, and thus it was that in 1471 Regiomontanus finally settled permanently at Nurnberg. Bernhard Walther, the rich patrician, became his pupil and patron. Together they equipped the first European observatory, for which Regiomontanus himself constructed astrological instruments of an improved type described in his posthumous *Scripta* (Nurnberg, 1544). His observations of the great comet of January 1472 supplied the basis of much of our modern knowledge of cometry. A printing press was established in Walther's home by Regiomontanus and a series of popular calendars was promptly issued. Regiomontanus worked out the method of "lunar distances" for determining the longitude at sea and recommended and explained it in his Ephemirides. In 1472 he was summoned to Rome by Pope Sixtus IV to aid in the urgently needed reform of the calendar. There in Rome he died, most likely of the plague, on the 6th of July, 1476.

His greatest projects remained unfinished, the printing office was not continued, and his manuscripts were scattered. His own works were not actually printed until forty years later. He was never able to accomplish the complete translation of Ptolemy, and it was not until 1505 that an older Latin translation was printed in Venice. The first printed Greek edition of Ptolemy finally appeared in 1538.

It was not only through his printing works, but even more because of his practical astrological work that Regiomontanus attracted around him in Nurnberg a circle of admirers and students of the ancient science. They also provided money for the printing business. Among them were the patricians Willibald Pirkheimer and Bernhard Walther, both humanists well versed in Greek. Walther became his pupil in practical astrology and it was at his house that their first real observatory was constructed.

The two friends made many observations together, and after Regiomontanus' death Walther assiduously continued to observe the celestial bodies, so that by the time he died in 1504 he had made 746 measurements of solar altitudes and 615 determinations of the positions of planets, moon, and stars. It was the first uninterrupted series of observations in the new rising of European science. A century later Tycho Brahe and Kepler utilized this great piece of work as a basis for their tables.

The measuring instruments were made of wood after Regiomontanus' own design and were of very simple construction. First, there was the *Dreistab* (three-staff), also called *triquetrum*, which was described originally by Ptolemy. It consisted of a lath about nine feet long (with two sights to direct it toward a star). This was hinged at the top of a vertical pole, the lower end was pressed against a second lath, graduated and hinged at a lower place on the pole; the distance from this point to the lower end of the first lath indicated the inclination. This instrument was used mainly to measure midday altitudes of the sun; one inch on the divided lath corresponded to nearly one half a degree.

A more widely used device was the cross-staff for measuring the distance between any two celestial objects. Along a graduated lath, which the observer took in his hand and directed at the midpoint between the two objects, there was a cross-lath adapted to slide up and down, until its two ends, as seen from the lower end of the lath, coincided with the two bodies. The reading of the cross-lath combined with its constant length gave the angular distance between the two bodies being measured. For several centuries the cross-staff was the most common instrument for navigators to measure the altitude of the sun or a star above the horizon.

Afterward, in 1488, Walther made an *armilla*, also after Ptolemy's original description, on which after careful adjustment he could directly read the longitude and latitude of any planet. In an attempt to measure earth distances by time intervals he made use of clocks, although at the time they were far from perfect because they were regulated by friction only and not by an escapement. The care with which he made his observations was shown by the fact that he discovered the upward displacement of the sun near the horizon, which he rightly explained as due to atmospheric refraction. His carefulness was even more clearly shown by the accuracy he attained! His positions for the planets, measured by means of cross-staff and *armilla*, had a mean error of only five minutes, and the errors of his solar altitudes were usually below one minute. His younger collaborator Johannes Schoner, who continued his work, published all these observations later in a valuable set of tables.

Thus we see how in the fifteenth century astrological science took a new trend. In the preceding centuries the most highly praised scientists were scholars, not actual investigators. They reproduced science as they found it, but did not produce any new science. Books and writings, not experiments and observations, were the source of their knowledge. Now, however, a new era opened up in which the actual observation of new phenomena became the source of the scientific progress.

So it was that by the close of the fifteenth century the original Greek ideas had been largely or completely recovered. They also became widely diffused through a number of countries with differing political and religious affiliations. These factors, together with a greatly improved physical sense, seem to have provided the foundations on which the extraordinary scientific developments of the next centuries were based.

It is clearly evident when one turns to the works of Copernicus that he possessed a far better developed physical sense than his Greek forerunners. Ptolemy had rejected the notion of a rotating earth on the ground that if the earth were rotating then bodies thrown upward from it would be found to lag behind. Copernicus dismissed this objection, arguing correctly that a body thrown up into the air possesses two essentially independent motions, a circular motion due to the rotation of the earth and a motion up and down.

Because we ourselves also possess the circular motion, we do not recognize it in the body; we recognize only the up and down motion. To the argument that the earth would fly asunder if it were spinning around, Copernicus answered by saying how much more certainly must the sphere of the stars burst asunder if they were spinning around. The distant stars would have to move at far greater speeds than the earth in order to make a complete revolution in only twenty-four hours.

Though Regiomontanus died at the age of forty, his scientific output was really overwhelming. Besides editing the books begun by Purbach, he authored a set of Tables of Sines, the study of comets, several books on trigonometry and trigonometric functions, and tables of stellar and planetary positions that were regarded by most astrologers of the time as greatly superior to the Alphonsine Tables and even to the later set of Prutenic Tables. Moreover, they contained Walther's and Regiomontanus' original and accurate observations.

The early Alphonsine Tables of astrological-astronomical data were compiled by, and under the supervision of, the king of Leon and Castile, Alfonso X (1223–1284), an enterprising scholar in astrology. After conquering Toledo from the Arabs in 1252 he gathered Jewish and Christian scholars to improve upon the values given in the Toledan Tables. These were compiled in Toledo by the Mohammedan astrologer Arzache (1080) for the purpose of correcting errors found in Ptolemy's original calculations. By the time of Alfonso new errors were even detected in these Arabic tables; hence in his effort to correct them Alfonso was also responsible for the publication of the *Libros del Saber,* a vast and valuable encyclopedia of astrological knowledge from Arabic sources. The Prutenic Tables were composed by Erasmus Reinhold in 1551 at the request of Duke Albert of Prussia, hence named Prutenic or Prussian, and were based upon the calculations from Copernicus' *De Revolutionibus* (see Chapter 13).

Besides numerous treatises on astrology, astronomy, geometry, improved instruments and physics, Regiomontanus also published many *Ephemerides,* calendars, and shorter letters on astrological matters. In 1468 he cast the horoscope of the new university of Pressberg, then under the reign of Matthias Corvinus, king of Hungary, where he lectured. He foresaw a great future for the university. Thorndike has said that no matter how good a mathematician Regiomontanus may have been he proved an indifferent astrologer at least on this occasion, for the new university was short lived. His correspondence on astrological subjects with James of Speyer, a famous astrologer, was of interest mainly because of the caution with which he discussed, or rather evaded, such dangerous questions as the effect of a possible conjunction on the birth and career of Christ. Regiomontanus merely referred to "the virtue of the great conjunction which predicted and signified" His coming. He did manage, however, to compute astrologically the day of the Passion. His *Ephemerides* are full of astrological material involving weather prediction—side by side with citing times for bleeding, planting, taking a bath, and cutting one's hair. His publishing house issued numerous astrological texts, many of which are still available and of great value.

It seems as if the writers who have stated a claim for Regiomontanus as a precursor of Copernicus have either not read his works at all, or have been content to read only the headings and first lines. For in his major works there was not one word in favor of any kind of motion of the earth. First there was an actual sneer at "certain of the ancients" who taught the rotation of the earth and imagined the earth was like meat on a spit and the sun like the fire, and who said it was not the fire that was in need of the meat, but the reverse. Likewise, he ridiculed the idea that the sun did not require the earth but rather the earth required the sun. After this attempt at humor the usual old arguments against such rotation were brought up: Birds and clouds would be left behind and buildings would tumble down. Truly this was not the language of a precursor of Copernicus.

And if anyone should say that these were perhaps the arguments of Schoner, and not of Regiomontanus, let him read the *Epitome in Almagestum* wherein the old arguments of Ptolemy were found. It is impossible to doubt that Regiomontanus rejected altogether the rotation of the earth. He also distinctly affirmed that the earth occupied the center of the universe.

Doppelmayr, who was the first to circulate the myth that Regiomontanus was the precursor of Copernicus, adds that Johannes Praetorius states in a manuscript found after his death that George Hartmann, a mathematician of Nurnberg (1489–1564), possessed a note written by Regiomontanus, from which he draws the conclusion: "Therefore it is necessary that the motion of the stars must be altered a little (*paululum variari*) on account of the motion of the earth."

But how was it possible to found any claim for Regiomontanus on evidence as vague as this, when it was distinctly contradicted by the published writings of the great astrologer himself? And what kind of a motion of the earth could he have thought of, which only affected the motion of the stars "a little"?

Even though Regiomontanus thought it necessary in the *Epitome* to put together the arguments against any motion of the earth, this does not prove a doctrine of that kind was current in his day. He only followed the example of Ptolemy in doing so. Yet he must have known of the mystical speculations of Cusa and may have thought it necessary to emphasize the works of Ptolemy. Regiomontanus would no doubt have been very much surprised if he were told that he should, some centuries after his death, be held up as an advocate of such a diametrically opposite opinion. Yet he was not the only great man who was proclaimed a precursor of Copernicus.

Since both the Copernican and the Ptolemaic systems are still valid mathematically, and even the bitterest opponents of the new system admitted that it would "save the phenomena," the truth or falsity of the heliocentric hypothesis was decided by other branches of science and by direct observation with telescopes.

Physical theory, most naturally, was the first to be brought into the discussion. Here again the answer was equivocal. Both systems involved assumptions that seemed difficult to reconcile with common sense and reason. Intelligent, unprejudiced men could justly ask themselves whether the terrific speed assigned to the heavenly spheres by the old cosmology was inherently any more improbable than the vast distance and incredible magnitude of the fixed stars implicit in the new theory. The mechanical difficulties in the way of making truly workable the infinitely complex assemblage of over eight material spheres were no greater than those involved in accepting a threefold motion of earth. Even for conscientious empirical scientists a choice between the two systems made on the basis of mathematics and rational logic rather than on ascertainable facts was impossible.

We mentioned the mechanical, and the foremost student of this art was Leonardo da Vinci, who did not write in Latin. Not only that, he never published or even finished a book or literary composition. Of the collection of 120 notebooks he bequeathed to Francesco de Melzi hardly a quarter is still extant. These manuscripts were written in Italian, with his left hand and from right to left. They are difficult to decipher and have come down in a mutilated, dismembered, scattered, chaotic, and corrupt condition. They contain sporadic records of readings, observations, and reflections, with some sketches in the master's hand. They reveal his interest in nature as well as in art and mechanics. He considered a large and varied assortment of scientific problems, and they were based in large part upon the scientific writings of the preceding medieval centuries.

But at the same time they were apparently utilized by subsequent writ-

ers on astrological science. They constitute a good transition and introduction to the thought of the sixteenth century. Although more years of
the life of the great man were in the fifteenth century, his notebooks
and literary remains were penned largely in the sixteenth, and probably
exerted their influence after his death. Leonardo da Vinci was rational,
logical, and always sought ways to explain the universe. He felt that the
dark and light areas of the moon were bodies of water and land, since
water reflects light better than earth.

About the same time John Pico della Mirandola presented objections
to astrology. He was a scholastic disputant and humanist, but not a good
Hebrew scholar. Thus he did little but add Platonism and mystic theology
to medieval scholastic thought. His genius was precocious, and in life he
was an attractive, compelling personality. The works he left behind him
only fill a single large volume, yet they were about magic, the Cabala,
and astrology.

Perhaps the most startling were propositions that were condemned as
bordering upon heresy. One was the idea that there was no science that
gives us more certainty of the divinity of Christ than magic and
the Cabala.

Pico showed that his thinking was largely colored by astrology, that
he was favorable to natural magic, and that he had a penchant for such
occult and esoteric literature as the Orphic hymns, Chaldean oracles, and
Jewish Cabala. Among his conclusions were: (1) That every soul par-
ticipating in a Vulcanic intellect was sown in the moon, that from this it
follows why all Germans were of good stature and blond and most rever-
ent toward the apostolic see; (2) That just as Apollo was of solar intellect
so Aesculapius was of lunar intellect; (3) That the moon in the ascendent
gives health to the one born then; (4) From Hermes Trismegistus he
derived the idea that God announced the future to man in six ways
(dreams, portents, birds, intestines, spirit, and Sibyl); (5) He affirmed
that the soul lived a contemplative life with Saturn, a political and practical life with Jupiter, an irascible and ambitious life with Mars, a life of
concupiscence and pleasure with Venus, and with Mercury, a vegetating
and stupid existence; and (6) The first seven years of life were under
Mercury, the second seven under Venus, the third under Mars, the fourth
under Jupiter, the fifth under Saturn, and the rest of one's life was under
whichever planet predominated.

But by 1491 we find he had completely altered his favorable attitude
to magic. He belittled the supposed wisdom of the ancient Chaldeans
and Egyptians and referred to his former attachment to magic as an illness of adolescence. He even censured Albertus Magnus for venturing
to suggest in the *Speculum astronomiae* that books of magic should not be

destroyed but preserved on the chance they might some day be of use to the Church. He asks, why preserve books that had better never have been written? He even asserted flatly that magic was nothing other than a mixture of idolatry, astrology, and superstitious medicine, "which just as other superstitions we have confuted one by one in our books on the true faith against its seven foes."

The closing decade of the fifteenth century was marked by two events of importance in the history of astrology and the opposition to it. The most outstanding theoretical and literary attack upon the art since the treatises of Oresme and Henry of Nesse in the fourteenth century was launched in Italy by Pico. Almost simultaneous with it was the legal condemnation in France of Simon, or Symon de Phares, and certain astrological works in his library.

Pico selected only those persons and data that supported his contentions, suppressing any evidence to the contrary and misrepresenting the attitude of other famous persons. Pico contended that the signs of the zodiac were purely artificial and mathematical divisions and of no natural significance or virtue. He also regarded the figures that were traced to connect the stars in constellations as mere figments of the human imagination. He charged that the Arabic and medieval Latin astrologers invented invisible images in each decan and facies, which were not known to the ancient Greeks, Latins, Egyptians, and Chaldeans.

Pico's attacks were an appeal to reason, while the condemnation of Simon was a resort to force. Yet both depended on theological and ecclesiastical motive forces for their drive and support. Simon was a man of wide learning and considerable stature, who studied medicine at Montpellier and attended the Universities of Paris and Orleans. He was astrologer and physician to John the duke of Bourbon, and was requested by Louis XI to go to his court. He was reluctant and spent the next four years in search of medicinal herbs in the Alps, until the king died in 1483. Simon settled in Lyons to practice astrology and attained sufficient fame to attract the king of France, Charles VIII, who visited him in his study and watched him in the process of casting horoscopes and predicting. It was this royal visit, as well as his spreading fame, that brought him into direct conflict with the archbishop of Lyons.

This powerful churchman seized Simon's library and sent it to the faculty of theology of the University of Paris, and prevented Simon from practicing his art. He took his case to the Parliament of Paris in 1491, and there the case lingered, in spite of Charles the VIII's requesting Parliament to act speedily and favorably. Parliament did nothing, but in February of 1494 the faculty of theology reached the formal conclusion that astrology was to be condemned. They condemned horoscopes, nativities, interrogations, and elections. But somehow they excluded the annual predictions that were so very popular with the common people of the time. Eleven of Simon's books were ordered burned, and Parliament rejected Simon's appeal. They ordered that he and his books be handed over to the Bishop and inquisitor of Paris for further questioning. Some historians claim that Simon met his death at the hands of the Holy Inquisition. However, Thorndike does not seem to agree! Perhaps King Charles VIII was able to save him; even so an air of uncertainty now prevailed among the practicing astrologers. The Roman Church and free will were apparently in command of the rational soul of man.

Yet astrology was still the warp and the instruments, tables, calculations, and observations were the woof in the web of the seamless robe of queen Philosophy. Those historians of "modern science" who pick out merely the threads which seem to them to deserve the name of science can neither trace a connected development which was true to life and thought nor give a picture of the past with any claim to accuracy. They merely tear to pieces a unified fabric, which the ravages of time have already worn threadbare, and certainly they show no regard for how it was woven. Most of them even ignored a new disease which spread like a crown-fire over Europe after the return of Columbus.

Not so Girolamo Fracastoro, who was born in 1478 and died of apoplexy in 1553. He studied mathematics, philosophy, and medicine at Padua. Fracastoro's great medical and scientific poem, *Syphilis,* contained two traditional beliefs which science and medicine have since largely discarded: the use of compound medicines containing many ingredients, and confidence in the influence of the planets on human health and happiness. He attributed the outbreak of the *morbus gallicus* (syphilis) to a conjunction of Saturn, Jupiter and Mars in Cancer. He refused to regard the disease as contagious, holding that it attacked some persons who in no way had exposed themselves. He stated its spread was rather due to corruption of the air under the influence of the stars. True, Fracastoro did not understand the real causes of syphilis, but he reflected the general life and thought of the late fifteenth century.

Another who was true to his age and thought was Michel de Notredame, known in history as Nostradamus, seer and astrologer. He was born in St. Remy, France in 1503. Though his prophecies were styled in the language of most predictions, the fact remains many lent themselves to striking interpretations of happenings which occurred centuries after the stargazer's death. Even the names mentioned by the seer coincide at times with those connected to the predicted events.

During the four centuries since Nostradamus, whenever their minds were filled with foreboding, men have turned to this physician-astrologer to find in his rhymed predictions some hope or solace. Nostradamus had followers who firmly believed he predicted events into the fortieth century. In his own time, in the sixteenth century, he was both honored and feared.

Nostradamus was the second of three sons; his father was an educated man and a notary public. His younger brother became an attorney, was a member of parliament and wrote a history of the poets and troubadours of the area. As a boy, Michel was studious and possessed a remarkable memory. His learned grandfathers taught him Latin, Greek, Hebrew, astronomy and mathematics. They sent him to Avignon to study philosophy and on to Montpellier's famous school of medicine. One of his grandfathers was physician to Rene of Anjou, Count of Provence, titular king of Naples, Sicily and Jerusalem. The other was physician to Rene's son Jean, Duke of Calabria. Good King Rene, as he was called, maintained a chivalric tradition; he loved food, wine and knightly balladry, dabbled in Eastern science, and attracted Arab scholars and Levantine merchants to his court. According to some accounts, the court physicians Pierre de Nostredame and Jean de Saint-Remy were Jewish. Their son and daughter, Nostradamus' parents, embraced Catholicism when Provence fell to the French crown after Rene's death. Nostradamus traced his own ancestry to the Hebrew tribe of Issachar, traditionally gifted in prophecy and in the Cabala.

Michel was twenty-one and in his second year of medical studies when an outbreak of plague swept through southern France and the school was closed. The young student set out to help the stricken, avoiding the cities where noted physicians were bleeding victims in the usual therapy of the time. He tramped through the countryside and treated the sick in villages and farmhouses with such success that his reputation spread before him and he was welcomed as far west as Bordeaux.

As a medical novice, he was very secretive about his methods of treatment. Years later, when he was again called upon to treat the plague, he remarked that the standard methods were of no value for this disease. It is now thought that since the cause of death from plague was the loss of body water, Nostradamus saved lives simply by abstaining from the conventional bloodletting and laxatives. His medical mission continued for four years, and when the plague subsided, he returned to Montpellier and passed his examinations. He was invested with the four-cornered hat, ermine-trimmed robe, golden girdle and ring of the physician.

At the demand of his fellow students he was appointed to the faculty, but he was restless and after a brief period of lecturing he resigned and again took to the road. His fame as a plague physician brought him many patients and invitations to settle in city after city. He stopped in Agen as a guest at the chateau of the leading family, fell in love with a young lady of the town, married her and established himself as a practicing physician. When three years later his wife and two young sons died of an unknown illness, he set forth again to seek consolation in solitary travel. For the next ten years, Nostradamus wandered through southern France and Italy. In his journal he evaluated the state of hospitals and medical practice in the cities through which he passed. His outspoken criticism of mercenary physicians and ill-administered pharmacies brought him many enemies. For three years, he worked with a physician of repute in research, and then spent some time in Milan, Genoa, Venice, and other cities.

The relative secrecy of these travels was ascribed to the hazardous new studies in which he was engaged. In this period, scientific investigation was readily linked with the black arts and subject to inquiry by the Holy Inquisition. Chemistry was generally understood as alchemy; judicial astrology was accepted as "celestial science," the geocentric universe of Ptolemy was still unquestioned. Copernicus' description of the solar system, although not yet published, may have come to Nostradamus' ears from the astrologers and physicians in Italy.

Nostradamus' astrologic calculations of later years revealed he measured planetary movements from equatorial rather than zodiacal armillas. He calculated from elliptic rather than circular orbits and took account of the law of gravitation. These are indications that as an astrologer he may have been far in advance of his time. In 1543, he returned to southern France in search of a permanent home. He declined invitations from Marseilles and other cities, settled in Salon, and found a second wife, Anne Ponsard Gemelle. She came of good family and was very rich, so the couple moved into a house in the Place de la Poissoniere, with ample lands bounded by a mill on one side and another private dwelling on the other. Of his six children who were born to the couple, the eldest, Cesar, developed literary and artistic talents. Another son became a Capuchin friar and inherited some part of his father's prophetic gift.

In 1546 there was a fresh outbreak of the Black Death form of plague. Nostradamus was sent for by the town council of Aix and when the plague subsided, the citizens paid him royally for his nine months' work and awarded him a life pension. His good work was gratefully recorded in the municipal papers, but his unorthodox treatment gave rise to rumors of sorcery and charlatanism. In his own account of the plague, Nostradamus observed that neither bleeding nor medical cordials were effective.

His sole remedy was a candy made mainly of roses freshly picked at dawn, together with a distillation of green cypress wood, iris of Florence, clove, sweet flag and ligni aloes. The ingredients were blended, shaped into small patties and dried in the shade. He wrote: "All who carried it in the mouth were preserved."

Some said Nostradamus prophesied by witchcraft and cured by sorcery, that those whose lives he saved would pay the penalty in everlasting hell fire. But in a century when witch-burning was commonplace, no official doubt was ever raised during his lifetime of the respectability of short, plump, rosy-cheeked Dr. Nostradamus with his grandfatherly long beard, his cheerful good humor and rarely displayed temper. He was a devout Catholic with no sympathy for the free-thinking followers of Martin Luther. He prayed, fasted, gave generously to the poor, and was devoted to his comfortable wife Anne and his six children. The great seer wrote besides his predictions an often-reprinted work on cosmetics, perfumes, and the art of making jam with sugar, honey, and cooked wine. This indicates Dr. Nostradamus was also well-versed in the science of herbs and minerals, like his grandfathers.

His prophecies, which he called *Centuries,* were not published until 1555, long after his book on cosmetics. These predictions made an enormous impression, and people from all classes traveled to Salon seeking his advice. About 1550, he began to issue a series of annual almanacs, in which, one source said, "He adroitly mingled the true and the dubious, reproduced therein certain of his recipes and announced impassively the direst catastrophes for the new year." Finally he published his first book of prognostications as a collection of rhymed quatrains in groups of a hundred. He projected his prophecy over seven centuries, but later expanded it to twelve.

The next year a royal summons came for an audience with Henry II. The king was prompted by his queen, Catherine de' Medici, a delver in the occult and herself a skilled astrologer. The long journey was made painful for Nostradamus by his gout and arthritis, but what services he performed at court remain unknown. Probably he practiced judicial astrology and drew up decumbency charts (astrologic prognoses) for members of the court who were ill. He returned home laden with gold and appointments as the physician-in-ordinary and privy counselor to the royal family.

Catherine de' Medici, who was greatly attracted by occult science and magic, was eager to know the future of her three sons, who were living at Blois. Nostradamus was sent there to see them, and when he returned to Paris, he predicted all three would sit on a throne. He was not more explicit, for he often said it was harmful to know the whole truth. He was right, for they were to ascend, subsequently, to the same throne.

He had enemies at court and he suffered especially from those who feared his influence upon the queen. A poet, perhaps Jodelle, wrote an acid couplet against him, playing upon the seer's name (*nostra,* our):

> We give what is ours in giving lies;
> For to deceive is our business.
> And measuring out the false
> We give nothing else, but our very own.

The carpers were silenced when under strange circumstances King Henry died the following year. He was celebrating the wedding of his sister, Marguerite de France, with the Duke of Savoy, and a tournament was held. Henry invited the young Earl of Montgomery to cross lances with him. Montgomery first declined this honor, then finally yielded to the king's wishes. An accident occurred; the Englishman's lance pierced the grill of Henry's golden helmet and entered the king's eye, wounding him severely.

The verses in the book of Nostradamus' *Centuries* were recalled:

> The young lion will conquer the old
> In a single combat upon the lawn.
> He will pierce his eye in a cage of gold,
> Two wounds One, to die a cruel death.

> In the year when the one rules in France,
> The court will be utterly disturbed,
> The lord of Blois will slay his friend,
> The kingdom will be treated ill and double doubt.

Both combatants bore the device of the lion; the king wore a gilded helmet (cage of gold). Montgomery's lance struck below the king's vizor, shattered and drove a splinter into Henry's right eye and brain (lance and splinter, two strokes in one). Henry lingered in agony for ten days, bearing out Nostradamus' prophecy of a cruel death.

There was trouble because of the dying "one-eye." Henry died soon from his wound. But what did the other verse signify? The three young princes who were all to be kings, according to Nostradamus, met a sad fate. The first, now Francis II, was only sixteen, and he died a year later. The second, the ten-year-old Charles IX, ascended to the throne under his mother's regency. In 1564, she journeyed with Charles to the pest-stricken and desolate Salon, seeking Nostradamus' advice. Little is known of what the seer told the aggrieved mother. The Huguenot storm arose in France, dividing the kingdom under the rule of a mother and child. Bloody St. Bartholomew's Eve brought horror and hatred, and Charles died at twenty-two, leaving his land in disorder.

The last of the princes was crowned Henry III. He resided at Vincennes, and he loved sorcery and occult practices. Sometimes he retired to the Tower of Paris at Vincennes, and people whispered horrible tales about him. After his death, they found the tanned skin of a child and blasphemous implements of silver which his adversaries made public. For Catherine, Nostradamus prophesied a more promising future: She would mourn her husband for seven years, then enjoy a long life and regency; all of which came to pass.

In 1558, Nostradamus published the second, enlarged edition of the *Centuries*, dedicating the work this time to the king with a lengthy epistle which bristled with prophecies. He predicted wars, famines, pestilence, naval battles which would turn the seas red, strange birds crying in the air, an age of desolation by the Antichrist, followed by an age of gold and universal peace. He even foretold his own death to the day and hour, as was afterward asserted by his disciple Jean-Aymes de Chavigny, a doctor of law and theology. According to Chavigny, Nostradamus had written in the margin of the *Ephemerides* of Jean Stadius, beside the date June 30: *Here death is near.* On June 30, he summoned the notary and made his will, and told his pupil goodnight on July 1 by saying, "You will not see me alive at sunrise." The following morning, July 2, 1566, Chavigny found his master dead at his bench.

Nostradamus died a wealthy man, owning house and land, furnishings and assets of coin in gold. He was a precise man. He even described the money coin by coin in his will. He listed bequests to religious orders and to the poor, specified the number of gold coins each for his widow and three daughters, and left his books, letters, notes and manuscripts to the son who would prove to be the most studious.

As he had requested, so no one might walk over his grave, his body was buried upright within the wall of the church of the Franciscan friars in Salon. His wife affixed a marble tablet bearing his portrait, arms and epitaph in Latin:

Here lie the bones of the most illustrious Michel Nostradamus, whose almost divine pen, in the judgment of all mortals, alone was worthy to record, under the influence of the stars, the future events of the entire world. He lived 62 years, 6 months, 17 days. He died at Salon in the year 1566. Posterity, disturb not his rest. Anne Ponsard Gemelle hopes for her husband's true felicity.

Nostradamus ascribed his prophetic sight to a combination of judicial astrology, divine inspiration and continual calculation, then he added, somewhat ambiguously, since occult philosophy was not forbidden, that he was never persuaded to meddle. Like all oracles, Nostradamus elected to baffle his interpreters with puns, anagrams, and a deliberate scrambling of chronologic order. The result has been a 400-year game in which each player reads into the quatrains the events of his own time. The same verses were deciphered by nineteenth century experts as referring to Napoleon, by twentieth century readers to Hitler, and earlier renderings as pointing to Cromwell. A single quatrain meant to one reader the St. Bartholomew's Eve massacre of 1572 and to another the death of Mussolini in 1945.

Another verse is read to mean Cromwell's death and the return of the monarchy, or alternatively Hitler's supposed death and his return. One interpreter sees fighting around Rome at some unspecified time where another beholds an accurate forecast of the Maginot Line. One understands a literal account of a freak human birth where another reads a vision of supersonic weapons. Nostradamus did refer to "Armies fighting in the air," which prophecy of airplanes was also made by Leonardo da Vinci.

Nostradamians have tackled the prophecies with the tools of cryptology, numerology, astrology, and pyramidalism (prophetic lore based on measurements in the pyramids). Verses are often read as prophecies of the American Revolution, the glorious future of "Hesperia" (Land of the West) or the United States, New York City's water pollution, an earthquake which will one day shake Manhattan. Interpreters in the years 1940–1945 found numerous verses predicting Pearl Harbor and the conflict with Japan.

Prognostications of events which are still to come are less comforting: in store are natural catastrophes and political calamities which will involve all the world's leading cultures, the rise of a world leader whether savior or tyrant, finally a date for Judgment Day in the year 7000.

> Men who come after may see and know
> That these events have certainly come to pass,
> Although they are veiled in cloud: but when
> the time comes for the removal of ignorance,
> Then all will be made clear.

> After my earthly death, my write shall do more
> Than when I was among the living.

In the next chapter we must consider an important subject we have neglected so far. While not presented in its true chronological pattern, the subject of "comets" needs a chapter all of its own, for they were awesome fearful objects in the sky until the middle of the eighteenth century.

ELEVEN

The Problem of Comets

Today modern astrology usually reads a comet as of the nature of a Mars-Uranus conjunction, for we do know much about comets now. But let us look back into time and history, and we will see this was not always the case. Comets were fearful omens of dire disaster. Why were they so fearful? This chapter will explain how the fears developed and how they finally were overcome.

Suppose we are living many years ago. One very dark night we see people gathering together in excited groups. They are all looking up into the sky, so we look up. There among the stars is a strange thing—a thing we have never seen before. It is not a star or a planet or a moon, but a hazy ball of light. Stretching from it in a great curve across the sky is a long, shining tail. The people are pointing to the strange sight and whispering to one another.

"It looks like a great serpent," one says.

"Or a dragon!" says another, and hides his face.

"I think it is shaped like a mighty sword," says another, "and it is going to bring a great war!"

"No! It means we shall all be sick!" another whispers in a low tone.

"But, I know it will kill the crops," suggests another.

"It is the end of the world," cries an old man. "God is going to destroy the earth because we were all so wicked, and worshipped Satan."

And we are frightened, for no one can tell us where the starry thing came from or what it is. They just tell us it is a comet.

One man says: "I talked to a man who studies the stars, an astrologer. He has been watching this comet for many nights, but tonight it is

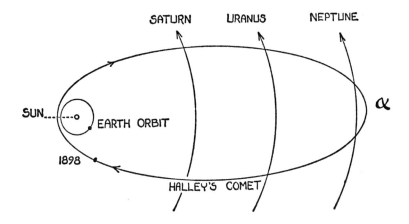

The orbit of Halley's Comet. It takes seventy-six years for it to orbit around the sun and out to beyond the orbit of Neptune.

> Of all the comets in the sky
>   There's none like Comet Halley.
> We see it with the naked eye
>   And periodi-cally.
>
> The first to see it was not he
>   But yet we call it Halley.
> The notion that it would return
>   Was his origi-nally.
>
> —Sir Harold Spencer Jones

larger and brighter than ever before. He said it was getting closer and closer and will hit us. When my grandfather was young a comet came, and the king died the same year."

Everyone agrees, "A comet is always a bad sign!"

We go to bed worried about what will happen. The next evening we look anxiously up at the sky. The comet is a little dimmer and smaller. The night after, it is even fainter. In a week or two we cannot see it at all, and in a month it is almost forgotten. But some people became sick and died, the crops were not so good as usual, and wars were reported some place nearby; we and the people recalled the comet and knew it was a warning of just these bad things.

Comets were unusual and spectacular phenomena, especially impressive in times when artificial illumination was only a rosin-wood torch. They seemed to appear without warning, and were seen and feared for so many centuries they cannot be assigned any specific place in the history of astrology. Since the story must be included somewhere, it might as well be here and now. Before Halley (1705) comets were "omens and portents in the sky" to almost everybody; after Halley they slowly became predictable astrological phenomena. But even as late as 1832, the newspapers of the world called the appearance of a comet a disaster and started a new wave of comet fear.

The beginning of this comet story is not only remote but confused. The first two important names are those of Appollonius of Myndus (270 B.C., also called Appollonius the astrologer) and Epigenes. Both of these men claimed to have studied astrology with the Chaldeans. They therefore also claimed to know the opinions held by the Chaldeans about comets. Appollonius was reported to have stated the Chaldeans considered comets to be like planets, but moving far from the earth most of the time and therefore completely invisible. Epigenes was reported to have said the Chaldeans thought them to be "fires produced by a kind of eddy of violently rotating air." If these two statements of what the Chaldeans thought came to us via two different classical sources, it would be possible to select the more likely one on the basis of the reliability of one of the two authors. But both these statements came from the same source, namely Seneca, a contemporary of Pliny the Elder.

Aristotle accepted the belief that comets were atmospheric phenomena. Of course he gave reasons; some were what was said among the Chaldeans, others were evidently his own. Some Greek philosophers, Anaxagoras and Demokriton, for example, had taken comets as astronomical phenomena like the planets. But this could not be true. In the first place, no planet was ever observed in early Greece except the known five (Mercury, Venus, Mars, Jupiter, and Saturn), and they all were often seen above the horizon at the same time. Comets were visible in addition to them, and comets were seen outside the zodiac. And this was impossible for planets. Also, they "vanished without setting, gradually fading away above the horizon . . . without leaving a star." If they were like planets, one should see these comets without any tails. They just did not fit into the astrological picture anywhere and thus were not astronomical phenomena.

Without any real intention of doing so, Aristotle started two thousand years of comet fear, because he considered them to be "weather signs" which indicated strong and dry winds. His own reasoning was that such winds produced comets as a by-product, but later on comets were thought to cause the winds together with the bad things strong winds produce, such as floods and fires.

Pliny the Elder, in his *Natural History*, accepted Aristotle's interpretation of comets as atmospheric phenomena. As was his usual habit, he enumerated the various names given to comets, based on appearance: "The kind named *Cerastias* has the appearance of a horn and *Lampadias* is like a burning torch; *Hippias* is like a horse's mane. There was one where the appearance of a mane was changed into that of a spear; it happened during the 109th olympiad, in the 398th year of the City. The shortest time during which any one of them has been observed to be visible is seven days, the longest 180 days."

The peak of European comet fear coincided with a never-yet-repeated abundance of large visible-to-the-naked-eye comets. The list for the fifteenth and sixteenth centuries was as follows; one in 1402, one in 1403, one in 1449, one in 1456 (Halley's), two in 1457, and one in 1472. The next century brought one large and bright comet in each of the following years: 1500, 1506, 1531 (Halley's again), two in 1532, and one each in 1533, 1538, 1539, 1556, 1558, 1569, 1577, 1580 and 1582. Such great numbers of bright comets during the fifteenth and sixteenth centuries naturally resulted in the making of many lists. Just how many frightened burghers and curious clergymen made comet lists for their private use, we will never know. The first one printed was compiled by the Paris physician Antonius Mizaldus (Antoine Mizuald) and appeared in Paris in 1544 under the title *Cometographia*. It was by no means a complete record of the appearances of comets, but after each listing of a comet it listed the disasters it supposedly caused.

The climax of fear was reached with the very large and bright comet of 1680, which produced the usual rash of pamphlets of all sizes, all degree of superstition, and in all European languages. In addition, there were two new innovations. A medal was struck to commemorate the event, and at Rome the news was that, while the comet was seen in the sky, "a virginal hen" laid an egg with the picture of a comet on its shell! That comet egg was even pictured and seriously discussed in the French *Journal des Savans* (dated January 20, 1681).

In America, the puritanical preacher Increase Mather grabbed at the 1680 comet as an excuse for a hell-fire sermon called "Heaven's Alarm to the World."

The Great God, when he made the world, placed the stars in heaven, to be for signs as to events that in the ordinary course of nature should come to pass. (Gen. I:14).

There are also extraordinary stars sometimes appearing in the heavens . . . blazing stars called comets, from the streamlike long hair which attends them. Such a star is prodigious and a fearful sight . . . As for the sign in heaven now appearing, what calamities may be portended thereby. . . .

Judgments, which are God's sharp razors on mankind whereby he doth shear down multitudes of sinful people, draw near. . . . And it may be He is declaring to that generation of hairy scalps who go on still in their trespasses that the day of the Calamity is at hand. I am persuaded that the floods of great water are coming. I am persuaded that God is about to open the windows of heaven and to pour down the cataracts of his wrath ere this generation is passed away. . . . Let everyone that is godly pray unto the Lord before the floods of great waters come nigh unto us.

In Holland and France the reactions were less old-fashioned. The simpler flocks of Calvinists were generally as susceptible as those of Increase Mather, but the Dutch elite were contemptuous of the comet as a portent of fear. In France, the famous letter-writer Madame de Sevigne was lightheartedly skeptical. The Protestant professor of philosophy, Pierre Bayle, delivered a violent attack on astrology in his *Pensees diverses*. This attack was inspired by the comet and by the fact, as he admitted, that France was over-run by astrologers. He suspected, like some astronomers of the time, that comets might be periodic, and this hypothesis would knock the bottom out of comet superstition. Of course, it was proved correct when Halley's comet returned at the end of 1758, as predicted by the followers of Newton and Halley. Bayle's book was widely circulated, and his equally famous colleague, Fontnelle, chose the favorite French weapon of mockery. He staged a comedy entitled simply *Le Comete*. In the next generation Voltaire dismissed comets and astrology with complete contempt in his *Dictionnaire Philosophique*.

The same abundance of comets which led to these outbursts—in retrospect fairly amusing—of superstition and commercialism exploiting the superstition, paved the way for a scientific attack on the comet problem. Careful observation came first by Johann Muller, who called himself

Regiomontanus, when in 1472 he observed a bright comet. With the aid of a colleague, Bernhard Walther, he measured its positions in the sky, and these measurements were good enough for Halley to use them in calculating the orbit.

The first important discovery concerning comets was made by Girolamo Fracastoro, who as a young man may have met the young Copernicus in Padua during the years 1501–1506. He announced in a book published in Venice in 1538 that the tails of comets were always turned away from the sun. Still, since comets were long believed to have a special significance for kings, we must consider the various treatises and predictions which were elicited by the comets of 1456, 1468, and 1472. Some indication of the astrological propensities attached to the leading rulers of that period also must be considered. The emperor, Frederick III, the duke of Milan, Lorenzo de' Medici, and the kings of France and England, along with several popes, were involved in the prognostications.

In 1456, one of the periodical appearances of Halley's comet was noticed by the chroniclers of the time and observed in more scientific fashion by the Florentine astronomer, Toscanelli. The universities took cognizance of it, and a *Judgment* based upon the comet was written at the university of Vienna. In a collection of fifteenth century astrological tracts from the library of the elector of the Palatinate, which were largely of German authorship, was one on the same comet. Later in this manuscript was a prediction for the preceding year consisting of nine chapters dealing with the weather, conjunctions of the planets and eclipses of the sun and moon, when to take medicine, diseases, crises good and bad, war and peace, religion, and the grain supply. There were also judgments in verse and prose for the year 1456 and its conjunctions of Saturn and Mars, and of Saturn and Jupiter.

Two comets appeared at Rome in 1456, with the last of the two in June, and Pope Caliztus III, alarmed about it, ordered prayers for many days to avert the wrath of God, and bells were rung to summon all to pray against the tyranny of the Turks. The comet of 1472 inspired even more treatises than those of 1456 and 1468. John of Glogau in his astrological *Summa* spoke of "the great comet," and it inspired Pietro Bono Avogaro to write a long treatise on comets. The comet is generally dated as appearing in January, although we are told that when a comet appeared on February 21, 1472, certain astrologers predicted pestilence as a consequence. Among the numerous treatises evoked by the comet of 1472 was one which John de Bosis wrote while a lecturer on astrology at Bologna.

Though not always strictly grammatical, John's treatise was well expressed and arranged. He first listed some twelve efficient causes of the comet which included the positions of the planets on September 28, October 28, November 27, and January 10. First was the conjunction of Saturn and Mars on August 12. Second was the position of other ponderous planets in trine. Saturn was descending in both its eccentric and its epicycle. Mars and Jupiter were descending in their eccentrics and ascending in their epicycles, while Venus was descending in both its eccentric and in its epicycle. A third thing he noted as a cause was that in the above conjunction Mars applied itself to the fixed stars. Fourth, there was the marvelous arrangement of the planets on August 14 when Saturn, Jupiter, Mars, Venus, and Mercury were all in aerial signs and in an aspect of friendship with the moon which was in a fiery sign.

Coming to the importance of this comet, John devoted a whole page to the pope. Those who predicted his ruin did so more from anger than from a thorough examination of all the essential astrological factors. He concluded that the supreme pontiff was in danger of diseases of the spiritual members from melancholy and phlegm and that he would probably have trouble with infidels. The emperor should also beware of danger to his life. As for the other parts of Europe, John addressed the king of Poland, and made dire predictions for France, Italy, the Turks, and various other happenings in the air and on earth.

We know a good deal more about comets nowadays. First of all, we know they are very light things made of dust and gases rolled into a huge ball of the very loosest kind, hardly able to hang together. When the head of a comet came between us and the sun a few years ago, we saw right through it and could not tell it was even there. A comet is the lightest thing you can imagine, although it may be as big as our earth or many times bigger.

But if the comet itself is light, think what its tail must be. For its tail is made of the very lightest parts of the comet. It is made of the thinnest of thin gases sweeping out from the comet, sometimes for millions of miles.

Those tails are interesting things. No two of them are ever alike. Sometimes they are big, sometimes they are little, sometimes the tail is just a feather of light or a sort of brush that can hardly be seen. Again, it may be a marvelous banner brilliantly glowing and stretching over a great part of the sky. But two things are always true; first, the tail grows longer and brighter as the comet comes closer to the sun, and then fades and grows shorter as the comet goes away again.

Second, the comet's tail always stretches away from the sun; so, while the comet is going toward the sun, its tail is behind it where a good tail belongs; but when the comet is on its way back into outer space, its tail stretches out in front, hurrying on before it. Maybe we should not call it a "tail" at all, but stick to the old Greek word for hair, from which "comet" comes. If you think of a woman's long hair streaming out behind her in the wind as she rushes in one direction, and then as she turns and runs with a strong wind, her hair streaming out in front of her, it will give you the idea of a comet's tail and how it streams out ahead or behind.

We told how comets used to frighten people because nobody knew when they were coming, and nobody knew what they were. The other things in the sky have always been comfortably regular. The sun rises every morning and sets every night. It rises farther north in the summer and farther south in the winter; but it is always the same. The moon grows from a crescent to a full moon through two weeks and wanes away during the next two weeks. The stars always keep the same pattern as they seem slowly to wheel around the North Star. They rise a little earlier each night, but this is regular and expected.

The planets wander about a bit in the sky, but they are always there, and long ago men learned what to expect of their wanderings. Only eclipses and comets came unexpectedly. That is why they were so feared! People were badly frightened when the sun or the moon seemed to be blotted out in an eclipse, and terrified when a comet came into sight with its long, shining tail. They sometimes thought the sky was cracking open, or the gods had put a "sign" in the heavens to warn them of disaster.

Terrible things have sometimes happened at about the time a comet was seen or a little while afterward. Of course, such things kept happening whether there was a comet in the sky or not. There have been wars and earthquakes and eruptions and sicknesses year after year. But when these things happened at the time of a comet, people thought the comet made them happen or the comet was a warning they were going to happen.

About seventy years after Christ was born, for instance, soldiers were fighting against the city of Jerusalem. A great comet appeared in the sky. Its tail made it look like a brilliant white and gleaming sword. The people were immediately frightened. They thought this meant the city would surely be taken by the soldiers, and of course it was.

Again, nearly nine hundred years ago, Duke William of Normandy—later called William the Conqueror—crossed with his soldiers over into England to fight the English king, Harold. In the midst of the battle, a big comet appeared in the sky with a gorgeous shining tail. Duke William looked at it and thought it was a good sign. "It means we shall win!" he said. King Harold looked at the same comet, but he decided it was a bad sign. "It means we shall lose," he moaned. King Harold's men were discouraged and they did not fight well. William's men were sure of winning, so they fought bravely. King Harold was killed, and William the Conqueror became the king of England. Perhaps the beliefs of those two kings changed the history of England—and just because of a comet.

About four hundred years ago there was a comet which was red. It must really have been quite beautiful, but the people thought it terrible, "It is the color of blood!" They imagined they saw dreadful pictures in its shape, thinking they saw hatchets and swords and men with their heads cut off, all in the red tail of the comet, even as we imagine that the clouds make pictures. This comet stayed in the sky for a long time, and some people were so frightened they fell sick; some even died. Many believed it meant the world was coming to an end.

Then came a time, about two hundred years ago, when another comet appeared; and this was during the lifetime of two great English astrologer-scientists who were interested in studying the heavens. They were Edmond Halley and Isaac Newton. Instead of being frightened by this brilliant comet, Newton and Halley took its appearance as the fine chance to study how comets move and what they really were.

They found that comets are pulled by the sun just as the earth and the other planets are, that they obey the same laws. Then Halley had a bright idea: "I do not believe the comets are all different. I think that maybe the comet we've looked at tonight is the same comet that people saw a long time ago. Maybe all the comets are going around the sun, just as our earth is, but traveling in a different kind of curve so they go away out into space, far out of sight, and then come sweeping back closer to the sun and to us."

Edmond Halley is now widely remembered for a bright comet named after him and also, perhaps, for the very considerable efforts he made in the publication of Newton's *Principia*. By his own account he was born on October 29, 1656, and he was therefore almost fourteen years younger than Newton. He was born near Shoreditch which was a hamlet just outside London. While he was still young his family moved to Winchester Street in London. His father was fairly rich, owning some property in London, having a profitable business as a soap-boiler and acting as a food salter. Although he suffered the loss of many of his properties in the great fire of 1666, his business ventures prospered and the family remained solvent.

Halley decided at the age of sixteen that he was going to be an astronomer and by the age of twenty he thought it was time he launched out on his own. He considered his most useful study would be to make a catalogue of those stars visible only in the southern hemisphere and he set about discussing the project with John Flamsteed. Flamsteed was the moving figure behind the building of the Royal Observatory at Greenwich in 1675 under Charles II, and was appointed Astronomer Royal. Flamsteed supported Halley's proposal and royal support was given to Halley.

In November 1676, without even his Bachelor's degree, Halley set sail, arriving in St. Helena at the end of the following February. Halley returned to England in 1678, arriving in May, and he spent the summer preparing his observations for publication. When they came out as *A*

Catalogue of the Southern Stars, Halley immediately became widely known. Flamsteed referred to him as the southern Tycho, and the King, to whom he presented a chart of the stars with one of the groups plotted named Charles' Oak, provided a mandate to Oxford University commanding that the degree of Master of Arts be given to Halley. The Royal Society elected him a Fellow and success seemed to be his.

During 1680 Halley toured the continent with a friend, and observed a large bright comet from the Paris Observatory; then, after spending about a year in Italy, he returned to England in January 1682. In 1705 Halley published his book *Synopsis of Cometary Astronomy* which contained the prediction that in December 1758 the bright comet which was seen in 1531, 1607, and 1682 would reappear. This prediction was correct and conclusively proved the point that comets were indeed celestial bodies. But it did more than this, for Halley made his predictions by computing the orbit of the comet using Newton's law of universal gravitation and the facts as laid down in the *Principia.* Thus his success brought new proof of the correctness of Newton's theory. Yet final confirmation of Halley's work arrived sixteen years after his death and over fifty years after the publication of his book. So it was only on its merits as a treatise on comets and their orbits that it was accepted at first. No one before had ever suggested comets obeyed the same basic laws as the planets or that they performed orbits around the sun. Halley's book was a really important contribution, since it stood even without final proofs.

None of the planets go exactly in circles—they all travel in ellipses. Most of the ellipses, though, are so nearly circles that you cannot tell much difference. Pluto travels in a rather long ellipse, so it is sometimes much closer to the sun than at other times, yet even Pluto's ellipse would seem round beside a comet's. Newton figured out the kind of ellipse the bright comet was following. Halley figured out when that comet must have been seen before; then he looked through the books and histories and found a comet looking just like this one that appeared regularly every 575 years.

A few years later another comet came, and the two men figured out the path of this one. "This comet ought to come back much oftener than the other," Halley said. "It should return about every seventy-six years." Again he looked for everything people had written about comets. Sure enough, he found out seventy-six years before there was a comet which looked just like the one he was seeing. Seventy-six years before that, in the midst of a war between the Turks and the Christians, a similar comet was seen and the frightened people prayed, "Lord, deliver us from our enemies the Turks, and from the Devil, and from the comet!" When Halley kept figuring back and back, he found this very same comet must have been the one

King Harold and William the Conqueror had seen when they were fighting the Battle of Hastings!

So Halley announced this comet, which since his time is called "Halley's Comet," would appear again in 1757. By then Halley himself was dead, but other astronomers watched for his comet. They watched night after night. But no comet! Finally, two years late, it came back in March, 1759. There it was, slowed down by coming too close to Jupiter. It has been back twice since Halley's day, and it will be back again in 1987.

After Newton and Halley made their discovery that comets follow the same laws as the sun, moon, and planets, astrologers looked forward to the coming of comets so they could study them. The astrologers were not afraid any more than you are when you see the moon. But many people were still frightened! Halley explained how comets come and go. When they got over thinking a comet was a good sign, or a bad sign, or a warning from God, they were afraid one would bump into the earth and smash it to pieces.

"But what about its tail?" people said. "Maybe it is made of poison gases. Maybe our earth will go through a comet's tail some day, and we'll all be poisoned and killed!" Well, we have been through a comet's tail. Some think we plunged through one about eighty years ago—and nobody knew the difference. Perhaps there was a slight glow in the sky at night, but that was all there was to it. Yet, on the appearance of the great comet of 1880, we find an educated man like the diarist John Evelyn writing of comets: "They may be warnings from God." In Germany, on the same occasion, we find professors and Lutheran ministers stressing the length of the comet's tail and regarding it as a rod of chastisement which God has put in his window—"and all the children fear, but he has in mind only the mischievous."

Erhard Weigel, a professor of mathematics whose astrological views admittedly were a little eccentric, interpreted the vanishing of one comet when about to enter the Milky Way as a warning to parents to feed their children on the milk of true piety. The astrologer-astronomer William Whiston (who succeeded Isaac Newton at Cambridge in 1703) gave a lecture in 1736 predicting an eclipse of the moon, accompanied by the appearance of a great comet. This would occur at precisely five A.M. on the following Thursday. These portents, Whiston told his audience, would herald the return of the Messiah to earth, and the world would end on the next Friday, by fire and earthquake. Indeed a comet did appear at about the appointed time. The prediction was fairly widely publicized, the city of London was thrown into panic, and thousands of people fled the city.

If the Reverend William Whiston did not cause this new comet fear, he at least kept it alive. When Halley constructed his comet table he attempted to show other comets might have regular periodicities. Halley found there were comets in 43 B.C., 531 A.D., 1106 and 1680. The older ones were poorly observed, but the time interval was just about 574 years. Halley himself did not consider the case completely established, but Reverend Whiston did. Whiston was both a minister and a professor of mathematics, and he came to the conclusion that the comet of 1680 had a period of exactly 574 years. Then he went even further, calculating earlier dates from this assumed period. He published a book called *The Cause of the Deluge Demonstrated* (London 1711). The comet supposedly approached the earth very closely and caused the Great Flood. Nobody knew all the dates involved were fictitious and that the Biblical flood was actually a local event. What mattered was that a clergyman stated that the greatest catastrophe ever known was literally and physically caused by a comet.

Biela's comet was due in 1832 and Professor Olbers of Bremen announced that on October 29 the head of the comet would go through the earth's orbit. Olbers saw this as a most interesting astronomical event, but to the newspapers of the time it spelled catastrophe. They were not yet used to the word "orbit" and did not realize the earth would be 50 million miles away at another point on its orbit. The director of the Vienna Observatory quickly issued a pamphlet in which he explained what was really going to happen. What is amazing was that the pamphlet accomplished its purpose. The public accepted the fact that a misunderstanding of terminology caused a false alarm. Of course nothing happened when Biela's comet crossed the earth's orbit in 1832, and nothing happened when Halley's comet reappeared in 1835.

Nothing could show the ridiculousness of this second wave of comet fear (the fear of the consequences of a collision) more clearly than the fact that the impact of a small short-period comet, such as Enke's or Biela's, would cause only a local disaster, and if the area of impact were in the middle of Greenland, Antarctica, or Central Australia, the inhabitants of North America or Europe would only learn about it from fancy astronomical observations.

So much for comets. Now let us go on with the history of astrology and talk about four important men. Bacon, Fludd, Lilly, and Culpeper lived about the same time as Tycho, Kepler and Galileo, but they were more concerned with predictions than with calculations or planetary systems.

TWELVE

Attacks and Defense

The name Bacon is one for us to reckon with. Not only do we have the legacy of Roger Bacon as he marched through the pageant of history with strange new ideas, but we also have Francis Bacon, one of the few great architects of ideas and words among all the English speaking people. And a few natives of Virginia may remember reading of "Bacon's rebellion" with its implications and sidelights on the history of our country.

Francis Bacon was born a little more than 400 years ago, in the third year of Queen Elizabeth's reign, to be exact, January 22, 1561. He was born into one of the great periods of Western History, and was destined to be one of the great actors on its scenes and one of its great victims. He was a victim of his own waywardness and ambitions, his love of luxury and admiration, and his exaggerated drive for superiority. Bacon saw clearly there were vital interrelations of all kinds between science and public affairs, and that these questions dealt not only with economy, with power and with prestige, but also with moral and ethical questions which now come to threaten man in his quest for survival in the 1970's.

Poet, lawyer, philosopher, statesman, Bacon's greatest legacy to modern science was his ruthless attack on scholastic mumbo-jumbo and his championship of scientific observation. In later centuries he was highly praised for having the intellectual courage to challenge Aristotle's teachings and advocate the empiric accumulation of knowledge. The last five years of Bacon's life were spent mostly at his writing desk, in literary work more valuable than his political activity. One winter while driving near Highgate, he wished to investigate the effect of snow on preserving meat. So he bought a chicken and stuffed it with snow; but in the cold weather he caught a chill that developed into bronchitis. He died a few days later on April 9, 1626.

Bacon's direct accomplishments in science were only a few. But he connected terrestrial and celestial phenomena, suggested the prediction of comets, and saw the relationship between moon and tides. He conducted experiments showing the compressibility of water, and worked out a theory of hearing. But his indirect influence in the formative period of science was enormous, for he awakened other men to the great possibilities in the new scientific approach to man's conquest of nature. He was the most powerful influence in breaking the dead grip of dogma and antiquarian authority on his age.

To the moon Bacon attributed such influences as eduction of heat and induction of putrefaction, increase of moisture, excitation of the spirits in the human body—of which lunatics were a crucial result—and affecting the winds and the weather. "New moons presage the dispositions of the air, but especially the fourth rising of it, as if it were a confirmed new moon. The full moon likewise do presage more than the days which come after."

He felt there might be other secret effects of the moon not yet brought to light. Bacon expressed doubt as to "a sympathy between the sun, moon and some principal stars and certain herbs and plants."

He affirmed that winds both preceded and followed planetary conjunctions, unless the conjunction was with the sun, in which case there would be fair weather.

At the rising of the Pleiades and Hyades come showers of rain, but gentle ones; after the rising of Arcturus and Orion, tempests. Returning and shooting stars . . . signify winds to come from that place whence they run or are shot. But if they fly from several or contrary parts, it is a sign of great approaching storms of wind and rain.

Bacon followed Pliny in locating rich soil at the ends of the rainbows. Astrology was discussed at length by Bacon in De augmentis scientiarum, where he declared that it was full of superstition but should be censored rather than rejected. He discarded the reign of the planets in turn over the hours of the day, although he admitted they got their names in this manner. He would also drop horoscopes, astrological houses, and the emphasis upon the hour of birth or the time for initiating an undertaking or making an inquiry. In other words, he opposed nativities, elections and interrogations.

He granted the celestial bodies exerted other influences than those of heat and light. He had no doubt that the moon in Leo had more power over terrestrial bodies than when in Pisces, or that a planet was more active when in its apogee, and more communicative when in its perigee. Prediction of comets, the weather, epidemics, wars, schisms, and folk migrations he thought entirely possible. His final word was that even elections were not altogether to be completely rejected. In his discussion about the length of human life according to the time of birth, he "omitted for the present" horoscopes and other astrological data.

Bacon's life, looked upon from our distance, contained the essence of tragedy. We perceive both the tragedy of success and the tragedy of failure in Bacon. We are fascinated by all the intrigues, the scandals, the corruption, and the impediments in his path as he yielded to the great heady lust for power. He sought power which Queen Elizabeth gave him grudgingly, if at all, and sought advancement from her in vain. But he stayed in politics with the idea of securing the power which was needed to fulfill his grand scheme of a scientific program.

Some people falsely believe that Bacon wrote all of the work of Shakespeare, but this claim, rather curiously, first arose eight generations after both were dead and buried. If this idea contained any truth, or even any common sense, man being what he is, it would have been advanced by living men who remembered both Shakespeare and Bacon.

Shakespeare must have been a great fortune-teller! But he restricted all his predicting to the characters in his plays. However, this makes him no less great as an astrologer. To make his characters use astrology correctly, he needed to be a master of the art of prediction himself. This was a need for him not only as a playwright, but as a stockholder in the theatre as well, for he knew the knowing audience would recognize any errors he made. His astrological references needed to stand up to the groundlings at the Globe as well as to the courtiers at Whitechapel. All were familiar with the influence of the stars.

Shakespeare was a man of the Renaissance, and his astrological knowledge seems strange to us today, for we seem to pass over it while we are being captivated by his plots. We overlook the technical astrology for the drama and poetry.

If ever lovers' stars were crossed, they were for Romeo and Juliet. How impossible it would be for a modern actor of today to please an Elizabethan audience in either role. The Elizabethan actor did not need to search for motives; they were all provided by the planets and written as such into the plot by Shakespeare.

We have forgotten Fortune's Wheel, and the four humors of the body; and many people ignore astrology. But in Shakespeare's day, the stars were the place for action on the stage, and they were the basis of all character. The delay of Friar John's letter in *Romeo and Juliet* was determined by the malefic influence of the planets.

Romeo believed it was his horoscope which brought about the tragedy of his life and he felt he was star-crossed. He thought his world-wearied flesh would find relief only in the apothecary's poisonous potion, which would shake him free from the yoke of inauspicious stars. When Romeo discovered Juliet dead, he blamed his unlucky stars and decided only the poison would release him from their baleful influence.

Shakespeare's plays show that human beings were merely helpless puppets of the planets. The theme runs through the thirty-six dramas from *Titus Andromacus* to *The Winter's Tale*. All sorts of references were made by the characters of Shakespeare's plays to astrology and numerology. These characters displayed a vast knowledge of the stars and planets, the effects of meteors, comets, solar and lunar eclipses, and aspects. The cast of characters reflected William Shakespeare's mastery of the occult, since they were knowledgable of the malefic influence of the Dragon's Tail, the rulership of Mercury over thieves and lying, the stultifying effect of moonlight, the generosity of Jupiter, and the judicious punishments of Saturn.

An even greater disdain for scientific learning was well expressed in Johannes Kepler's controversy with Robert Fludd, the English follower of Paracelsus. Fludd insisted nature should be grasped in mystic immediacy, not through the abstractions of thought.

> The commonplaces of the mathematicians are concerned with quantitative shadows; the chymists and Hermeticists embrace the true marrow of natural bodies.

Against this view Kepler vigorously defended the true aim of science as the expression of the real relations of things in an abstract mathematical form. Kepler claimed that to seize the essences of things except by means of their relations and properties was quite impossible; without mathematics even the eye of the mystic is blind.

> I seize, as you say, reality by the tail, but I hold it in my hand. You may continue to clutch at its head, if only you don't do it merely in dreams. I am satisfied with the effects, that is, with the motions of the planets.

> But if you can find in their causes themselves such transparent harmonious relations as I have found in their orbits, I wish you luck in this discovery and myself in its understanding, so soon as I am able to understand it.

Kepler wrote about Fludd:

He greatly delights in the dark riddle of things, while I try to bring into the light of the intellect things themselves involved in obscurity. The former is the familiar of chymists, Hermeticists, and Paracelsists; the latter is the possession of mathematicians.

As we shall see later on (in the next chapter) Kepler was a logical realistic mathematician and not a mystic.

But Fludd was a Rosicrucian and alchemist. He was born in 1574 at Milgate House, in the parish of Bearsted, Kent. His father was Sir Thomas Fludd, a knight who enjoyed the patronage of Queen Elizabeth, and served her for several years as "Treasurer of War in the Low Countries." At the age of seventeen Robert entered St. John's College, Oxford, and five years later he took his degree as a Bachelor of Arts. Shortly afterwards, on deciding to take up medical science, he left England and went to study on the continent. Going first to Spain, he travelled to Italy, and even stayed for some time in Germany. There he supported himself by acting as pedagogue in various noble households. But soon he was home again, and in 1605 Oxford conferred on him the degrees of Bachelor of Medicine and Doctor of Medicine. Five years later he became a Fellow of the College of Physicians, and was now thoroughly trained for the medical profession.

Fludd went to London and took a house in Fenchurch Street, where he soon gained an extensive practice. His success was not due only to his genuine skill, but also to his having an attractive and even magnetic personality. But busy as he was, he found the time to write at length on medicine and become an important and influential member of the Fraternity of the Rosy Cross. About the same time he commenced alchemistic experiments, and preached the great efficacy of the magnet, of sympathetic cures, and of the weapon-salve. He declared his belief in the Philosopher's Stone, the universal alkahest and the *elixir vitae*. He maintained that all things were animated by two principles—condensation (the Boreal), or northern virtue; and rarefaction (the Austral), or southern virtue.

Fludd asserted the human body was controlled by a number of demons, each disease having its own peculiar demon, each demon his own particular place in the frame of humanity. To conquer a disease—say in the right leg—you must call in the aid of the demon who ruled the left, always proceeding by this rule of contraries.

Fludd embraced the doctrines of the Rosy Cross Brotherhood with all the eagerness of his dreamy intellect. Several German writers made an attack upon them, so he published a defense (1616) called *Apoligia Compendiaria Fraternitatem de Rosea-Cruce Suspicionis et Infamiae Maculis*

Aspersam Abluens. This soon gave him a widespread reputation as one of the apostles of the new fraternity. He met with the usual fate of all prophets, and was lustily belabored by a host of enemies. Fludd retorted to his opponents in an elaborate treatise, *Summum Bonum, quod est Magiae, Cabalae, Alchimiae, Fraturum Roseae-Crucis Veroroum, et adversus Mersenium Calumniatorem.* Later he made an attempt to identify the doctrines of the Rosicrucians with what he was pleased to call the Philosophy of Moses in a treatise entitled *Philosophia Mosaica, in qua sapientia et scientia Creatonis explicantur* (1638). He also wrote numerous treatises on alchemy and medical science, and founded an English school of Rosicrucians. Fludd was one of the high priests of the Magnetic Philosophy, and learnedly expounded the laws of astral medicine, the doctrines of sympathies, as well as the fine powers and marvelous effects of the magnet.

When two men approached each other—such was his theory—their magnetism was either active or passive (positive or negative). If the emanations which they sent out were broken or thrown back, there arose antipathy, or *Magnetismus negativus;* but when the emanations passed through each other, positive magnetism was produced, for the magnetic rays proceeded from the center to the circumference. Man, like the earth, had his poles or two main streams of magnetic influence. Like a little world, he was endowed with a magnetic virtue which, however, was subjected to the same laws as the magnetic power of the universe.

Fludd died in 1637 at a house in Coleman Street, to which he moved a few years before. But before his demise he won a fairly wide reputation by his chemical ability and had issued a considerable number of occult books.

Alchemy was combined with astrology in this manner: The ancient Chaldaic Pantheism, the doctrine of an *anima mundi,* or "soul of the world," with indwelling spirits in all things, was applied to whatever could be extracted from substances by fire (such as "spirit" of wine, "spirit" of nitre, or the various essences and quintessences). The seven planets (the sun, the moon, Mars, Mercury, Jupiter, Saturn, Venus) corresponded to the seven days of the week and to the seven known metals (gold, silver, iron, quicksilver, tin, lead and copper). As these metals were supposed to be generated in the bowels of the earth, the special aim of alchemy was to find the fecundating or germinal substance under its appropriate planetary influence.

Fludd's basic philosophy may be summarized as follows: Light emanating through the Sephiroth was the chief agent of all things, and its union with ethereal spirit constitutes the World Soul (of which all individual souls are particles). The empyrean heaven was angelic nature itself, the flower and purer portion of ethereal spirit illuminated by divine light. There were nine orders of good angels and nine classes of bad angels. On the fourth day the sun was formed in the middle of the ether, then Mercury from the sun and the inferior region. Thirdly Venus was formed from reflexion between the sun and Mercury. Jupiter was formed fourth from reflexion between sun and fixed stars. Mars was fifth, from reflexion between the sun and Jupiter. Saturn was sixth, from reflexion between Jupiter and the fixed stars.

As there were nine orders of angels and nine classes of demons, also there were nine elemental regions arranged in groups of three each. Pure earth, minerals and vegetation made up the lower region; fresh water, salt water and the lowest of the three regions of air constituted the middle group; the highest consisted of the middle and upper regions of the air, and of fire. Man the microcosm corresponded to three heavens; the intellect in the head, to the empyrean; vitality and free will in the heart, to the ether; natural functions in the abdomen, to the elemental spheres. While the superior of formal Diapason was divided harmonically from the sun to the supreme hierarchy of angels, the inferior or material was divided arithmetically from the earth to the sun.

Fludd has been characterized as "a philosopher, astrologer, physician, anatomist, physicist, chemist, mathematician and mechanician," and credited with "a rare gift of observation in the exact sciences." But he still thought it possible and advisable to combine with science and medicine not only the cloak of religion but also the occult science which had come down from the past: magic and Kabala, astrology and alchemy, physiognomy and chirmancy, geomancy and weather signs. Before he died, the greatest astrologer of the seventeenth century was born.

The Englishman William Lilly (1602–1681) was an astrologer, not an astronomer. But he was able to read and assimilate the information from books on astronomy which were translated from Latin into English. As a professional astrologer he wrote and published the earliest almanacs of prophecies. His most famous book, *Christian Astrology*, modestly treated of in three volumes, was largely concerned with expounding interrogations, and Lilly always emphasized questions concerning thefts and hidden property.

He drew up a horoscope in order to catch a thief who stole money from one of his clients. He made the following judgment on a horoscope which he cast for King Charles I: "Luna is with Antares, a violent fixed star which is said to denote violent death, and Mars, which is approaching Caput Algo, which is said to denote beheading, might intimate that." Two years later the King suffered precisely this predicted fate. Some of Lilly's predictions got him into serious trouble. He accurately predicted the great fire of

A prophetic woodcut entitled "The Great Fire of London," from William Lilly's *Monarchy or No Monarchy in England*, published in 1651, fifteen years before the plague and fire.

London and after the actual event in 1666 a committee of inquiry into the causes of the fire was appointed by the House of Commons. Lilly was suspected of complicity and was summoned before the committee, but was finally acquitted. A typically indefatigable man of the Renaissance, Lilly later turned his attention to medicine and earned a license to practice. He used much of astrological knowledge in the treatment of patients.

The popularization of astrology in the 16th and 17th Centuries did little to cleanse its soiled reputation. Penny almanacs and handbooks were produced in the first half of the 16th Century. These kept the man in the street happy with garbled astrological nostrums pirated from the authoritative textbooks of Ptolemy and Albertus Magnus which were translated into English. Astrology on this low level was hardly to be taken seriously and so received a considerable amount of criticism.

William Lilly was born April 30, 1602, at Diseworth, Leicestershire, the son of William Lilly, a yeoman farmer. A rival astrologer, John Heydon, insisted in his *Theomagia*, 1664, that Lilly's father was "a laborer or ditcher." In 1613 he was sent to the grammar school of Ashby-d-la-Zouch where John Brinsley the elder was chief master. According to his own story, Lilly learned Latin, some Greek, and a little Hebrew. He became an efficient writer of Latin verse and a good Latin conversationalist.

When sixteen years old he was "exceedingly troubled in his dreams concerning his salvation and damnation." His father's poverty ridden circumstances forced him to earn his own livelihood from an early age. On April 3, 1620, he left Diseworth for London, with a recommendation to Gilbert Wright, a native of Market Bosworth, who resided "at the corner house in the Strand." There seems no reason to doubt Lilly's statement that Wright gave him immediate employment as a domestic servant. Wright lived on rents derived from property in London, but could neither read nor write. He soon found the youth useful in helping him with his business accounts. Wright's wife, a believer in vigils, died in 1624, of a cancer in the breasts, and Lilly acted as nurse and amateur surgeon through the long, severe illness.

In February 1625 Wright married again, but he died on May 11, 1627, and Lilly accepted the offer of marriage made by this recent widow. They were married the following September and "the corner house in the Strand" was then his permanent London residence. Being well provided for by his wife, he spent his time in fishing, or hearing Puritan sermons. It was in 1632 that Lilly first turned his attention to astrology. A friend introduced him to Arise Evans, an astrologer residing in London's Gunpowder Alley. Evans found Lilly an apt pupil who bought all the old books on the subject belonging to William Bedweel, "lately dead," and read them day and night. Within six or seven weeks Lilly could "set a figure." He soon knew the chief astrologers of the day in the various parts of England and gave many details concerning their modes of life in his autobiography. In October 1633 his wife suddenly died.

In 1634 a scholar pawned with him for forty shillings a manuscript copy of the "Ars Notoria," which taught him the doctrine of the magical circle and methods of invocating spirits. Soon afterward Vacy Ramsey, the king's clock-maker, announced there was much treasure buried in the cloisters of Westminster Abbey. He obtained the permission of Dean Williams to make a search for it. Ramsey invited John Scot who "pretended to the use of the Mosaical rods" (divining rods) and Lilly to assist him. One dark cold winter's night the three, with some thirty spectators, "played the hazel rod round about the cloisters. Upon the west side the rods turned one over another." The laborers were ordered by Lilly to dig beneath the spot. A coffin was found at a depth of six feet, which seemed to the three too light to merit serious attention. On passing into the abbey, a blustering wind arose, which threatened to blow down the west end of the church. Lilly managed to dismiss the demons, who were thus marking their displeasure. He attributed the failure and fiasco to the irreverent laughter of the spectators.

On November 18, 1634, Lilly married a second wife, Jane Rowley, who brought him 500 pounds in gold and a shrewish temper. After teaching astrology to many promising pupils, and practising the art himself with success, he fell a victim to severe hypochondriacal melancholy. In the spring of 1637 Lilly went to Hersham, near Walton-on-Thames, and remained there five years. In 1639 he wrote a treatise upon *The Eclipse of the Sun in the Eleventh Degree of Gemini 22 May 1639*, which he presented to his friend, William Pennington of Muncaster, Cumberland. In September 1641 he returned to London, noting there was money to be found there. In 1643 he attended Sir Sulstrode Whitelock, M. P. during a severe sickness, and claims to have foretold his patient's complete recovery.

In April 1644 Lilly published his first almanac, which he entitled *Merlinus Anglicu Junior, the English Merlin revived, or a Mathematical Prediction upon the affairs of the English Commonwealth,* and sold the first printing within one week. From then on he prepared an almanac each year until his death. In 1644 he began issuing a long series of pamphlets of prophecy. On June 22, 1644, appeared *The English Merlin Revived or his Predictions upon the affairs of the English Commonwealth, and of all or most Kingdoms of Christiandom, this present year 1644.* Here Lilly's arts and divinations enabled him to foresee nothing more novel than "a troubled and divided court, an afflicted kingdome, a city neere a plague, and Ireland falling into discontent." In July he published *Supernaturall*

Sights and Apparitions seen in London, June 30, 1644, interpreted. In the same year (1644) Lilly printed a *A Prophcy of the White King and Dreadfull Deadman explained.* The first part, drawn from an old manuscript in the Cottonian Library, was published before by many other astrologers. But the obscure and meaningless sentences were paraphrased by Lilly to apply to Charles I. A fuller commentary by Lilly on these predictions appeared in 1646.

In 1645 a rival almanac-maker, Captain George Wharton, attacked Lilly as "an impudent, senseless fellow." Wharton was a pronounced Royalist, and in order to answer him with better effect, Lilly, who disclaimed any earlier interest in politics, promptly became a parliamentarian. The quarrel lasted long, and in many pamphlets issued in 1647 and in the following years Wharton claimed to expose Lilly's errors. On the day of the battle of Naseby—June 14, 1645—Lilly published his *Starry Messengers, or an Interpretation of that strange Apparition of Three Suns seen in London 19 November 1644 being the Birth of Prince Charles.* His reflections in this pamphlet and in his almanac for 1645 on the commissioners of excise taxes led to Lilly being summoned before the parliamentary committee of examinations, but the charge was not pressed. In 1646 he published nativities of Laud and Strafford, and in 1647 he published the work which he prized, *Christian Astrology modestly treated in three books,* dedicated to Whitelocke. This book he made his master textbook for his pupils. He asserted his fame reached to France, Italy, and Germany, and denied he received at any time money from the parliament.

In 1647 Jane Whorwood, Oxfordshire, a devoted partisan of the king, consulted Lilly about the possibility of the king escaping from Hampton Court prison and remaining concealed in some part of the country. Lilly suggested a place in Essex, twenty miles from London, and received twenty pounds. Fairfax suspected Lilly was applying his art improperly and ordered him to come to Windsor. Fairfax entreated him to discontinue his astrological practices unless he could convince him they were lawful, and agreeable to God's word. Hugh Peters supported Fairfax's arguments, but this appeal did not stop Lilly from procuring a saw and some acid to send to the imprisoned king. Meanwhile Lilly was ostensibly serving the parliament as a spy. In 1648 he obtained political information from France for which he was paid fifty pounds, and a pension of one hundred pounds which was paid him for two years. He attended the king's trial, and on January 6, 1648, he published *A peculiar Prognostication astrologically predicted according to art, whether or no his Majestie shall suffer Death this present yeare 1649; the Possibility thereof discussed and divulged.*

In August 1648 Lilly was ordered to the army engaged in the siege of Colchester. He was expected to encourage the soldiers with predictions of a speedy victory. In 1651 he stirred up new attention by his *Monarchy and no Monarchy,* in which he asserted England should no more be governed by a king, and added sixteen hieroglyphical engravings, two of which he declared portrayed the plague and fire of London (see drawing). An Appendix included "Passages on the Life and Death of King Charles," which reappeared in a revised form in Lilly's *True History of King James the First and King Charles the First.*

In 1652 he purchased a house and land at Hersham, and in his almanac for 1653 he declared the common people and the soldiers would quickly combine to overthrow the parliament. For this political prediction he was summoned before the committee of ministers. The speaker, Lenthall, earlier and privately pointed out to Lilly the offensive passages, so Lilly was dexterous enough to present the committee with amended copies when he appeared. He was detained in jail for thirteen days and released. On February 16, 1653, Lilly's shrewish wife died, and he "shed no tears." In October 1654 he married for the third time, to Ruth Needham.

In 1652 Lilly published his *Annus Tenebrosus, or the dark year, together with the short Method how to judge the Effects of Eclipses,* and dedicated it "to the commonwealth of England." His bold claim to be treated as a true scientific investigator aroused Thomas Bataker in 1644 to vehemently denounce him as an imposter, so Lilly retorted with similar frankness in his next year's almanac. In 1653, a violent attack was published by Thomas Bataker, B.D., *Against the Scurrilous Aspersion of that grand Imposter Mr. William Lillie,* of whom he writes: "There needs not much skill in his pretended art, to discover the vanity of it." In 1655, Lilly was indicted for having unlawfully given judgment about the recovery of stolen goods. For such service he received half-a-crown. He was acquitted, despite the presence among the judges of many who felt he was an obnoxious imposter.

At the Restoration Lilly was taken into custody, and was examined by a committee of the House of Commons about his knowledge of the details of Charles I's execution. He asserted that the executioner was Cornet Joyce and he was soon set at liberty. Pepys describes a pleasant evening spent with Lilly and his friends at his house in the Strand on October 25, 1660. There were many other attacks on Lilly. And, though eight years later (in 1663) he was appointed church warden of Walton-upon-Thames, this respectable position did not save him from being summoned (October 1666) before a committee investigating the causes of the Great Fire of London. But this turned out to be an advertisement for his astrological arts. "Having found, Sir, that the City of London should be sadly afflicted with a great plague, and not long after with an exorbitant fire, I framed these two hieroglyphics . . . which in effect have proved very true."

At the trial (April 1667) of Rathbone and others who were charged with having set fire to London, it was stated September 8, 1666, was the day selected for the attempt, because Lilly designated it in his published predictions "a lucky day" for such a dirty deed, but then the fire of London broke out on September 2, 1666.

Lilly moved to Hersham and studied medicine with such success his friend, Alias Ashmole, induced Archbishop Sheldon to grant him a license to practice, which was done on October 11, 1670. From then on he combined the professions of physician and astrologer, and every Saturday rode over to Kingston, where "the pooerer sort flocked to him from several parts." As a public astrologer, Lilly anticipated many astrological journalists of our own day. In 1644 Lilly wrote: "Saturn in the fifth house causeth more abortives than usually have been, the destructions of many men's son or children, much tergiversation with Ambassadors and foreign Agents, and that they perform not what may be expected from them."

Lilly died of paralysis at Hersham on June 9, 1682, and was buried at the chancel of Walton Church where Ashmole set up a black marble monument. His astrological apparatus passed into the hands of John Case, the astrologer, who bought Lilly's London practice. Before his death Lilly gave Coley the copyright of his almanac, and Coley continued it under its original title, adding the words, "according to the method of Mr. Lilly." In 1683 Coley issued *The great and wonderful Predictions of that late famous Astrologer, William Lilly, Mr. Partridge, and Mr. Coley.*

His predictions, as a rule, were so vaguely worded as to be incapable of any practical interpretation, but comets and eclipses gave him opportunities of terrifying his credulous patrons and he occasionally stumbled in his numerous prophecies onto something which was accurate. Two printed letters addressed to him by clients—one from Roger Knight, inviting Lilly's opinion as to the success of a love-suite, and enclosing eleven shillings, and another from Vincent Wing, the mathematician, making an inquiry respecting some stolen property, and begging one line of commendation for his "Harmonicon Celeste" in the *Anglicus* for 1651—illustrate the confidence people had in Lilly. Wood boldly describes him as an imposter, and Pepys related how he and his friends laughed at Lilly's prophecies. His published writings mainly consisted of astrological predictions and of vindications written in answer to the attacks made upon them by rival practitioners of the art. His *Christian Astrology* was long the authority in astrological literature, and was reprinted as an *Introduction to Astrology* with a preface by Zadkiel in 1852.

Lilly's name was illegally affixed to many cheap books dealing with fortune-telling, the interpretation of dreams, and the like. Of these the best known were the *Compleat and universal Book of Fortune*, London, 1728, and *A Groat's Worth of Wite for a Penny*, New Castle, 1729. Of course, Lilly had his rivals, and Gadbury (who we will tell of later) published a *Collectio Geniturarum*, which he described as "being of Practical Concernment unto Philosophers, Physicians, Astronomers, Astrologers, and others that are friends unto Urania" (Urania was the muse of astronomy). Here we have the facts about an often maligned astrologer. You must decide for yourself—was he the charlatan imposter his enemies claimed, or was he a scientific astrologer as he called himself? But let us go on to another astrological physician who also upset people and created enemies.

The belief mystically connecting mankind with trees and plants was and still is widely diffused over the world. These beliefs show considerable variation in the different countries and climates, but a brief description of a few of the better known plants and their legends will illustrate the employment of plants as astrological-medicinal agents. When we look at a medical dispensatory of the seventeenth century, such as *Culpeper's Complete Herbal* (still available), there is an amazing profusion of herbs, shrubs, and trees with their roots, barks, woods, flowers, fruits, and seeds, all reputed to be of medicinal value. Why, if all these plants are curative, are so few of them still in use? And if they were of no value, why were they used in the first place? The answer is twofold: prior to the eighteenth century, unbiased observation and experimentation played but a trivial role in the selection of plant remedies. Rather, certain plants were hit upon because of some uncommon or striking quality for which they were used in magical or religious rituals, and so were later credited with medicinal properties.

In 1649 Nicholas Culpeper incurred the wrath of the Royal College of Physicians by writing his treatise on astrological botany, *The English Physician Enlarged,* and by translating the "Pharmacopoeia" into English and publishing it in his *Physical Directory.* This was the golden age of the astrologer-herbalist. The medical man of this period was so imbued with the thought that all diseases were to be cured by botanicals, that he spent his time in the field and had little time left for his patients. These studies advanced botany and created the Botanical Gardens of Edinburgh and London. The "Physick Garden" or "Apothecaries' Garden" led to botanical fellowships under the resonant title of "Socii ierantes." These probably inspired Linnaeus, since he instituted a "herborizing" society at Upsala, whose members were summoned for excursion and "sampling" (collecting trips) by a trumpet and horn.

According to the *Dictionary of National Biography,* Culpeper was born in London and studied at Cambridge where he got a knowledge of Latin and Greek. He studied old medical writings pertaining to apothecary. In 1640, Culpeper set himself up as an astrologist and physician in Red Lion Street, Spitalfields. He worked in the poorer sections of London and was not strict about collecting his bills, which made him very popular with his clients. He was not at all popular with the medical profession, however, after he translated into English the *Pharmocopoeia* of the College of Physicians. The wrath of the professional hierarchy of London descended on Culpeper with this publication, for the Royal College prevented general disclosure of their secret formulae by publishing it in Latin. Culpeper, who was not a fellow of the College, probably considered his translation a righteous deed. In the third edition of *A Physical Directory: Or a Translation of the Dispensatory Made by the College of Physicians of London, And by them imposed upon all the Apothecaries of England to make up their Medicines By,* he replied as follows to the castigation of the College.

And now at last, (to let your blasphemies and my own Medicines alone) I seriously advise you to consider what will become of your souls another day: How will you answer for the Lives of those poor people that have been lost, by your absconding Physick from them in their Mother Tongue? Are you a College of Physitians or no? Do you know what belongs to your Duty or not? Wherefore did K. Harry the Eighth give you your Charter? to hide the knowledge of Physick from his Subjects yea, or no? Do you think you shall be called to an account for what you have done? I would have said for what you have left undone: Is not omission of good as great a sin as commission of evil? Look to it, look to it, For (as the Lord lives) I pity you, nay weep for you too: I tell you truly (and I am not ashamed of what I tell you) God hath given you what you desire, you are a Colledge of Physitians; You have Honor and Command, Learn to know yourselves; . . . Do not think that I delight to oppose you; if you do, you are mistaken. Conscience dictated a few visions to my eyes, which were not supernatural: All the sick People in England presented themselves before me, and told me, They had Herbs in their Gardens that might cure them, but knew not the Vertues of them; For the Colledge of Physitians were so Proud, so surly, and so Covetous, that Honesty went a begging in Amen-Corner, and could find no entertainment.

Culpeper, the leading physician of the time, suggested the small triangle of bone in the skull, known as "os triquetum," was excellent, when crushed, for falling sickness. Also, he sang the glories of rubbing human fat on "limbs falling away in flesh." He also suggested the dried blood of a young man as a plaster for ulcers, and recommended an eye salve made of one-half of a human brain mixed with honey. Menstrual blood was also used to kill insects and even quell storms at sea, while rinsing one's mouth with his own urine cured the toothache. Culpeper accomplished in a short life the preparation and translation of a prodigious number of texts on the treatment of disease, several of which were more popular in the home than as reference works in the physician's library. He prepared so many tracts that the presses seemed inadequate to handle the volume, and a number of manuscripts remained unpublished at his death.

As a physician-astrologer, Culpeper interpreted the influence of planets, stars, and comets on medicinals. Since astrology was the vogue for centuries, even the revival of critical scientific inquiry during the Reformation could not immediately shake off its influences. It was not unusual for the alchemist and the physician to pay homage to astrology, as noted in another of his popular herbal treatises entitled, *The English Physician Enlarged with Three Hundred and Sixty-Nine Medicines Made of English Herbs, that were not in any Impression until This. Being an Astrological-Physical Discourse of the Vulgar Herb—of this Nation, containing a complete Method of Physic, whereby a Man may preserve His Body in Health, or cure himself, being-Sick, for Three-pence Charge, with such Things only as grow in England. They being Most fit for English Bodies.* In such category, the botanical, the place of growth, the time of year it reached maturity, and its preparation for use were described, concluding with the diseases for which it was of value. Almost any excerpt may be reproduced as an example. There were thirty-nine herbs listed as useful in gout; in most instances, they were to be used as topical ointments. Pellitory of the Wall was described as useful for tussis, dyspnea, oliguria, ulcer, calculus, alopecia, hemorrhoids, and gout.

It is under the dominion of Mercury. The dried herb Pellitory made up into an electuary with honey, or the juice of the herb, or the decoction thereof made up with sugar or honey, is a singular remedy, for an old or dry cough, the shortness of breath, and wheezing in the throat.

In explaining the influence of heavenly bodies on herbs and disease, Culpeper presented his thesis of domination:

What Planet causeth the disease; what part of the body is afflicted by Disease, and by what Planet the afflicted part of the Body is governed; as the Brain, by Herbs of Mercury, the Breast and Liver, by Herbs of Jupiter; the Heart and Vitals, by Herbs of the Sun, etc. Suppose diseases by Herbs of the Planet opposite to the planet that caused them—as, for instance, diseases of Jupiter, by Herbs of Mercury, and the contrary; disease of Mars, by Herbs of Venus, and the contrary. A way to cure Diseases by simpathy, and so, every Planet cures his own disease; as the Sun and Moon, by their herbs cure the eyes; Saturn the spleen; Jupiter the Liver; Mars the gall and diseases of Choller; and Venus, diseases in the instruments of Generation.

The various other plants were under certain planets and heavenly bodies as well. In *Planets and Plants*, the great astrologer states:

Celandine: This is an herb of the Sun, and under the celestial Lion; it is one of the best cures for the eyes; for the eyes are subject to the luminaries; let it be gathered when the Sun is in Leo, and the Moon in Aries.

Cucumbers: There is no dispute to be made, but that they are under the dominion of the Moon, though they are so much cried out against for their coldness, and if they were but one degree cooler they would be a poison.

Peach-tree: Lady Venus owns this tree, and by it opposes the ill effects of Mars; and indeed for children and young people, nothing is better to purge cholera and the jaundice; than the leaves and flowers of this tree, being made into a syrup or conserve.

Nettle: This is an herb Mars claims dominion over. You know Mars is hot and dry, and you know as well that winter is cold and moist; then you may know as well the reason by Nettle tops, eaten in the spring, consume the phlegmatic superfluities in the body of man, that the coldness and moistness of winter has left behind.

Wild carrots: Wild carrots belong to Mercury, and therefore break wind, and remove stitches in the sides, provoke urine and women's courses, and help to break and expel the stone.

Houseleek: It is an herb of Jupiter; and it is reported by Mezaldus, to preserve what it grows upon from fire and lightning.

Lettuce: The Moon owns it, and that is the reason it cools and moistens what heat and dryness Mars causes, because Mars has his full in Cancer: and it cools the heat because the Sun rules it, between whom and the Moon is a reception in the generation of men.

Hellebore: It is an herb of Saturn, and therefore no marvel if it has some sullen conditions with it.

Saffron: It is an herb of the Sun, and under the Lion, and therefore you need not demand a reason why it strengthens the heart so exceedingly.

Lily of the Valley: It is under the dominion of Mercury, and therefore it strengthens the brain, recruiting a weak memory, and makes it strong again.

Artichokes: They are under the dominion of Venus, and therefore it is not wonderful if they excite lust.

The English Physician Enlarged (1653).

In the same work other plants of interest are assigned as follows:

To the Sun: The olive, peony, vine, and walnut.

To the Moon: Water-cress, water lily, pumpkin, turnip, sea holly, willow, and white rose.

To Mercury: Mushrooms, lavender, and parsley.

To Venus: Apple and cherry, gooseberry, raspberry, strawberry, primrose, sorrels, wild thyme, and violet.

To Mars: Chives, onion, mustard, radish and horse-radish, hops and peppers, tobacco, honeysuckle, wormwood.

To Jupiter: The oak and the orange, peas and dandelion.

To Saturn: Holly and ivy, hemlock and nightshade, poplar, quince and yew.

Although this combination of astrology and medicine was away ahead of his day, Culpeper served medicine by translating several treatises from Latin into the vernacular, thereby making the text available for those not schooled in the ancient language. (Two centuries were to elapse before English replaced Latin as the language of medical communication in England.)

The times in which Culpeper lived were troublous; the darkest known to man. They were just before the "great dawn" of Science! We must bear in mind that in his boyhood James I was King; that Charles I was executed the year his "Dispensatory" was published; and Cromwell was active the year of his death.

It was a period during which party conflicts embittered men's tongues and sharpened their pens. Culpeper was ever on the side of the Parliamentarians and in 1643 he entered the army. Here ill luck pursued him, for he was wounded by a shot in the chest. His health did not recover and he abandoned the profession of arms and returned to his studies.

It might be interesting to learn something of the neighborhood in which Culpeper lived. His works were dated from "Spittle Fields, next door to the Red Lyon." "Spitalfields" originally was the plot of ground to the northeast of old London, belonging to the ancient church and hospital of Our Blessed Lady.

It was established in the reign of Henry III, since called "St. Mary Spittle" outside Bishopsgate, for the use of regular canons.

While distinctively a monastery, it provided also for poor travellers and persons in sickness and distress. At the time of its seizure and dissolution by Henry VIII, it supported 180 beds, "well furnished for receipt of the poor of charity; for it was an hospital of great relief."

The monastic buildings were later destroyed, and by the end of the next century numerous houses were built on the site of the hospital. A public square which Henry VIII granted to the Artillery Company, known as Spital Square, was maintained and used by the gunmen of the Tower. It was known as the Artillery Grounds at the time Culpeper set up medical practice. But, in 1540, it was abandoned for a new field in Finsbury.

In the meantime, the many "fair houses" in the district were abandoned as "the lodgings of worshipful and honorable men," and fell into decay and squalor. It was into this region that Culpeper emigrated. The whole district later on became devoted to home and workshops of the silk weavers, French refugees from the Revocation of the Edict of Nantes. The district has since been known as the silk weavers' quarters.

Although Nicholas Culpeper was an outstanding type of "Our fathers of old," who preferred to "look at the stars when a patient is ill," he also possessed a fair measure of their excellent heart and their excellent courage. For this he surely deserves to be remembered among those who with tireless industry and unconquerable resolution have labored unceasingly upon many fields to promote the happiness of their fellow-men ungrudging of their own.

Culpeper was intensely personal in all his publications, so we find facts relating to his life in prefaces and introductions as well as here and there throughout the treatises. He must have been attractive in his personal character, as may be learned from a narrative of his life and from a "Nativity" calculated by John Gadbury, a brother astrologer, prefixed to his *School of Physic* published in 1659. Gadbury knew Culpeper very well for a number of years, so though the nativity was "calculated" after Culpeper's death, it was done in the light gained by experience during his life, and therefore, is not of the type of the ordinary natal prophesies.

Now we are at last ready to discuss the giants of astronomy, men who actually observed the stars and made great changes in the cosmic universal view of Ptolemy. In the next chapter will be discussed Copernicus, Tycho, Brahe, Kepler, Galileo, and Newton. All were astrologers, even if modern astronomy tries to claim differently.

THIRTEEN

The New Giants

It is a historic fact the Copernican system was first publicly announced, if not precisely under astrological auspices, at least to an astrological accompaniment, and was for long after associated with astrology in many men's minds. Indeed, this astrological accompaniment was somewhat of a new idea itself, since it represented the movement of the earth rather than the motion of the stars as influencing the course of human destiny. In the thirteen centuries following Ptolemy, only a few significant observations were made by European astrologers. The Arabs brought the Hindu system of numbers to Europe and introduced algebra. They kept alive the works of the Greeks and provided continuity between Ptolemy and the concepts of the Renaissance and the great Copernicus.

Copernicus was born in the year 1473, about twenty years before Columbus discovered America. He was the man who upset Ptolemy's ideas which people believed for so many hundreds of years. He started a great change in people's thinking when he gave to the world a whole new picture of the universe and the places of the sun and the earth and the planets. Copernicus was a great astronomer and astrologer, the kind of man who wanted to know about everything and understand everything. When he was young he went to the university. He studied Latin, medicine, and prepared to enter the church as a priest. But most of all he liked to study the stars, for he thought there was nothing quite so interesting as the way they behaved, and he spent much of his time watching them. He learned Ptolemy's explanation of their movements. As he studied more about the stars and planets, he found they did not seem to behave quite the way they should according to Ptolemy's explanations.

He studied at various universities until he was more than thirty years old, first at the Polish University of Bologna, and then Ferrara and Padua in turn. His was a prolonged education, but a cultivated man of those days regarded all knowledge as his province, and did not limit his education to acquiring skill in one particular calling. In this spirit Copernicus acquired a profusion of knowledge in the classics, in astrology, mathematics, astronomy, medicine, law, economics, and of course in theology. This he did not let lie idle, but put it to full use even after he reached a high position in the Church. We read of his curing the poor as well as sick fellow-ecclesiastics, writing on economics, advising the Polish government on questions of currency, making his own scientific instruments, writing poetry, and even painting, at least to the extent of one self-portrait. He achieved success as an administrator, as an estate manager, and as a diplomat at a minor peace conference. Like Leonardo da Vinci before him, he was a man of wide knowledge and of varied attainments, but his main interest was ever in mathematics and astrology. These subjects figured largely in the teaching of the medieval universities and we find Copernicus attending lectures on Euclid, on spherical geometry, on geography, on astrology and on Ptolemaic astronomy.

When he could find any spare time, however, he spent it thinking and studying and watching the stars and planets. The more he watched them, the less satisfied he was with Ptolemy's explanation of the way they moved. It seemed a clumsy, made-up story which was not quite real.

Copernicus studied Greek, learning from what he read that long before Christ there were some great thinkers in Greece who had believed that the sun and not the earth was the center of all the universe and that the earth and the rest of the planets moved around the sun. But since no one had been able to prove these ideas, people had forgotten about them. They believed, instead, the teachings of Aristotle and of Ptolemy. This was still the official astronomy and astrology of the universities and of the Church, but a number of advanced thinkers were already feeling quite skeptical about it, advocating something more like the heliocentric astronomy of Aristarchus. Another man who thought this way was Domenico Novaro, who was Professor of Mathematics and Astronomy at Bologna while Copernicus studied there and who remained his friend after he left the university.

The writings of the Pythagoreans now were accessible to European scholars, and they proclaimed that the ultimate truth about the universe must consist of simple, elegant and harmonious relations. Novaro thought the Ptolemaic astronomy much too cumbersome to comply with this criterion. Copernicus looked up and studied all the old ideas which were forgotten for almost two thousand years, and then watched the sky. This

was not easy, since besides having very little time, Copernicus had little
to work with. His instruments were not good and he did not have enough
of them. But he was not discouraged, and made the best use of what he
did have.

Since telescopes were not yet invented, he cut some narrow holes or
slits in the walls of his home. As the stars moved across the sky during
the night, Copernicus sighted through these slits. He measured how high
the stars were above the dark horizon and how far they were from each
other. He carefully checked over old star maps and noted the paths of
the moon and the planets among the stars. He found they were not always
where they should be according to Ptolemy's idea of their motions. He
found the things he was seeing and learning showed more and more clearly
the ideas of Aristotle and Ptolemy were wrong and the ideas of those early
Greeks were more nearly right. He longed to find some clear and simple
plan of the movements of all the things that shine in the sky—something
which would explain the mysterious ways in which they seemed to move.

"Suppose Aristarchus and those other ancient Greeks were right, after
all; suppose we are looking out at the stars from a moving earth, as they
said—would that make things any clearer?" he thought. If the sun and
the stars are standing still and if the earth is spinning, the sun and stars
will seem to rise and set. If the earth is going around the sun, the stars
will seem to be in a different part of the sky at different times of the year.
If the other planets are going around the sun, the way the earth does, they
will have special paths in the sky.

But Ptolemy's way of explaining these things was very confusing, and
his explanation does not quite work. In the dedication of his great book
Revolutionibus Orbium coelestum to Pope Paul III, he recalled "according
to Cicero, Hicetas had thought that the earth moved . . . and according
to Plutarch others had held the same opinion." This led Copernicus to
long meditations on the subject, which ultimately resulted in the system
he proposed. Copernicus began his discussion by remarking:

> every change of position which is observed is due to the motion either of
> the observed object or of the observer, or to motions of both. . . . If the
> earth should possess any motion, this would be noticeable in everything
> that is situated outside the earth, but would be in the opposite direction,
> just as though everything were traveling past the earth.

The relation is similar to that of which Aeneas says in Virgil: "We sail
out of the harbour, and the countries and cities recede."

Copernicus next suggested the apparent daily revolution of the "sphere
of the fixed stars" can be explained on these lines: The earth, and not this

sphere of stars rotates once a day. This opinion was held by the Pythagoreans, Heraclides and Ecphantus, and by the Syracusan Nicetas, who
assumed the earth to be rotating in the center of the universe. He continued:

> It would thus not be strange if someone should ascribe to the earth, in ad-
> dition to its daily rotation, another motion also. It is said that the Pythago-
> rean ·Philolaus, no ordinary mathematicist, believed that the earth rotates,
> that it moves along in space with various motions, and that it belongs to the
> planets; wherefore Plato did not delay traveling to Italy to interview him.

The Ptolemaic system placed the earth at the center of the universe and
supposed the sun to move around it in a circular orbit. This was a very
artificial arrangement, but its very artificiality provided a clue to its true
meaning. When a child sits in a whirling merry-go-round at the fair, distant objects and spectators seem to the child to advance and recede alternately—as a result of the child's own motion. If the child moves in a circle
of a thirty foot radius, then outside objects will appear to the child to
move in circles of thirty foot radius, and at every moment they will all
appear to be in corresponding positions in these circles. The apparent motion of many objects is a sort of "reflection" of one's real motion, namely,
that of the child on the merry-go-round.

Copernicus thought the apparent motions of the planets in their epicycles could be explained on similar lines as reflections of one real motion
of the earth around the sun. If so the whole motion of the solar system
was one of the earth and planets moving in circular orbits around a fixed
central sun, so the earth was simply one "wanderer" of many. He said,
"The sun, as if sitting on a royal throne, governs the family of Stars which
move around it." It was not a new hypothesis, being identical to the one
Aristarchus proposed 1800 years earlier. What Copernicus did was to show
that the old system of Aristarchus could explain the observed motions of
the planets, or rather it would produce precisely the same appearances in
the sky as the complicated epicycle motions of Ptolemy.

The earth is not standing still. The sun and the stars are not going
around it. The earth is swinging around the sun, spinning as it goes. Copernicus was so sure he was right he dared to attack the ideas of Ptolemy
and to tell the people they were wrong. Copernicus sent a brief summary
of his conclusions to his astronomical friends under the title *Commentariolus,* but he shrank from the task of preparing the whole work for publication. Ten years elapsed before he consented to do this. But he did give
permission to Georg Joachim (Rheticus), who resigned from the Chair of
Mathematics at Wittenburg, to prepare a short summary of the contents of

the book, which was published in 1541 under the title *De Libris Revolu-tionum Narratio prima*. Copernicus subsequently handed over the text of his whole book to Rheticus, who revised it and prepared it for the press. The printing was completed only just in time for the author to handle the book as he lay on his death bed.

About the time of the *Commentariolus*, another problem was troubling the priests of the Church. Their calendars were no longer right with the seasons. For over a thousand years almost the only real use made of astron-omy was to figure out the dates of the big church holidays like Easter. But now holidays that had come in the spring came around before winter was quite over. The time for harvest festivals came before the wheat rip-ened. It was clear that the calendars must be changed. Since the sun, the moon, and the stars are the real calendar, the Church called in Co-pernicus to help them fix up the calendar because he knew so much about these things. He said people must first watch the sun and the moon more carefully and write down exactly where they were at different times.

Copernicus figured out just when people could expect the sun and moon to be in certain places in the sky. They worked so carefully people began to realize Copernicus was a great astronomer and began to believe his ideas. But most of the common people still thought they were ridiculous. They could see that the earth was standing still, and they could see the sun swing up in the east every morning and drop in the west every night. Copernicus did not wish to print his discoveries because he was afraid people would misunderstand him. Also, he did not want to arouse the Church against him. But he wrote down his ideas and his proofs, and showed them to his friends.

Many people saw his writings, and some said it was a very interesting idea. Others believed that perhaps he was even right. A few were amazed by his charts—they were so simple and clear; these people were sure he was right. More and more people wanted him to give his ideas to the rest of the world, to publish them in a book. Even the pope at Rome, the head of the Church, heard of his work and said it should be published. Finally, when Copernicus was an old man, he gave in. In his dedicatory letter to the pope, Copernicus explained why he hesitated so long before he published his theories to the world: "I considered what an absurd fairy tale people would consider it, if I asserted that the earth moved. . . . The scorn which was to be feared on account of this novelty and absurdity of the opinion impelled me for that reason to set aside entirely the book I had already drawn up."

Notwithstanding this clear statement, it has often been asserted Coper-nicus held back his book from a fear it might incur the displeasure of the Church. It is hard to find any evidence for this. Copernicus made no secret of his conclusions!

He quite frankly said in *De Revolutionibus Orbium Celestium* (1543):

> First and above all lies the sphere of the fixed stars, containing itself and all things, for that very reason immoveable; in truth the frame of the universe, to which the motion and position of all other stars are referred. Though some men think it to move it some way, we assign another reason why it appears to do so in our theory of the movement of the earth. Of the moving bodies first comes Saturn, who completes his circuit in 30 years. After him, Jupiter, moving in a twelve year revolution. Then Mars, who revolves biennially, Fourth in order an annual cycle takes place, in which we have said is contained the earth, with the lunar orbit as an epicycle. In the fifth place Venus is carried round in nine months. Then Mercury holds the sixth place, circulating in the space of eighty days. In the middle of all dwells the Sun. Who indeed in this most beautiful temple would place the torch in any other or better place than one whence it can illuminate the whole at the same time? Not ineptly, some call it the lamp of the universe, others its mind, others again its ruler—Trimegistus, the visible God, Sophocles' Electra the contemplation of all things. And thus rightly in as much as the Sun, sitting on a royal throne, governs the circumbient family of stars. . . . We find, therefore, under this orderly arrangement, a wonderful symmetry in the universe, and a definite relation of harmony in the motion and magnitude of the orbs, of a kind it is not possible to obtain in any other way.

The first copy of his book was brought to him when he lay in bed, paralyzed, half-blind, dying. Perhaps it was better he could not read it. Some one slipped in a paragraph at the beginning saying the great discovery was only a theory, only an interesting idea, so it should not be taken as the actual truth or a true picture of things as they really are. Only a few mathematicians and astronomers expressed their confidence in the new structure of the world, while the majority of men remained hostile or indifferent until the telescope of Galileo provided visual confirmation of its accuracy some sixty-six years later. Even then, one of Galileo's colleagues refused to look through the telescope, on the ground he saw no reason for reopening a question which already was settled by Aristotle. He was perhaps exceptional, but many felt genuine objections to the new doctrines on religious grounds.

The great astronomer Kepler, himself a convinced Copernican, later wrote: "It must be confessed that there are very many who are devoted to Holiness, that dissent from the judgment of Copernicus, fearing to give the Lye to the Holy Ghost speaking in the scriptures, if they should say that the earth moved and the Sun standeth still." Even in 1669, the year in which Newton became Professor at Cambridge, the university hired Cosimo de Medici to give a series of dissertations against the Copernican astronomy.

And in the eighteenth century, Assini (1625–1712), the Director of the Observatory of Paris, taught the Copernican doctrine as a convenient but false hypothesis. For a long time the new American Universities of Yale and Harvard taught the Ptolemaic and Copernican systems on a parallel footing, implying they were equally tenable. It was not until 1822 that the Roman Church gave formal permission for the Copernican systems to be taught as the truth.

On December 14, 1546, three years after the death of Copernicus, Tycho Brahe was born. In many ways he was the opposite of Copernicus. Copernicus was a great mathematician and a great theorist, but was weak as a direct observer. Tycho was weak as a mathematician and theorist, but great as an observer. In fact, he was one of the greatest observers, perhaps the greatest, of all time. He was a Dane, the son of a Danish nobleman, although his birthplace, Knudstrup in Scandia, now belongs to Sweden. A solar eclipse which occurred on August 21, 1560, while he was a student at the University of Copenhagen, made a great impression on him and gave him a keen interest in astrology. He began to study the works of Ptolemy and attempted simple observations with crude instruments of his own making. After studying mathematics and astronomy at the Universities of Leipzig, Wittenberg, Rostock, and Basle, he made a European tour, and met the Landgrave of Hesse, who was an enthusiastic astrologer. The Landgrave must have been impressed by Tycho's ability, for he persuaded the King of Denmark, Frederick II, to take the young astrologer under his royal patronage.

In due course, Frederick granted Tycho a yearly pension and the island of Huen in the straits between Copenhagen and Elsinore. There he built himself an observatory which he called Uraniborg, and furnished it so magnificently and equipped it so sumptuously his pension soon proved inadequate. But he was clever and had it supplemented by further grants from the king. When Frederick died in 1588, Tycho's income was reduced and he left Uraniborg in 1597. Two years later, the German Emperor Rudolph II invited him to Prague, granting him a pension and a castle to use as an observatory. But Tycho's real useful life was over. Before he settled down to serious work he was struck down by a sudden illness and died on October 24, 1601.

Tycho opposed the doctrines of Copernicus because he thought they were contrary to sound physics and to the clear word of Scripture. The massive solid earth just did not move in space. He was also influenced by

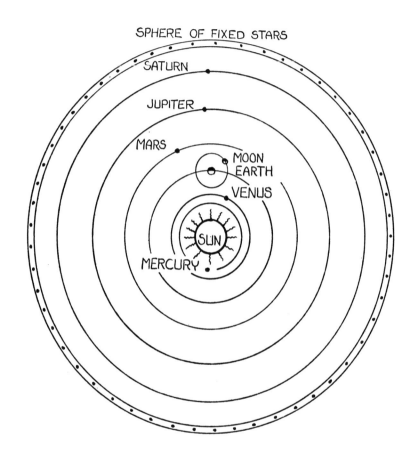

The plan of the universe of Copernicus. In the Copernican system only three classes of motion need be recognized:

a. the earth's diurnal motion about its own axis from west to east.
b. the moon's orbital motion from west to east.
c. the orbital motion of all planets (including the earth) from west to east. Mercury is at its extreme easterly position (maximum elongation) as an evening star, Venus is at its extreme westerly position (maximum elongation) as a morning star. Neither of them can ever be seen on the meridian after dark.

the Ptolemaic objection that the stars did not change their relative positions in the sky. This they would have to do if the earth was in actual motion. And so he set to work to improve the Ptolemaic system according to his own ideas. He kept the earth for the center of his universe and the Aristotelian sphere of fixed stars for its outer boundary. The sun still circled around the earth, but the other planets—Mercury, Venus, Mars, Jupiter and Saturn—all circled around the sun in epicycles. This gave the same apparent motion for the sun, moon, and planets as either the Copernican or the Ptolemaic systems. So direct observation could not decide between the two systems. But Tycho's system plays a serious part in the history of astrology, because all later developments were made by believers in the Copernican cosmology.

Tycho's real service to astrology was as an observer rather than as a theorist. He introduced a new standard of accuracy into astrological calculations. He attained this in two ways—by the use of better instruments, and by the use of better methods. It may seem an easy matter to obtain greater accuracy by making larger instruments, but actually the situation was not quite so simple. The larger an instrument is, the more it bends under its own weight. A stage is soon reached when the bending more than neutralizes the advantages gained by the increased size of the instrument. Tycho was able to employ large instruments because they were of a clever and novel design. They were especially planned to escape this objection. Today, the importance of precision in scientific observation and experiment is taken for granted. The most exact and delicate measurements, the most sensitive instruments, capable of measuring millionths of an inch or velocities of hundreds of thousands of miles a second, have been developed. Tiny discrepancies, which have been revealed by carrying such measurements "to the next decimal place," have led to great discoveries. This factor was virtually unrecognized in Tycho's day, so his own observations were miracles of accuracy.

Copernicus would have been elated to be correct to ten minutes of arc, but Tycho's observations, made without a telescope, could be trusted almost to minutes. In 1893, Sir Oliver Lodge wrote, "for certain purposes connected with the proper motion of stars they are still appealed to." The conclusions Tycho drew from his own observations were sound. Yet it remained for a greater man to interpret them.

Kepler's work would have been incomplete or impossible without that of Tycho. Kepler was a theoretician, at times to the point of absurdity. It was the direction provided by Tycho's facts and the knowledge that he could rely on them implicitly, which led him after many years of work to the conclusions embodied in his laws of planetary motion. Tycho saw the advantage of taking a great number of observations, all of the same quality, then averaging the result. This made accidental errors more likely to be averaged out.

Using these methods, Tycho determined the more important constants of astrology with a new greater accuracy, as well as made fresh determinations of all stellar positions. These were published in the *Star Catalogue* of 1602. Probably his observations on the positions of the planets were his best work; not for any use he made of them, but for the part they played in later developments in astrology. He handed them over to Johannes Kepler, an assistant whom he engaged just before his death. But Tycho was an improver rather than an originator; he plays a great part in the history of astronomical technique, but figures little in the history of thought. Nevertheless, some of his work reached out beyond the merely technical problems of astrology. On the evening of November 11, 1572, he observed a bright new object in the constellation of Cassiopeia. To Tycho it was "a miracle indeed, either the greatest of all that occurred in the whole range of nature since the beginning of the world, or one certainly that is to be classed with those attested by the Holy Oracles, the staying of the sun in its course in answer to the prayers of Joshua, and the darkening of the sun's face at the time of the Crucifixion."

If this new object belonged to the solar system, it would have appeared to move against the background of the fixed stars. As Tycho could observe no such movement, he concluded the object must belong to the "sphere of Fixed Stars." In brief, it must be a star! The Aristotelians taught everything in these outer regions of the space was perfect, and therefore unchanging: "All philosophers agree, and facts clearly prove it to be the case, that in the ethereal region of the celestial world no change, in the way either of generation or corruption, takes place; but that the heavens and the celestial bodies in the heavens are without increase or diminution, and that they undergo no alteration." Tycho, by showing from direct observation these regions were no more immune from change than the regions nearer to the earth, dealt a shattering blow to Aristotelian cosmology.

The work of Tycho represented a new outlook—a change as radical in its way as that of Copernicus, for, surprising as it may seem now, the idea that before describing phenomena one should know as accurately as possible what those phenomena were, was almost unthought of in the sixteenth century. Tycho was thoroughly modern, in his day almost unique, in realizing the value of precision in measurement. Dreyer, his excellent modern biographer stated that Tycho's accuracy, but for the invention of the telescope, could hardly have been exceeded by his successors. Certainly without Tycho's work there would be no Kepler's laws, and possibly Newton would have been unable to formulate his law of gravitation.

On his island, Huen, the main building, known as Uraniborg, was nearly in the center of the island and was built in the Gothic Renaissance style then becoming popular. It was at the first the only astronomical building in the world, but in 1584 a second observatory was erected to the south, known as Stierneborg. To this island astrologers from all over Europe came to work with Tycho, and the work done there was the basis of modern astronomy and, of course, astrology. Tycho's innovations consisted first in the great size of his instruments. Secondly, in his improved method of graduation; he was the first to use the method of transversals in which the main graduations were made alternately on each of a pair of parallel lines, the successive marks being joined diagonally so as to form a zigzag pattern. Thirdly in a greatly improved method of constructing and arranging his "sights." And finally, in the practice already mentioned of determining as precisely as possible the errors of his instruments.

His most outstanding contributions included far more accurate observations of the positions of the heavenly bodies than any previously made, the first observations of the effect of atmospheric refraction on apparent positions, and the discovery of the third and fourth inequalities (known respectively as the "variation" and "annual equation") in the moon's motion as well as the fluctuation in the inclination of the moon's orbit to the eclipse. It was customary to make occasional observations of the positions of the planets; Tycho observed them regularly and systematically before and after opposition. This systematic observation combined with the care and accuracy with which the observations were made, enabled Kepler to deduce his three laws of planetary motion and so to lay the foundation of celestial mechanics.

As a man Tycho was not altogether lovable or admirable. He was overbearing, and failed to carry out the extremely light obligations which the generosity of the king placed on him in return for his privileges. Of his utterly selfless devotion to astrology, however, there is no doubt. It must be recorded in his favor that in an unfortunate dispute with Kepler, who was in general a far more noble-minded man, it was Tycho who appeared in the more favorable light. Also, while at Huen it was his habit to give away medicines which he made through his lifelong love of alchemy. He made a practice of preparing them and placing considerable trust in them. Tycho was fond of mystery and display. His observatory at Uraniborg abounded in mechanical devices and mystical means of communication with which he liked to confound his visitors. He wrote tolerable verses, some of which, along with his paintings, adorned the walls of his observatory.

A typical example of the ornate character of the building was the ceiling and walls of the study at Stierneborg, which showed the Tychonic

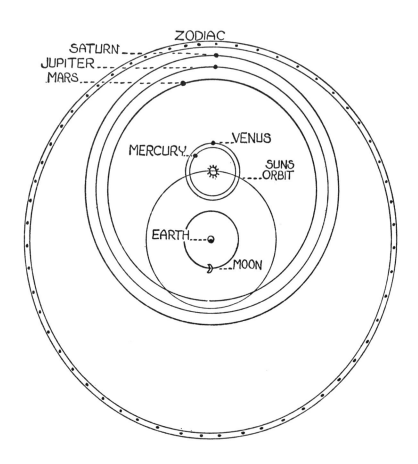

Tycho's scheme of the solar system. Tycho Brahe's system looks strange to us mainly because we know it to be wrong. Actually it was a very interesting idea. Considering that true distances in the solar system (except for that of the moon) were not known and that nobody in pretelescopic times could have any idea about the sizes of the planets, and considering especially that the rival Copernican system was not the one we now call by that name, but the one Copernicus wrote, it is quite understandable that Tycho could think he had found the answer.

system of the world and the portraits of eight astrologers, ending with Tycho and "Tychonides," a successor yet unborn. In the inscriptions underneath, Tycho leaves his own work to the judgment of posterity, but the hope was expressed that Tychonides might be worthy of his great ancestor. There also was a dwarf called Jep, who Tycho used to feed with an occasional morsel at the table, like a dog. Jep was supposed to be clairvoyant and to make remarkable prophecies.

But now let us turn to the south of Europe, to a summer morning in 1633. A seventy-year-old man clothed in sackcloth stands in a room in the Convent of Minerva in Rome, his face pale, his weakened limbs trembling, and hears his fate pronounced by the cardinals of the Inquisition. For having espoused the Copernican doctrine that the earth moves around the sun, contrary to what was taught in the Holy Scriptures, Galileo Galilei is condemned of heresy, but his life is spared, provided that with a sincere heart he abjure and curse the heresies he cherished against the Church. Thus ended temporarily a long struggle between the dogmas of a crumbling medieval world and a representative of the new science of the Renaissance.

This great astrologer and experimental philosopher was born at Pisa on the 15th of February 1564. His father was an impoverished descendant of a noble Florentine house which changed their surname of Bonajuti to Galilei. From his earliest childhood Galileo, the eldest child of the family, was remarkable for his intellectual aptitude as well as for mechanical invention. His favorite pastime was the construction of original and ingenious toy-machines; but his application to his studies was equally great. His father desired Galileo should apply himself to medicine and placed him at the University of Pisa. He accordingly entered there on the 5th of November 1581 and immediately attended the lectures of the celebrated physician and botanist, Andrea Cesalpino.

The natural gifts of the young Galileo seemed equally ready to develop in any direction towards which choice or hazard might incline. In 1581, while watching a lamp set swinging in the cathedral of Pisa, he observed that whatever the range of its oscillations, they were invariably executed in equal times. He at first applied the new principle to pulse measurement, and more than fifty years later used it in the construction of an astrological clock. Up to this time he was entirely ignorant of mathematics, his father having carefully held him away from a study which would lead to total alienation from medicine. In 1585 he withdrew from the university, because of lack of money, and returned to Florence, where his family resided. We next hear of him as lecturing before the Florentine Academy on the site and dimensions of Dante's Inferno. Shortly afterwards he published an essay about his invention of the hydrostatic balance.

In 1588 he wrote a treatise on the center of gravity in solids, which obtained for him, together with the title of "the Archimedes of his time," the honorable if not lucrative post of mathematical lecturer at Pisa. During the next two years (1589–1591) he carried on a remarkable series of experiments in which he established the first principles of dynamics and earned the undying hostility of bigoted Aristotelians. From the Leaning Tower of Pisa he afforded to all an eye-witness demonstration of the falsehood of the dictum that heavy bodies fall with velocities proportional to their weights. With perfect logic he demolished all the time-honored maxims regarding the motion of projectiles. He continued to challenge Aristotelian dogma in his eighteen years at Padua University. He finally resigned his post to return to Florence under the protection of the Medici Duke Cosimo II, who appointed him court mathematician.

The keen sarcasm of his polished writing and speaking was not calculated to soothe men already smarting under the deprivation of their most cherished false illusions. The death of his father caused family cares and responsibilities to fall upon him; thus his nomination to the chair of mathematics at the University of Padua, secured by the influence of the Marchese, was welcome both as affording relief from money problems and as opening a field for scientific astrological research. His residence at Padua over a period of eighteen years from 1592 to 1610 was a course of uninterrupted prosperity. His lectures were attended by persons of distinction from all parts of Europe, and such was the charm and appeal of his demonstrations that a hall capable of containing 2000 people was assigned to him for the accommodation of the overflowing audiences.

His invention of the proportional compass or sector—an implement still used in astrological drawing—dates from 1597; and about the same time he constructed the first thermometer, consisting of a bulb and tube filled with air and water and terminating in a vessel of water. Galileo seems to have adopted the Copernican theory at an early period of his life, and was deterred from avowing his opinions—as is proved by his letter to Kepler of August 4, 1597—by fear of ridicule rather than of persecution. The appearance, in September, 1604, of a new star in the constellation Serpentarius afforded him an opportunity which he eagerly took. With it he made an onslaught upon the Aristotelian axiom of the incorruptibility of the heavens.

The discovery of a novel and potent implement of research in the shape of the telescope placed at his command startling and hitherto unsuspected evidence as to the constitution and relations of the heavenly bodies. Galileo was not its original inventor, for that honor must be assigned to Johannes Lippershey, an obscure optician of Middleburg. A rumor of the new invention reached Venice in June 1609, which set

Galileo on the track. After one night's profound meditation on the principles, he succeeded in producing a telescope of three-fold magnifying power. After this first attempt he rapidly improved until he attained a thirty-two power instrument. His instruments, which he manufactured with his own hands, were soon in demand all over Europe.

Two lenses only—a convex and a concave—were needed, and this simple principle is still employed in the construction of opera-glasses. Galileo's new instrument for study of the heavens formed a new era in the history of astrology. Discoveries followed with astounding rapidity and in bewildering variety. In the Palace of the Doges in Venice the senators and nobles, resplendent in their silk togas against a lustrous background of canvases by Titian and Tintoretto, gathered on a summer day in 1609 for a demonstration of "Galileo's gun," a satin-sheathed leaden tube about two feet long and less than two inches in breadth, with a lens at each end. The hardiest members of the assemblage clambered up the steep steps of the campanile of San Marco and were astounded to see through the tube the campanile of the church of Santa Guistina in Padua, thirty-five kilometers away.

Less than a year after this triumph Galileo disclosed to the world in his book *Sidereus nuncius* the startling discoveries he made as the first man in history to look closely at the heavens. In his dramatic report on his astronomic observations through the telescope he told how he was overwhelmed to find more than 500 new stars distributed among the old ones within one or two degrees of arc. His telescopic view resolved the murky old philosophic disputes about the nature of the Milky Way into a clear picture of many stars grouped together in clusters. He exposed the falsity of the ancients' description of the moon as a perfect body, noted that it was pitted and pocked very much like the earth, accurately estimated the altitude of the highest lunar mountains at four miles (which he mistakenly believed was higher than any earth mountains), and reported the previously unobserved phenomenon of "earthshine," a secondary illumination of the darkened regions of the moon by sunlight reflected by the earth.

As his most important discovery he announced the sighting of four planets in orbit around Jupiter, which he named *sidera medicea* in honor of his Florentine patrons. With this evidence of the existence of other satellites besides the moon he attempted to rally support for the Copernican heliocentric theory; he offered further evidence of the earth's motion after his discovery of the phases of Venus, which could not be explained under the old Ptolemaic geostatic cosmology. These epochal discoveries set off a wave of enthusiasm for astrology: poets expressed their awe at the vast universe opened to the eye and mind, painters found new themes in the fresh vision of heavenly bodies, the astronomer Kepler hailed the telescope as more precious than the scepter, and had Galileo's book reprinted in Germany within a year; within five years a translation appeared in China. But the discovery which was to be most important in itself, and most revolutionary in its effects, was that of Jupiter's satellites, first seen by Galileo on January 7, 1610.

Before the close of 1610 the memorable cycle of discoveries begun in the previous year was completed by the observation of the triple form of Saturn, of the phases of Venus, and of the spots on the sun. In the spring of 1611 Galileo visited Rome, and exhibited in the gardens of the Quirinal Palace the telescopic wonders of the heavens to the most eminent personages at the court. Even in the time of Copernicus some well-meaning persons suspected a discrepancy between the new view of the solar system and certain passages of Scripture—a suspicion strengthened by the anti-Christian inferences drawn from it by Giordano Bruno. But the question was never formally debated until Galileo's brilliant disclosures enhanced by his formidable dialectic and zeal. These irresistibly challenged the attention of the authorities. Many scientists and academicians treated the new discoveries with extreme skepticism; even Kepler refused to acknowledge the existence of Jupiter's satellites until their discoverer lent him a telescope which enabled him to see for himself. Entrenched in the universities were rabid followers of Aristotle who denied the validity of Galileo's observations inasmuch as the Greek philosopher had not mentioned them. Clavius, author of the Gregorian calendar reform, scoffed at the reported discovery of Jupiter's satellites and asserted they must have been placed in the telescope by its builder. A monk named Sizy took issue with Galileo on theologic grounds and asserted the satellites of Jupiter were incompatible with the doctrines of the Holy Scriptures.

Against his detractors, who accused him of impiety by advocating views contrary to Holy Writ, Galileo ardently defended the compatibility of his scientific views with true Christian faith in a series of brilliant articles, the *Letters of Sunspots*, the *Letter to Castelli* and the celebrated *Letter to the Grand Duchess Christina*. He argued "Nature is inexorable and immutable, therefore nothing physical which sense-experience sets before our eyes, or which necessary demonstrations prove to us, ought to be called in question (much less condemned) upon the testimony of biblical passages which may have some different meaning beneath their words. For the Bible is not chained in every expression to conditions as strict as those which govern all physical effects; nor is God any less excellently revealed in Nature's actions than in the sacred statements of the Bible."

But when formal charges against Galileo were made to the Inquisition, several friendly cardinals urged the increasingly ardent defender of the

Copernican system to keep silent in public. In 1615 a group of eleven theologians pronounced Galileo's heliocentric conceptions absurd and heretical. Cardinal Bellarmine admonished him not to hold, teach or defend the condemned opinion of Copernicus, and Copernicus' book *De Revolutionibus*, which was approved years before by the pope to whom it was dedicated, was now condemned and prohibited until properly corrected by reliable authorities. Galileo received a semi-official warning to avoid theology, and limit himself to physical reasoning. "Write freely," he was told by Monsignor Dini, "but keep outside the sacristy." Unfortunately, he had already committed himself to dangerous grounds.

On February 24, 1616, the consulting theologians of the Holy office studied the two propositions—that the sun is immovable in the center of the world, and that the earth has a diurnal motion of rotation. The first they called "absurd in philosophy, and formally heretical, because expressly contrary to Holy Scripture," and the second they said was "open to the same censure in Philosophy, and at least erroneous as to faith." Two days later Galileo was by command of the pope summoned to the palace of Cardinal Bellarmine. There he was officially admonished not thenceforward to "hold, teach or defend" the condemned doctrine. When the author of a poetic tribute to Galileo's discoveries, Maffeo Cardinal Barberini, was elevated to the papacy in 1623 as Urban VIII, the philosopher sought a relaxation of the restrictions imposed on him by the Church. Urban VIII agreed that he could write about the Copernican system so long as he treated it as a hypothesis and not as reality. Galileo used the Church printer to publish the *Dialogue* in Florence in 1632.

Within a few months the Church suppressed the *Dialogue*, which it had examined and approved before publication, and summoned the author to Rome for trial before the Inquisition. Still unresolved are the real reasons for the reversal of the Church's position. Some interpreters suggest that the pope was affronted by the transparent device Galileo used to weight the dialogue in favor of the Copernican system: All the arguments against it were advanced in the most naive and unconvincing manner by a philosopher appropriately named "Simplicio."

Applause from every part of Europe followed the publication of the *Dialogue*. It would be difficult to find in any language a book in which animation and elegance of style are so happily combined with strength and clearness of scientific exposition. Three interlocutors, named respectively Salviati, Sagredo, and Simplicio, take part in the four dialogues of which the work was composed. The first-named expounds the views of the author; the second was an eager and intelligent listener; the third represents a well-meaning but obtuse Peripatetic, whom the others treat at times with undisguised contempt. Salviati and Sagredo received their names from two of Galileo's early friends, the former a learned Florentine, the latter a distinguished Venetian gentleman; Simplicio ostensibly derived his from the Cicilian commentator of Aristotle, but the name was doubtless instigated by a sarcastic regard for the double meaning of the word.

The ebb and flow of the tides were, Galileo asserted, a visible proof of the terrestrial double movement, since they resulted from inequalities in the absolute velocities through space of the various parts of the earth's surface, due to its rotation. To this notion, which took its rise in a confusion of thought, he attached capital importance, and he treated with scorn Kepler's suggestion that a certain occult attraction of the moon was in some way concerned in the phenomenon. On June 22, 1633, the papal court pronounced sentence of imprisonment against Galileo, who kneeled and abjured his "errors and heresies about the earth's motion." In the realm of legend is the famous remark he is said to have uttered under his breath, "Eppur si muove!" (But it does move!)

The Vatican placed Galileo in the custody of his friend, Ascanio Piccolomini, Archbishop of Siena, but after a few months confined him to his own villa in Arcetri near Florence, apparently to enforce a stricter seclusion than was imposed in Siena. Despite his complaint of declining mental powers, the seventy-year-old completed the definitive summation of his views in *Discourses and Demonstrations Concerning Two New Sciences,* and smuggled the manuscript through a friend in Venice to the publisher Louis Elzevie in Leyden; when it appeared in print in 1638, he pretended not to know how the manuscript reached Holland.

The Church took no formal notice of this transgression, but maintained a strict surveillance over the scientist. He was permitted to leave Arcetri only twice in the last eight years of his life, once to visit the Comte de Noailles at Poggibonsi, and once to consult the best physicians in Florence. The inquisitor reported to his superior that he found Galileo totally blind, suffering terribly from hernia, in constant pain which prevented him from sleeping more than an hour at a stretch, and "so prostrate that he looks more like a corpse than a living person." The philosopher, who was carried into Florence for treatment under threat of excommunication if he mentioned to anyone his condemned opinion of the earth's motion, sent a second request to the Vatican, for permission to be carried to hear mass at a little church twenty paces from his house.

His last telescopic discoveries—that of the moons diurnal and monthly librations—were made in 1637, only a few months before his eyes were forever closed in hopeless blindness. In his seventy-eighth year, while working on an analysis of the nature of the force of percussion, Galileo

was stricken by a fever accompanied by palpitations of the heart. After
two months of illness he died on January 8, 1642.

In accordance with his request to be buried in the family vault in the
church of Santa Croce, the body was carried from Arcetri to the church.
The Court of Tuscany ordered a great public funeral and voted 3000
crowns for a marble mausoleum. The Grand Duke yielded to pressure
from the Vatican to lay aside the project for a public funeral oration and
for interment in a mausoleum; instead the remains were quietly buried in
a corridor of Santa Croce. A devoted disciple, Vincenzo Viviani, planned
to do public homage to his master's memory by covering the facade of his
own house in Via dell'Amore with laudatory inscriptions, but half a century elapsed before he dared emblazon this challenge to the Inquisition.
Viviani also made provision in his will for the erection of a suitable monument to Galileo in Santa Croce when permission could be obtained. This
was accomplished in 1737 under the pontificate of Clement XII.

The idea of a universal force of gravitation seems to have hovered on
the borders of this great man's mind without ever fully entering it. He
perceived the analogy between the power which holds the moon in the
neighborhood of the earth and that which compels Jupiter's satellites to
revolve, and the attraction exercised by the earth on bodies at its surfaces.
But he failed to conceive the combination of central force with tangential
velocity, and connected the revolutions of the planets with the axial rotation of the sun. This notion, it is plain, tended more toward Descartes'
theory of vortices than towards Newton's theory of gravitation. More valid
instances of the anticipation of modern discoveries may be found in his
idea that a small annual parallax would eventually be found for some of
the fixed stars. He also felt the extra-Saturnian planets would at some future time be found to exist and he was convinced light travels with a
measurable—although in relation to terrestrial distances, infinite—velocity.

In order to form an adequate estimate of the stride made by Galileo
in astrology, it would be necessary to enumerate the confused and erroneous opinions prevailing on all such subjects during his time. His mind
was eminently practical. He concerned himself above all with what fell
within the range of exact inquiry, and left to others the larger but less
fruitful speculations which can never be brought to the direct test of experiment. In his fight for recognition of the truth of the Copernican system
he exposed the conflict, which Copernicus left unresolved, between that
system and Aristotelian physics. Aristotelian philosophy envisaged the
heavenly bodies as composed of "incorruptible" ether in contrast to the
earth composed of four "corruptible" elements (Earth, Air, Fire, Water).
It had distinguished between the "natural" circular motion of the heavenly

bodies and the "natural" downward motion of heavy bodies and upward motion of light bodies on earth.

By his observations of such celestial flaws as moon craters and sunspots, Galileo destroyed the fiction of an imperfect earth immobilized at the center of a perfect universe; and through numerous experimental observations combined with reasoning he discovered the law of acceleration and grasped intuitively the true principles of motion which Isaac Newton developed and formulated in the basic laws of inertial physics and astrology. His keen intuition of truth, his vigor and yet logic in argument, his fertility of illustration and acuteness of sarcasm, made him irresistible to his antagonists. The fleeting triumphs of scornful controversy have given away to the sedate applause of posterity. Galileo's revolutionary views that well-defined mathematical laws govern the physical movements of all bodies stimulated the modern new approaches in astrology.

When he was totally blind, Galileo wrote to a friend: "These heavens, this earth, this universe, which by wonderful observation I had enlarged a thousand times beyond the belief of the past ages, are henceforth dwindled into the narrow space which I myself, occupy. So it pleases God, and it shall therefore please me also." Kepler would carry on the fight where Galileo left it and describe the elliptical orbits of the planets.

Kepler's chief claim to memory lies in his careful enunciation of the basic laws of planetary motion. The whole of his life was one long story of domestic trouble, ill-health, and financial worry. Yet, through all this, he displayed a genius and an enthusiasm for mathematics and astrology which led him to the highest pinnacles of scientific achievement. Yet, Kepler was denied the great joy of any direct astrological observations. In his youth a serious illness permanently injured his eyesight and telescopes and other instruments of observation were for him "the forbidden fruit." He conquered, but his victory was won on the battlefield of mathematical geometry and statistics with the aid of his careful calculations, his drawing instruments, and above all his wonderful perseverance in the face of repeated failure.

Johannes Kepler was born at Weil in the Duchy of Wurtemberg on the 21st of December 1571. His father was an idle, unreliable soldier of fortune, while his mother, the daughter of a burgomaster, was ignorant and of violent temper. She was a true child of Saturn with the disposition of a shrew. Johannes was a sickly child, so an attack of smallpox, which nearly killed him at the age of four, left him with a disabled constitution. He went to a local school at a very early age, but it was not long before the first check to his studies appeared. It seems his father became surety for a friend who proved to be a defaulter. As a consequence he lost what little money he possessed and was obliged to keep a shabby tavern. So we see the sorry spectacle of a future professor of astronomy and astrology withdrawn from school at the age of nine and employed as a pot-boy in his father's inn.

For three years this state of affairs continued, but eventually, owing to kind friends, young Johannes Kepler was able to attend school at Marlbronn. His ability in mathematics enabled him to pass on, at the age of seventeen, to the University of Bugingen. Fortunately for the world, he came under the influence of Michael Maestlin, then professor of mathematics at the university, who soon detected Kepler's great genius. Maestlin was an outspoken convert to the Copernican doctrine of the solar system. Its simplicity made a powerful appeal to Kepler's imagination. He was its vigorous defender in many a lecture and debate. When in 1594, a professorship of mathematics fell vacant at the University of Graz in Styria, it was immediately offered to Kepler who accepted it without hesitation. From the point of view of pay and prestige, astronomy was none too highly rated in the universities, as the professors were expected to devote more to the revelations of astrology than to anything else.

The best recognized function of German astronomers was the construction of prophecying almanacs, greedily bought by the credulous public. Kepler found the first duties required of him were of an astrological nature, so he set himself with characteristic alacrity to master the rules of the ancient art as laid down by Ptolemy and Cardan. He sought in the events of his own life a verification of the theory of planetary influences. But, his thoughts were already working in an even higher sphere. He early came to the settled conviction that for the actual disposition of the solar system some abstract intelligible reason must exist. This, after much meditation, he believed himself to have found in an imaginary relation between the "five regular solids" and the number and distances of the known visible planets, aside from earth. It was because of these facts, and because of his bitter recollections of the acute poverty of his childhood, that Kepler was so eager in accepting the professorship.

In 1597, at the age of twenty-six, Johannes Kepler married a lady from Styria. It is not known whether or not he thought with her dowry she might ease his financial position. She was twice married before to very wealthy men, and be that as it may, it was not too happy a union. There were three children of the marriage, and Kepler's financial cares were considerably increased in consequence.

The first works executed by him were an homage to the astrological proclivities of the emperor. His purpose of preserving and purifying the grain of truth which the science contained was strengthened. Indeed, the doctrine of "aspects" and "influences" fitted excellently with his mystical conception of the universe, and enabled him to discharge with sincerity the most lucrative part of his professional duties. Although he strictly limited his prophetic works to the estimate of tendencies and probabilities, his forecasts were none the less in great demand. Shrewd sense and considerable knowledge of the world came to the aid of stellar lore in the preparation of "prognostics" which earned him much credit with the vulgar as well as with the learned. He drew the horoscopes of the emperor and Wallenstein, as well as of a host of lesser magnates.

"Nature," he wrote, "which has conferred upon every animal the means of Subsistence, has given astrology as an adjunct and ally to astronomy." He wrote a treatise on the "great conjunction" of the year 1603 and he published his observations on a brilliant star which appeared suddenly and remained visible for seventeen months. While sharing the opinion of Tycho as to the origin of such bodies by condensation of nebulous matter from the Milky Way, he attached great mystical significance to the coincidence in time and place of the sidereal apparition with a triple conjunction of Mars, Jupiter, and Saturn.

Kepler knew the six planets were at successively greater distances from the sun. Indeed, he knew the farther a planet was from the sun, the slower seemed its motion. It was Kepler's strong feeling there was some governing scheme. His first theory, developed at Graz, was fantastic! He was a keen student of geometry, but his mathematics in those early days was tinged with mysticism. Between these six planets there are five spaces, and for some reason or other Kepler felt this held the clue which he was seeking. The five spaces led him to think of the five symmetrical solid figures—the tetrahedron, the cube, the octahedron, the dodecahedron, and the icosahedron. Accordingly his scheme took the following form: beginning with a sphere to represent the earth's orbit, he drew around it a dodecahedron, and around this another sphere to represent the orbit of Mars; about that a tetrahedron, and around that a larger sphere for Jupiter; about that a cube, and around that a final sphere for the orbit of Saturn. Returning to the sphere representing the earth's orbit, he drew within that an icosahedron, and inside that another sphere for Venus; inside this was an octahedron, and finally inside that a sphere for the orbit of Mercury.

Kepler's delight is worth quoting. "The intense pleasure I have received from this discovery can never be told in words. I regretted no more the time wasted; I tired of no labor; I shunned no toil of reckoning, days and nights spent in calculation, until I could see whether my hypotheses would agree with the orbits of Copernicus or whether my joy was to vanish into air." Kepler published his theory in 1596 in a book called *Mysterium Cosmographicum,* and it brought him the enthusiastic applause of a wondering world. Of more immediate importance to Kepler, however, was a cordial invitation which he now received from Prague from the great astrologer, Tycho, who was destined to affect his whole future career.

Tycho was not a true follower of Copernicus, but he had sound advice to offer to Kepler: "Do not build up abstract speculations concerning the system of the world, but rather lay a solid foundation in observations and then by ascending from them, strive to come at the causes of things."

Kepler paid his visit, studied the records, and did not hesitate to abandon his theory when he realized it was not consistent with the accurate observations of Tycho. But he earned the respect of his host, and when his professorship became exceedingly uncomfortable owing to a religious change in the regime of the university, Kepler gladly accepted the offer of a post as imperial mathematician to King Rudolph II in 1601, his duties being to assist the great Tycho Brahe. This was a wonderful combination of talents. Tycho was a splendid observer, but a poor mathematician. Kepler was a splendid mathematician, but a poor observer. Both had unbounded enthusiasm for their work and admiration for each other. What they might have achieved together had the alliance continued! But it was not to be! Tycho never completely recovered from the disappointment of his dismissal from Uraniborg, and he died soon after Kepler joined him.

All this time Kepler was in serious and continuous financial straits, and periodically he was seized with illness. Tycho's generosity tided him over his troubles, but at his colleague's death they broke out again. Bohemia was in a sorry state at the time; misgovernment and wars brought the national exchequer to a low state and Kepler's salary was more often promised than paid. A solemn duty was entrusted to him by Tycho on his deathbed. Tycho, engrossed in the preparation of an elaborate set of planetary tables, charged Kepler to complete them, and they were to be known as the "Rudolphine Tables," in honor of their patron. They entailed enormous work and considerable expense, but since money was scarce and involved a delay, Kepler devoted the time to other matters.

In 1604, he published a work called *Paraliponema in Vitellionem*, about the theory of lenses. The telescope was recently invented, and Kepler clearly saw the necessity for such investigations as it permitted. He tried to work out a relation between the angle of incidence and the angle of refraction. Kepler's great influence on his contemporaries in the realm of mathematics, and particularly in geometry, must be mentioned. This branch of mathematics suffered some neglect at the expense of a great advance in algebra, the theory of equations and trigonometry. The seventeenth century revival in geometry was largely due to the influence of Kepler.

Meanwhile, Kepler's financial worries and domestic miseries were continual. His salary was always in arrears, and his wife was suffering from long fits of despondency, and finally in 1612 a series of misfortunes produced a crisis in his affairs. His patron, King Rudolph, died and his poorly paid salary ceased entirely. Within a very short time all his children fell ill with smallpox. A few days later his wife and one child died. When his fortune seemed at its lowest ebb, he was offered a professorship at the University of Linz, and without hesitation he accepted it. Off to Linz he went with his two remaining children, leaving a sum of 8,000 crowns of back salary still due him. There was little money in a professorship, so at Linz, he published a sort of *Old Moore's Almanac*, told people's fortunes, and generally practised the arts of the astrologer in a way which in these days would have earned for him a great following.

Having settled in Linz, Kepler did a bold thing in view of his unhappy experience of married life. He deliberately looked around for a second wife, and he set about it very thoroughly and most scientifically. There were, it seems, no less than eleven candidates for the privilege, and Kepler, mathematician to his finger-tips, carefully set forth his estimate of the merits and demerits of each! And then carefully cast their horoscopes! He was honest in all this and free from any mercenary motives. In fact, he chose the poorest of them all—an orphan girl without a dowry. It turned out a much more satisfactory marriage than his first one. Judging from the fact that his wife bore him seven more children, his continuously scanty resources must have been taxed to the utmost in his efforts to pay his way. Always something seemed to turn up to increase his difficulties. Thus, about this time, news reached him that his bad-tempered old mother had managed to get herself accused of Sorcery in Wurtemberg. She was found guilty of witchcraft and was condemned to imprisonment and torture. Kepler hurried off to Wurtemberg to intercede on her behalf. Although he failed to obtain her release, he at least saved her from torture. It took him another twelve months, however, before he could get her released from prison. She died shortly after, bellicose and mean to the last—a true child of Saturn.

Kepler was applying his mind to the problem of the solar system, and one by one, at long intervals, he gave to the world his three wonderful laws of planetary motion. Nor did Kepler forget his promise to Tycho Brahe to complete the Rudolphine Tables of planetary motions. Year after year he worked at these, all the time puzzling as to how to raise the necessary funds for their publication. Time and again he applied to the court for assistance. And always without result! Kepler never abandoned his determination, and at last, tired of further waiting, he determined to find the money himself. How he succeeded remains a mystery, but it was asserted he accumulated a secret hoard of money, the fruits of years of successful fortune-telling as an astrologer. But it is difficult to believe he deliberately and unnecessarily subjected his wife and children to years of miserable poverty in the accumulation of such a private hoard.

The Rudolphine Tables were published, and handsomely, in 1627. They were of the utmost importance, and their accuracy rendered them indispensable to the navigators of the seventeenth century.

The publication of the tables left Kepler a broken man. The long strain of ill-health, poverty, worry, and constant study began to have its effect. At last, in November 1630, in his sixtieth year, while on his return from a fruitless mission to Prague for the purpose of recovering the money so long due to him, he caught a chill and died. He was buried in St. Peter's Church at Ratisbon, and little was done to perpetuate his memory. A century ago a proposal was made to erect a marble monument to his memory, but nothing was ever done. It matters little one way or the other whether Germany, having refused him money during his life, should, a century and a half after his death, offer him a stone. It matters little indeed. Kepler's monument is not of stone, and it stands in those brilliant laws of planetary motion which gave to the world for the first time a complete view of the cosmic scheme.

"There were three things," he wrote, while still at Linz, "of which I pertinaciously sought the causes why they are not other than they are: the number, the size, and the motion of the orbits." He fully realized the fundamental importance of his self-imposed task, and of his book, *Treatise on the Motions of the Planet Mars,* he took care to "warn-off" the anti-Copernicans: "If any one be too dull to comprehend the science of astronomy, or too foolish to believe in Copernicus without prejudice to his piety, my advice to him is, that he should quit the astronomical school, and condemning, if he will, any or all the theories of philosophers, look to his own affairs, and leaving this worldly travail, go home and plough his fields." Kepler's materials were Tycho Brahe's observations, and his own knowledge of geometry. His was the method of trial and error, and every conceivable relationship between distance, the rate of motion, and the path of the planets he tested in the light of Brahe's results, only to reject them one after the other. Through all he saw one ray of hope: "I was comforted and my hopes of success were supported, as well, by other reasons which presently follow, as by observing that the motions in every case seemed to be connected with the distances, and that when there was a great gap between the orbits, there was the same between the motions."

Like Copernicus, Kepler followed in particular the movement of the planet Mars, this being sufficiently rapid to provide data for testing purposes. What was the correct orbit of Mars? He soon convinced himself that if it were a circle, then at any rate the sun could not be at its center.

After much labor he got one step farther, as he noticed that when the planet's distance from the sun diminished, the planet went faster, and when the distance increased, it went slower. This gave him the idea the planet must sweep out equal areas in equal intervals of time. Suppose, therefore, he were to represent the orbit by a circle, with the sun not at the center, would the planet under such conditions sweep out equal areas in equal times? He tested it for innumerable positions of the sun, but it never quite fit. He next tried an oval orbit, but this, too, never quite fit the facts. At last, however, he hit upon the right solution. Why not try an ellipse? He tested it, and it fit beautifully!

At last the long-sought secret was his, for the path of the planet is that of an ellipse with the sun at one focus, and the variations in speed are such that in equal times the planet sweeps out equal areas. An Ellipse represents the orbit of any planet.

The Master Laws of Kepler are as follows:

Law 1. All the Planets move around the Sun with elliptic orbits with the Sun at one focus.

Law 2. The radius vector or line joining the Planet to the Sun sweeps out equal areas in equal times.

Law 3. For all Planets, the square of the time of one complete revolution (or year) is proportional to the cube of the mean distance to the Sun.

The character of Kepler's genius is difficult to estimate, for his tendency towards mystical speculation formed a fundamental quality of his mind along with a strong grasp of positive scientific truth. Without assigning to each element its due value, no sound comprehension of his modes of thought may be attained. His idea of the Universe was a Pythagorean and Platonic, for he started with the conviction that the arrangement of its parts must correspond with certain abstract conceptions of the beautiful and harmonious. His imagination, thus kindled, animated him to the severe labor for his great discoveries. His demonstration that the planes of all the orbits pass through the center of the sun, coupled with his clear recognition of the sun as the moving power of the system, entitled him to rank as the founder of modern physical astronomy and astrology.

The relations imagined by him of planetary movements and distances to musical intervals and geometrical constructions were discoveries no less admirable than the achievements which secured his lasting fame, and the harmony of the heavens was reborn. Outside the boundaries of the solar system, the metaphysical side of his genius, no longer held in check by experience, fully asserted itself. The Keplerian cosmos like the

Pythagorean, was threefold, consisting of the center or sun; the surface, represented by the sphere of the fixed stars; and the intermediate space, filled with ethereal matter. He mentioned the sun's axial rotation as the physical cause of the revolutions of the planets. This was soon confirmed by the discovery of sun spots. The suggestion of a periodical variation in the ecliptic and the explanation of the solar atmospheric effect of the radiance observed to surround the totally eclipsed sun were other great theories of Kepler.

What Copernicus started in Poland with his heliocentric world, what Kepler revealed to be the correct shape of planetary orbits by his calculations in Austria, what Galileo strengthened by his observations in Italy, still needed a synthesis. This was made in England, and the man who made it, Sir Isaac Newton, was born in the year of Galileo's death on December 25, 1642, at Woosthorpe near Grantham. Newton was a premature baby and his mother sometimes said later he was so small at birth she could have hidden him in a one-quart mug. He was not expected to live for more than a few hours; yet actually he lived for eighty-four years and three months. At the age of fourteen he disappointed his mother by thinking about mathematics instead of doing his farm chores. Newton's uncle, William Ayscough, was a member of Trinity College and solved the family problem when Isaac was eighteen by sending him back to school to prepare for college. He received his Bachelor of Arts degree at Cambridge in 1665 and was elected a Fellow of the Trinity College two years later, at the age of twenty-five.

His main work was *Philosophia Naturalis Principia Mathematica*, published in 1687, the final outcome of the speculations he began to make in 1666 when he wondered whether the earth's cosmic pull might not "extend to the orb of the moon." On December 10, 1684, Dr. Edmond Halley had informed the members of the Royal Society that Newton had showed him a treatise entitled *De Motu* (On Motion). He requested Newton to send it to the Society to be registered. Newton did so and the treatise was registered in February 1685.

Then Newton had a great new idea: Gravitational and astrological force seemed to behave as if it were concentrated in the center of the attracting body and, therefore, for purposes of calculation, a celestial body could be treated as a point. But was this really correct? Or was it only due to the fact the bodies in the solar system are so far from one another they appear as points? Newton decided to work on this problem by assuming a small particle near a very large body (the sun) and calculating in detail what would happen. He had no preconceived opinion as to the probable outcome, but when he had finished his calculations he saw that the sum of the attraction of the particles composing the sun acted as if all

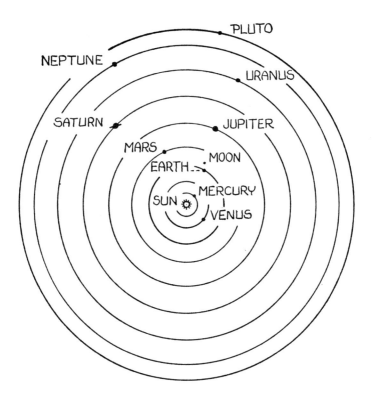

The modern system of the planetary orbits. Mercury, the smallest planet, is
closest to the Sun and rotates only once on its axis in every trip around the
Sun. A day and a year would be equal on this planet, the equivalent of 88
Earth days. Venus, about the same size as the Earth and often called its twin,
revolves around the Sun once in every 225 days. Swinging in a wider orbit
is the Earth and its satellite, the Moon. Mars has polar caps of ice and snow
which grow and diminish seasonally, and there are dark areas, believed by
many to be vegetation, which change color accordingly. A Martian year is
about 686 days; two satellites orbit around this planet. Jupiter, the largest
planet, spins so fast on its axis that it is flattened out at its poles. This planet
can boast of twelve moons. Saturn is circled by three rings which are made
up of millions of small satellites. Nine moons also circle the planet. The three
planets farthest from the Sun were all discovered after the invention of the
telescope. Uranus has five satellites and takes about eighty-four years to complete
its orbit around the Sun. Neptune is so far out from the Sun that surface
temperature is around 300° F. below zero. Pluto, discovered in 1930, has
the most eccentric orbit of all the planets and takes 248 years for one trip
around the Sun.

the mass of the sun were concentrated in the sun's center. Hence any celestial or astral body, provided only that it was spherical could be treated in calculations as a point.

In March 1686 he began writing the three books in the form in which the *Principia* was finally published. The first is entitled *De Motu Corpoum*, which he finished on April 28, 1686, and showed to the Royal Society the same day. The short time required for the writing proves that all the ideas presented were already in Newton's mind for a long time. The second book, which deals with the motion of bodies, but in a resisting medium, was finished on June 20, 1687. In the letter to Halley announcing this, Newton added: "The third I now design to suppress. Philosophy is such an impertinantly litigious lady that a man had as good as be engaged in lawsuits as have to do with her." Halley may have conceded there was some truth to the argument, but he would not accept the final conclusion. So on September 6, 1687, the third book, *De Systemate Mundi*, was presented to the Society, and the whole work was published immediately.

At about this time it occurred to Newton that the number of mathematical operations was insufficient for many purposes. Kepler, incredible as it may seem, did most of his work using only elementary algebra, addition, and multiplication, and only late in his life was to profit from the introduction of logarithms. Henry Briggs, who "invented" the system of logarithms based on the figure 10 and who calculated the first table of such logarithms, died at Oxford in 1630, the same year Kepler died at Regensburg. But while the logarithms saved enormous amounts of work and time in calculations, they did not enable the mathematicians to accomplish anything which had not been done before. In 1665 Newton conceived "fluxions," which we now call calculus. It was his second mathematical discovery, as he had already developed the "binomial theorem." And in 1666, Newton said, he began to "think of forces and gravity extending to the orb of the moon."

At the same time he began thinking about optics and the problem of colors. For half a dozen years he devoted most of his efforts to a study of optics. This resulted in a very important invention, a new type of telescope. It seems logical to assume Newton's optical studies were prompted by the defects of the telescope of his time.

When Newton bought a glass prism at a fair in Stourbridge in 1666, he saw how a ray of sunlight was spread out by the prism into a ribbon of rainbow colors. After some study of this phenomenon he arrived at the conclusion that light consists of rays which are "differently refrangible." When Newton was interested in a natural phenomenon his preoccupation was total and complete. His friend Dr. Edmond Halley once asked how he made his discoveries. Newton's reply was: "By thinking about the problem unceasingly." His thoughts about colors led to a short paper entitled "New Theory about Lights and Colours," which he read to the Royal Society on February 8, 1672. This, of course, had nothing to do with astrology and celestial bodies, but it was an interesting piece of work.

Sir Isaac Newton's *Principia* marked the beginning of what should be known as the "Celestial Century." In the following five-score years astrologers and astronomers were more active and achieved better results than ever before. During this century we have seen that Dr. Edmond Halley predicted the periodicity of his comet and noted three bright "fixed" stars—Aldebaran, Arcturus, and Dirius—had shifted position since the time of Hipparchos. During this century Giovanni Domenico Cassini began publishing the first nautical almanac; Immanuel Kant wrote his *General Natural History of the Heavens*, evolving the first of the modern cosmological theories; Charles Messier compiled his famous catalogue of "nebulosities"; and the two "transits" of Venus, those of 1761 and 1769, provided measurements on which good calculations of the size of the solar system could be based. The Celestial Century culminated with the first discovery of a major planet since pre-Babylonian times. This was the discovery of Uranus by William Herschel, which we shall discuss in the next chapter. This was the century during which astronomical discoveries crowded one another in a way which will probably happen again between 1969 and 2020 A.D.

Newton states the three laws of motion. These are of vital importance to modern astrology.

1. Every body continues in its state of rest, or of uniform motion, in a right (straight) line, unless it is compelled to change that state by forces impressed upon it.

2. The change of motion is proportional to the motive force impressed; and is made in the direction of the right line in which that force is impressed.

3. To every action there is always opposed an equal reaction; or, the mutual actions of two bodies upon each other are always equal, and directed contrary parts.

These three laws, which are so simple and look almost obvious, at long last provided a firm foundation for astrological computation. The most important is the first one, which states the concept known as inertia. A body will remain at rest or in motion, provided that no external force acts upon it. All at once, the "primum mobile," the ultimate moving force which was assumed to be necessary, and which was both mysterious and annoying, was no longer needed. All the observed motions could be explained by an interplay of inertia and gravitational attraction. A satellite moves in an orbit around a planet because it had once received an impetus setting it in motion. If no other force were acting on the satellite, it would have kept on moving in a straight line. But there is another force—the gravitational attraction of the nearby planet—and this gravitational pull bends the straight line into a closed curve.

The same reasoning, of course, held for the orbit of a planet around the sun, and since gravitational attraction weakens with distance the difference in orbital velocity at aphelion and at perihelion could be explained. So could the variable astrological forces at trine, opposition and conjunction be explained logically as well. Nobody who reads this now can help wondering why the world had to wait for Sir Isaac Newton to advance the concept of inertia. Why had not one of the famous scholars of antiquity —say Archimedes—thought of it? The answer is probably that everyday observation and experience seems to contradict the idea. A cart, given a strong push, will roll along the road for a short distance and then come to a standstill. It seemed self-evident the cart stopped moving because the motive force was lacking. But the simple case of the cart which received a push is not at all simple.

The cart was being acted on by a number of hidden forces. There was the friction of the wheels against the road; there was the friction of the axles or bearings; and there was air resistance. But friction is ever-present on earth; nobody ever tried to conceive of frictionless motion, though many examples were moving overhead as celestial bodies. It is a bit more surprising that the astronomical and astrological thinkers a century before Newton, such as Kepler and Galileo, did not arrive at that conclusion, since they came so close to it. Galileo Galilei, in his second letter to Markus Welser on Sunspots, wrote: "Therefore, all external impediments removed, a heavy body on a spherical surface concentric with the earth will be indifferent to rest and to movements toward any part of the horizon. And it will maintain itself in that state of rest, it will conserve that; and if placed in movement toward the west it will maintain itself in that movement." This sounds as if Galileo was building up a generalization, but instead he restricted his remarks to rotating bodies, the rotation of the sun and the motion of the sunspots.

As for Kepler, he should have derived the inverse-square law of gravitational attraction from his own third law of planetary motion, but he did not go far enough. It is anybody's guess what he might have written in his unfinished *Hipparchos* had he lived. Some of Newton's contemporaries at least thought of the inverse-square law, and Robert Hooke, professor of geometry, loudly said so. As time went on Hooke's claims grew larger; at first he only claimed to have told Newton his idea about the inverse-square law. Later, Hooke, according to Hooke, supplied Newton with all of his ideas of celestial mechanics.

Newton, though understandably annoyed, tried to avoid argument by inserting a note of acknowledgment in his *Principia.* Hooke was not satisfied with this acknowledgment, but his complaints did not stop the spread of Newton's ideas. In fact, the time-lapse between the publication of the ideas and their general acceptance was surprisingly short. Nor did Newton himself have to wait long for rewards, though he fell seriously ill for two years in the interim period. He recovered from his illness, a nervous ailment, in 1694. During the following year he was elected a foreign associate of the French Academy of Science, which was a rare honor shared by only seven other men.

In 1695 he was appointed Warden of the Mint; the elevation to Master of the Mint followed in 1699. Newton moved to London and in 1701 resigned his professorship and his fellowship at Trinity College. In 1703 he was elected president of the Royal Society and was re-elected every year until his death in 1727. He was Sir Isaac for the last twenty-two years of his life, being knighted in 1705.

Most books on Newton deal with his work, not with the man; the one which tried to fill the gap is a small volume appropriately entitled *Newton: The Man,* by Lieutenant Colonel R. de Villamil, a retired officer of the Royal Engineers. The book was published in London after 1928 and sometime before 1933. Colonel de Villamil's reason for writing this book was that he had found a missing document. Since Newton died intestate, a careful inventory was taken of his property, but nobody knew whether the inventory still existed and where it could be found. Colonel de Villamil had the old court archives searched. So one day the "True and Perfect Inventory of all and Singular the Goods Chattels of Sir Isaac Newton" was found.

Though the "Inventory" was dirty, it could be cleaned up and proved to be legible. Colonel de Villamil said it was so complete that Newton's house, were it still standing, could have been refurnished as it looked at the time of Newton's death. The listing of Newton's belongings makes one thing clear. As a man of his official position and accompanying income, Newton led an extremely simple life. This was not from premeditated austerity, and the charge of the Abbe' Alari (the instructor of Louis XV) that Newton was stingy is exaggerated.

The abbe' reported when he was invited for dinner, "the repast was detestable" and he was served Palma and Madeira wines which Newton received as presents. This report was borne out by the fact that the "Inventory" valued the parcel of wine in Newton's cellar at only a few pounds. Newton did not dress well and he had no taste for wine or fine food, but he was very generous with other people. He simply did not care about luxuries for himself, so his furniture was simple and what was upholstered was all in crimson, a color he liked. He did not care for poetry or art, and he made fun of people who collected things. He seems never to have kept a pet. The frequently repeated story about a dog named Diamond is almost certainly a myth. The over-all picture which emerges, then, is of a man who lived for his thoughts and kept away from anything—the arts, collecting, pets, any kind of luxury—which might have distracted him. As a person he was generally friendly; as Master of the Mint he did his duty efficiently; as a mathematician and a physicist and an astrologer he was a genius. He did like books! The inventory takers counted 362 books in folio, 477 in quarto, 1057 in sizes smaller than quarto, and "above one hundred pounds weight of pamphlets."

Reading over the list of books owned by Newton one is amazed by the extraordinarily large number of works in Greek and Latin. Not only comparatively recent scientific and philosophical works written in the classical languages, but the true classics themselves. If anybody were to check the classical works then available in print against the catalogue of Newton's library he would probably find that Newton owned most of them. Interesting too is the large number of printed sermons; Newton was a serious man all his adult life. He once rebuked Halley for making a joke about some scientific matter. The absence of some types of books is also interesting, for there are no books dealing with plants, botany, or gardening; no books on art; no poetry is listed. The only language well represented in addition to English, Greek, and Latin was French, with many books on travel, history, and commerce.

By the time Sir Isaac Newton died many of the astrologers and astronomers who had been alive when the *Principia* started the Celestial Century had died too. With Newton went some of the greatest minds in Europe, but now the sun must stand while the earth goes around and around and around. In the next chapter we will tell of some practicing astrologers and some of the attacks made on astrology on the basis of rational thought and mechanistic science.

FOURTEEN

Decline and Rebirth

Well-nigh the last attempt upon a large scale to defend, rehabilitate and reconstruct judicial and genethliacal astrology was made by Jean Baptiste Morin in 1630. His *Astrologia Gallica* was a monumental work. The edition of 1661 was thirty-six folio pages and 784 more pages of text double columned. Morin tells us he was forced to study astrology unwillingly some forty years before by a bishop whose physician he was. For ten years he pursued it empirically and made no sense out of it, but finally he discovered the principles which satisfied every rational inquirer, and served to distinguish what was true and what was false. He declared these true principles of astrology were not stated by Ptolemy or anyone else until himself.

Just as Henri IV summoned the physician and astrologer, Lariviere, to the birth of Louis XIII, so at the birth of Louis XIV, Morin was concealed in the royal apartment to draw up the horoscope of the future Grand Monarque. Later he selected the favorable astrological hour and minute for the trips of M. de Chauvigny, secretary of state, as well as the times when he would be well received at foreign courts. He was sure that drawing up a horoscope for the exact moment of birth was accurate and scientific. But he rejected the employment of a figure for the time of conception.

The chief features of Morin's system are summarized thus: In place of the old distinction between superiors and inferiors, heaven and earth, celestial and sublunar, fifth essence and the four elements, he adopted a threefold division of elementary, ethereal and celestial. The planets were no longer simple bodies of a fifth essence, but compound bodies with the elemental qualities of hot, cold, dry and moist, as well as ethereal and celestial matter. Morin distinguished between their elemental action in heating, moistening and the like, and their influential action by virtue of their celestial nature. The first heaven or primum mobile was a simple body and acted as such, pouring out its universal force through the whole world. But it also had a second action, as it was divided into signs of the immobile zodiac. The "most solid" celestial heaven of the fixed stars had no sublunar influence, but the particular constellations and stars in it exerted virtues of their own. The ether of the ethereal heaven had no sublunar virtue, but the planets in it exerted a great influence. The signs signified more fully and efficaciously than did the planets. In particular, the degree of the sign on the eastern horizon at the moment of birth signified more efficaciously than the lord of the horoscope or the planet in the first house. Morin held it was enough to know the degree for the horoscope and that the exact minute of the degree was not essential.

This was in contrast to his contemporary Descartes, who asserted the idea that the physical world was sheer mechanism, and the ultimate laws of nature were simply the laws of mechanics. God was needed to create and start the motion. In the name of Descartes, it was proclaimed the Aristotelian world was dead! Not only were the "errors of the schools" rejected but also all the various attempts of the Renaissance to interpret Nature in the image of man were also rejected. The microcosm of man and the macrocosm of Nature were sharply split asunder by the Cartesian dualistic two-fold doctrine. It was paradoxical that Descartes exercised such a profound influence over even the men who found his approach most distasteful.

Some of them rejected the most important of Descartes' fundamental conclusions. Huygens, the Dutch astronomer and mathematician, admitted late in life that he could accept only a small part of the Cartesian physics. However, he said it was Descartes who had first opened his eyes to science in general. He also stated that it was Descartes who exposed the failures of the old philosophy.

In his *Principles* Descartes affirmed there were no qualities so occult, no effects of sympathy or of antipathy so marvelous or strange, that his principles of mechanics could not explain them, provided they were from a purely material cause. His chief explanation was that the long, restless, string-like particles of the first element, which existed in the intervals or interstices of terrestrial bodies might be the primary cause.

For those that form in each body have something particular in their figure that makes them different from all those that form in other bodies, and they may pass to very distant places before they encounter matter which is disposed to receive their action.

Descartes was so confident of his ability to think up a rational and mechanical explanation for all seemingly occult phenomena that he was likely to encourage rather than discourage the belief in them. Furthermore, his tendency to advertise the results of his method as marvelous as well as easy of attainment savored more of magic than of science.

A Discourse on the Influence of the Stars according to the Principles of Descartes was written by Claude Gadroys, in 1671. Gadroys claimed that it showed "that there goes out continually from the stars a matter by means of which may be explained the things which the ancients have attributed to occult influences." This matter was, of course, Descartes' first element. After chapters on the nature of the stars, the sun, fixed stars, and the planets, Gadroys told how the matter from the stars got to earth; and then discussed conjunctions, oppositions and aspects. He not only ascribed to them an effect on weather and health, but also broached the theme of talismans or astrological images.

Gadroys explained how the stars incline us, although they do not compel us, to this or that action through their effect upon the animal spirits, for difference in the animal spirits produced the diversity of inclinations. Descartes said that spirits differ in four ways as they were more or less abundant, their parts more or less gross, more or less agitated, and more or less equal. Their abundance excited love, goodness and liberality. If they were strong and gross, they made for confidence and boldness; if equally agitated, for tranquility; if unequally agitated, for desire, promptitude and diligence. If deprived of all these qualities, they caused malignity, fear, inconstancy and disquietude.

Sanguine humor was compounded of promptitude and tranquility of mind, and perfected by goodness and confidence. Melancholy humor was compounded of sloth and disquietude, and augmented by malignity and fear. Choleric humor was a compound of promptitude and disquietude, fortified by malignity and defiance.

Descartes stated it was important to note the positions of the planets at the moment of birth, because immediately thereafter the parts of the brain set themselves and conserved all through the course of life the first impressions which they received. The force of a star's impressions depended upon its finding in the child dispositions conforming to its quality. Each planet caused certain inclinations in men according to its distance from the sun and consequent solidity. Saturn, being far from the center of its tourbillon (the sun) was very solid and coarse. The planets were solid bodies which were governed by certain laws to which liquid bodies such as the sun and stars were not subject.

One of the working astrologers of these times was John Gadbury, born on the last day of December 1627, and educated at Oxford. He joined a merchant adventurer named Thorn in London, then married about 1648. He joined the Presbyterians, the independents, and the "family of love," and was associated with William Lilly for a time. In 1652 he returned to Oxfordshire to visit his grandfather, Sir John, and settled down to study astrology under Dr. N. Fiske.

In 1655 he presented to Sir John Curson the first of his long series of annual "Ephemerides." In 1665 he published *De Cometis, or a Discourse of the Natures and Effects of Comets, with an account of the three late Comets in 1664 and 1665, London's Deliverance from the Plague of 1665,* and *Vox Solis, or A Discourse of the Sun's Eclipse, 22 June 1666.* In 1666 Gadbury went to Westminister where he attended the abbey each Sunday. He was maliciously accused of debauchery in 1667, and of complicity in the murder of one Godden, who had recently indicted him at the court sessions.

By 1678 he possibly was received into the Church of Rome, but this is extremely doubtful. Yet he was suspected of participation in some "popish plots." He was the author of the humorous narrative ballad *A Ballad upon the Popish Plot.* Thomas Dangerfield, an enemy of Lilly's, had eight meetings with Gadbury in September 1679, at the house of Mrs. Elizabeth Cellier. Gadbury was summoned as a witness against Mrs. Cellier at her trial for sorcery and witchcraft. He testified for her, claiming to have known her ten or twelve years, which did not make William Lilly happy at all. Gadbury was taken into custody on suspicion November 2, 1679, but he denied the charge and obtained his release two months later. His enemies (especially Lilly) pretended that he had attempted to bribe his way out of jail.

Gadbury was falsely accused of being implicated in a plot against William III, and again was detained in jail eight or ten weeks. Partridge reproached him for ingratitude to Lilly, and accused him of being the author of the vindictive *Merlini Liberati Errata,* as well as *The Scurrilous Scribbler dissected; a Word in William Lilly's ear concerning his Reputation.*

Gadbury died near the end of March 1704, leaving a widow, and was buried in the vault of St. Margaret's Church, Westminster, March 28, 1704, as a Protestant. And so it went on through the seventeenth century —a whole pack of astrologers boasting and backbiting, and most of them, clearly, doing quite well for themselves with their predictions.

If the astrologers were fighting, the poets were not. John Dryden was the greatest writer of this Restoration period and not an unworthy successor to Shakespeare. Dryden was the true founder of English literary criticism and the Formulator of a new style of poetic expression, the heroic couplet.

With the Restoration came the reopening of the theaters, and quite naturally the young poet turned to the stage in search of fame and profit. After a false start with *The Wild Gallant*, he and Sir Robert Howard won a resounding success in serious drama with their joint effort *The Indian Queen* (1664). Dryden showed his comic abilities in *The Rival Ladies* (1664). The plague of 1665 was followed by the Great Fire in 1666, and Dryden, like the young William Shakespeare two generations before, now found himself denied access to the theater. He retired to the country, where at the Earl of Berkshires's estate he occupied himself with writing.

By 1668, Dryden was firmly established in reputation and finances. The way, of course, was not always smooth; in 1671 he was held up to scorn, as Bayes in the witty *Rehearsal*, while two years later he was involved in a rather indecorous controversy with the dramatist Elkanah Settle. Maybe this helped him to modify his own views; maybe he had grown tired of serious drama. Dryden was deprived of his laureateship in 1689, and entered upon a time of economic difficulty. Returning to the theater, he won some success, but nothing like that which greeted his early dramas. In any case, the theaters themselves were in a bad way and had little to offer. With his usual adaptability, however, Dryden discovered a fresh field of activity in the poetic translation of the work of Juvenal. It is his translation of the poet Juvenal which concerns us in the history of astrology.

In his longest satire, an attack upon the female sex, Juvenal finds one of the gravest faults of women to be their susceptibility to oriental cults— and to astrology.

> And Mankind, ignorant of future Fate,
> Believes what fond Astrologers relate.

A woman, says Juvenal, will consult an astrologer for the strangest reasons:

> From him your Wife enquired the Planets' Will,
> When the black Jaundice shall her Mother kill,
> Her Sister's and her Uncles' end would know;
> But, first, consults his Art, when you shall go.

In 1693, Dryden translated the following, on women to avoid:

> Beware the Woman, too, and shun her Sight,
> Who, in these Studies, does her self Delight.
> By whom a greasie Almanack is born,
> With often handling, like chaste Amber, worn;

Not now consulting, but consulted, she
Of the Twelve Houses, and their Lords, is free,
She, if the Scheme a fatal Journey show,
Stays safe at Home, but lets her Husband go.
If but a Mile she Travel out of Town,
The Planetary House must first be known:
And lucky moment; if her Eye but akes
Or itches, its Decumbiture she takes.
No Nourishment receives in her Disease,
But what the Stars, and Ptolemy shall please.

Juvenal, from *The Sixth Satire*

Dryden went on to say, according to the English Chronicles of 1186, that all Europe panicked at one time in that century because of a prediction by astrologers of an approaching conjunction of planets in the constellation Libra. The fact that the conjunction was to take place in an "airy" or "windy" sign was interpreted as signifying a terrific wind-storm.

But Dryden was not as cynical as Juvenal, for he wrote this epitaph for an admired young lady:

For sure the milder planets did combine
On thy auspicious horoscope to shine,
And even the most malicious were in trine.

Dryden slowly made his way toward the acceptance of astrology and mysticism, for his later works all contained an element of the occult.

The astrologers were still fighting among themselves, so we must look to a musician for the next part of our story. An organist who liked to look at the heavens at night, but who neither taught about the stars nor was an astrologer, made the next contribution to the art. Herschel used to spend night after night watching and studying the heavens just for his own personal pleasure. Perhaps because he was a musician he found true beauty and rhythm in their movements out in distant space, just as did Pythagoras.

One clear Tuesday evening in the spring of 1781, while he was "rummaging among the stars" with his telescope, he got a great surprise. He found something that he had never seen before—a round, flat cloudy thing. He kept watching it steadily. "It can't be a star," he thought, "for stars are so far away that there's no telescope big enough to make them look like more than points of light—and this has a definite shape."

He watched it longer. "It has changed its place among the stars! It is moving!" he exclaimed. "Now I know it's not a star. Perhaps it's a comet." Then he told the Astrologer Royal about his new find. It was not long before astrologers all over the world heard of the new discovery. They turned their telescopes on it and watched the slow motion of this strange new object in the sky. Some thought it was a comet; some, a lost star.

At the time in Russia there was an astrologer who proved that it was really another planet circling around our own sun, way out beyond Saturn. You can imagine Herschel's great delight when he found he was the very first known person in history to discover a planet. He wanted to name it after George III, who was the king of England. Other astrologers wanted to name it Herschel. But they finally all agreed to name it after one of the old Greek and Roman gods, like the rest of the planets. They called it Uranus after the God of the sky.

"Since Uranus is a planet," thought Herschel, "it probably has moons like our earth and Jupiter. I am going to see whether I can find them, too." So he watched his planet week after week, month after month, and year after year, hoping and hoping to find its moons. Then one clear winter night he was rewarded for his six long years of patient watching. He discovered what looked like a group of very faint stars. "If these are moons," he thought, "they will be moving around Uranus. Then tomorrow night I ought to see one of them here." So he made a map of the place where he thought this one certain moon should be. And sure enough, the next night it was actually where he predicted.

He thought Uranus had six moons, but later on it turned out he made a mistake. Only two of the faint objects he had seen were actually moons. The others were real stars far, far out in space. Later two more moons were discovered. When the astrologers actually measured Uranus with their telescope they found it was a huge planet, much bigger than the earth: but still not so large as Saturn or Jupiter.

Uranus was the first planet ever to be discovered with a telescope. The others—Mercury, Venus, Mars, Jupiter, and Saturn—were all known long before recorded history. Naturally astrologers everywhere watched the new planet Uranus very carefully. They wanted to know more about it —what its path was around the sun and how fast it was traveling. They figured out just where it should be on different dates. But Uranus did not behave quite as they expected it to. It did not keep exactly to the nice regular path they marked out for it. Finally they decided something must be pulling on Uranus from outside to make it wobble about.

Then some mathematicians became interested. "Tell us just how far out of its path it goes and in just what direction it wobbles and we will see whether we can figure out what is the matter," they offered. So the astrologers all measured carefully, and the mathematicians got the exact measurements. They figured and worked and wrote piles of papers covered with numbers. Many years went by and many people tried to solve the problems of why Uranus was pulled out of its path. Then in 1846, about sixty-five years after Herschel discovered Uranus, two mathematicians finally worked it out at about the same time. One was an Englishman named Adams, and the other was a Frenchman named Leverrier. They did not know anything about each other, but each set to work in his own country to figure out why Uranus behaved as it did.

After a great deal of figuring each one decided there must be another planet farther away from the sun even than Uranus, and that this planet must be pulling Uranus out of its path by gravitation. But where to find this other planet? That was what they must figure out next. Adams finished his work first and sent his figures to an English observatory to be checked. You would think the men there would have been very excited over the idea of seeing a new planet for the first time. But they were not! They put the figures aside, and it was not until some months later they finally began to search the heavens for Adams' new planet.

Leverrier was luckier. He sent his figures to an observatory in Berlin. The people in the German observatory were more fortunate than those in the English one because they were working on some star maps, which proved to be a great help in regard to this new planet. The very first night after the astrologer received Leverrier's figures he looked through his telescope and sure enough, there was a new planet, just where Leverrier said it would be. It is a twin planet to Uranus, and Leverrier named it Neptune after the God of the Sea.

It is an amazing thing that a planet could be found just by accident, the way Herschel, the musician, discovered Uranus; but it is even more wonderful that mathematicians could just sit down with pencil and paper and figure out exactly where a planet ought to be. Neptune was the first planet ever to be discovered solely by calculation. It is twice as far away from the sun as Uranus is—nearly three billion miles—and it is about thirty times as far from the sun as our earth. Like the earth, Neptune has only one moon. Its moon is larger than ours, but it goes around Neptune in less than six of our days; so a month on Neptune is not quite six days long. It takes Neptune so long to travel its great course around our sun that one of its years is as long as a hundred and sixty-five of our own.

Ever since Uranus and Neptune were discovered, men have been watching and studying these far-away planets. Then, a little over 130 years ago, some astronomers began to notice strange things about Uranus and Saturn. These two planets were not behaving as they were expected to. It seemed as if they were being pulled out of their regular paths. Then astrologers became interested, and began to work on this new problem. What and where was the thing in the sky that was pulling on Saturn and Uranus?

Apparent motion of the planets with the earth as the center of the horoscope.

The outer planets begin to retrograde at the left, continuing in opposition with the sun where they attain their greatest retrograde motion. From there, they retrograde more slowly until they reach the point marked D where the planets attain direct motion once more. The sun is closing the gap between itself and the planets in question. On the other hand, the two inner planets, Venus and Mercury begin to retrograde to the right of the sun, picking up speed as they cross the face of the sun (conjunction).

The outer planets retrograde for a different reason. Actually, all the planets go around the sun in the same direction (counterclockwise, or eastward); they never once actually stop and go backwards. To explain all this, look at the diagram and notice that the earth is drawn in the center. Since the earth's orbit takes it around the sun, it must at some time come between the sun and each one of the outer planets. It is at this point that the opposition of the planet occurs, and it is because of the greater speed of the earth's revolution that the outer planets appear to go backwards. It is like two trains going at different speeds in the same direction on parallel tracks. When the faster train passes the slower, the people looking out the windows of the fast train think the slower train is going backwards.

To explain the reason for the retrograde motion of Venus and Mercury, we must realize that these two planets are between the earth and the sun. When Venus and Mercury are between us and the sun, we see them in what appears to be a retrograde motion. When they are on the far side of the sun, they are in superior conjunction and go in direct motion. Mercury takes about 21 to 25 days to retrograde. This has a direct bearing on the speed of Mercury at the retrograde conjunction. If Mercury is taking long to retrograde, say 25 days, the speed at conjunction will be around 43′ daily motion. If Mercury completes its retrograde motion in 21 days, its speed at conjunction will be well over one degree per day and as high as 1° 23″. Venus does not vary so much, and its speed at retrograde conjunction is about 38′ per day.

Venus and Mercury must always retrograde through the same sign as the sun. If you add thirteen degrees to the sign Venus is in on the day it begins to retrograde, you will have the degree the Sun will be in when Venus turns back to direct motion. The greatest speeds, both in direct motion and in retrograde motion, are attained when they are in conjunction with the sun.

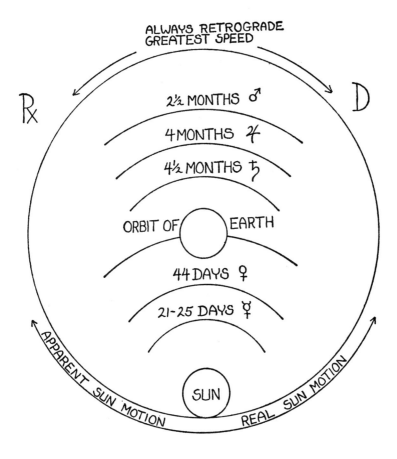

Dr. Percival Lowell, head of the famous Lowell Observatory in Flagstaff, Arizona, was a great philosopher as well as a great mathematician. He studied Mars a great deal and believed there were people living on Mars. He became tremendously interested in this new riddle of what was pulling on Saturn and Uranus. So he set to work trying to solve it, and spent years working and studying and figuring and watching. Finally in the year 1905, he made certain discoveries. From his calculations he was certain there must be another planet out beyond Neptune, and this new Planet was what was pulling on Saturn and Uranus. He called it "Planet X" and he was able to prove with his figures just why it must be a planet and where it was to be found.

He began to search for it, but he knew it would be terribly difficult to find such a far-away planet against a background of millions of stars. There was only one thing to do. He must get photographs. He set all his men in the observatory to work. They divided up into sections the part of the sky where they figured it must be. Then they took several pictures of each one of these sections. Two or three nights after they took the first set of pictures they would take a second set of pictures of the very same sections. Then they would look at the two sets of pictures, study them and compare them. They hoped to find one tiny point of light which changed its place in the sky between the first and second photographs.

This was a long, long task, for each little picture was exposed for three hours to let the light from the very faint stars make a record on the film. Dr. Lowell examined and compared all these photographs, and that was a longer and more difficult task than taking the pictures. Only a person like Dr. Lowell, who had the greatest interest and enthusiasm, would ever have tackled such a gigantic task. For about ten years he patiently photographed, studied, measured, hoping to find the planet which his figures told him was surely traveling around our sun out beyond Neptune. In 1916 he died and the search for the planet was stopped!

Fourteen years later the work of finding the planet was resumed. One small object was seen which shifted its position among the stars between the two times it was photographed. The distance it moved showed it was very slow-moving and very far away. They kept watching this new object and found out many things about it, such as its light was yellowish, not bluish like the light from Neptune. This means it had a very different kind of air or perhaps it had no air at all. They found that it was between forty and forty-three times as far away from the sun as the earth—so far away it gets only a little bit of sunlight and very, very little heat. They discovered that it takes this planet two hundred and fifty of our years to go around the sun.

Now in the old stories, the king of the Gods, Jupiter, had two brothers.

The signs and dates of the Zodiac.

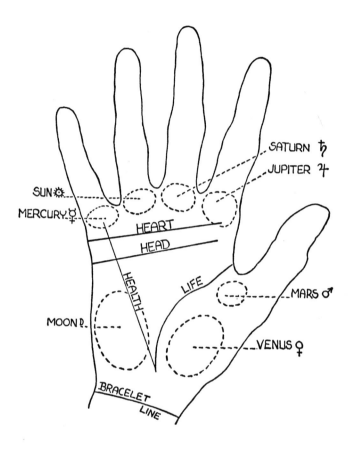

Modern day palmistry is closely related to astrology. For example, the Mounts at the base of the fingers are as follows: the Mount of Jupiter, which is contained between the base of the first finger and the Headline; the Mount of Saturn, between the base of the second finger and the Heartline; the Mount of the Sun, between the base of the third finger and the Heartline; and the Mount of Mercury between the base of the little finger and the Heartline.

The upper Mount of Mars is placed directly beneath the Mount of Mercury, and is bounded by the edge of the palm, the Line of Heart, the Line of Health and the Line of Head.

The Mount of the Moon rises beneath the Upper Mount of Mars, and is bounded by the edge of the palm, the Line of Head and the Top Bracelet on the wrist.

One was called Neptune and the other was called Pluto, so the new planet was called Pluto. From the earliest days of astrology, special note was given to the planets, "wanderers," which followed their own special paths among the fixed stars of the constellations that form the signs of the Zodiac. When Uranus was discovered, astrologers removed Saturn from Aquarius and put Uranus there instead. Jupiter was accorded similar treatment when Neptune was discovered, Jupiter had to leave Pisces, turning it over to Neptune. When Pluto was discovered the natural sequence would give it to Aries, but many astrologers said Pluto belongs to Scorpio. Then a dual rulership was adopted: Jupiter and Neptune together are co-rulers of Pisces, Saturn and Uranus are co-rulers of Aquarius, and Pluto and Mars rule Aries and Scorpio together.

Many of our best astrologers object to the word "ruler" being bestowed on a planet in relation to a sign. The signs of the Zodiac cover the universe. Each sign stretches for millions of light-years, distances so great they are hardly thinkable. On the other hand, a planet is a mere pinpoint in the sky in comparison with a sign. Yet these tiny points are often said to "rule" such immense vastnesses. It is often said that a term like "analogue" or "correlative" would be more appropriate for the planet's influence. In the current standard pattern a small, dead orb like the earth's moon is given "rulership" over a sign on an equal basis with the great and mighty sun itself: Sun rules Leo and moon rules Cancer.

Ptolemy gave all the planets signs to rule, beginning with Mercury in both directions; but he had only the visible planets to work with, causing considerable confusion when Uranus, Neptune and Pluto were discovered. Some of our best astrologers cast the entire Ptolemaic rulership pattern aside, using none whatever, or deciding on one of their own. The author can attest from his own experience and from reports of other practitioners that astrology is not entirely self-sustaining without some planetary rulership pattern.

One objection to the standard pattern is the fact that Saturn, the planet of death, is the ruler of Capricorn, the sign of fame and honor. Again, Mars is the planet of authority, the police, the armed forces and so on. Capricorn is the sign of authority; why then should not Mars rule Capricorn? Carl Payne Tobey, struggling with this problem, found a way to bring Mars to the tenth sign and Saturn to the eighth. By taking the northern view of the Zodiac as against the usual Southern view, and placing the sun (Leo) on the first house cusp, he had the moon (Cancer) on the second, Mercury (Gemini) on the third, Venus (Taurus) on the fourth, Pluto (Aries) on the fifth, Neptune (Pisces) on the sixth, Uranus (Aquarius) on the seventh, Saturn (Capricorn) on the eighth, Jupiter (Sagittarius) on the ninth, Mars (Scorpio) on the tenth. The eleventh and twelfth are for planets Y and Z which may be small asteroids. Tobey succeeded here in bringing Saturn, the planet of darkness, to the eighth, or House of Death; and Mars, the planet of authority, to the tenth, or House of authority. There are other suggested patterns extant, all in the process of testing with the purpose of finally completing the Ptolemaic system of planetary influence.

We have seen how the scientist of today and the philosopher of the eighteenth century hoped to prove that everything in the world moves according to unchangeable and predictable physical laws. The late eighteenth century was the last period in history when human omniscience was thought to be an attainable goal. Then, the people of Europe were enjoying an ever-increasing prosperity. Educated and imaginative men saw the world as a place for all types of pleasure. The eighteenth century was one of comedy into which, at its end, came a grim revolution both in France and America. It was into this century of comedy, laughter, and sensual pleasure followed by grim reality that the "Prince of Quacks," a charlatan and the world's greatest student of the occult, was born.

Count Alessandro Di Cagliostro, whose real name was Guiseppe Balsamo, lived from 1743 to 1795. He was and is considered the greatest mystic and impostor of all time. This opinion was fostered by Thomas Carlyle, the Scottish historian. However, recent research shows that Cagliostro was not quite the quack and scoundrel he was previously presented as being. This research shows he cast many of the most accurate astrological forecasts of all times. Cagliostro's father was of humble origin and died young, leaving Guiseppe's mother destitute. The boy went to the local seminary school in Palermo, but frequently ran away and was usually found in unsavory sensual surroundings. When sent to a Benedictine Monastery School, he was put directly under the supervision of the Father Superior.

It was from the apothecary (or druggist) attached to the monastery that he learned the principles of chemistry and medicine. He was more interested in learning astonishing and surprising alchemical combinations than gaining any factual knowledge of the subjects. After a few years, he fled the monastery and returned to Palermo. He associated with the same rascals, whores, and vagabonds as before, spending many a night in jail for drunkenness and venery. The young seer robbed his uncle of a large sum of money when the kind man tried to assist him to go straight. When he was only fourteen, he assisted in the assassination of one of the wealthy canons of the local Roman Church.

As he grew older, he also grew bolder, and grew tired of these childish excursions into crime. At the age of seventeen he laid the foundations for his fortune. In Palermo there lived a goldsmith called Marano, who was very superstitious and believed whole-heartedly in the effectiveness of magical occult powers. Cagliostro soon made his acquaintance and convinced him he was a "real master of magic" and a true alchemist. He convinced the old goldsmith that a large amount of buried treasure was in a field on the outskirts of town. Its exact location would only be found by the aid of certain magical incantations; for such occult mysteries, sixty ounces of the purest gold were needed as a lure to the spirit world. It was simple for Cagliostro to convince the superstitious goldsmith to furnish this large amount of gold for "bait." They went to the field together at midnight of the new moon and Cagliostro began his dreadful incantations.

These sacrilegious chants disturbed poor Morano so badly he fell prostrate upon the ground. He was quickly overpowered by the scoundrels gathered by Cagliostro for the occasion and the golden lure—all sixty ounces—disappeared. Cagliostro narrowly escaped capture by the local authorities and fled south to Messina.

In Messina, Cagliostro adopted the title of "Count" and met with Althotas. This mysterious prophet was dressed as an oriental with caftan and robes. Cagliostro and Althotas became fast friends and the "Count" took lessons from him in astrology, alchemy, and the other cognate occult sciences. Magic, to Althotas, was a fixed science with laws both discoverable and reducible to reason. Astrology was such a science, and its laws and truths were well known to the seer. Cagliostro was an apt pupil and soon was proficient in casting a horoscope. These two empiric mountebanks departed for Egypt.

Althotas and the Comte de Saint Germain were one and the same. Saint Germain was born in 1710 of obscure origin. Some say he was a Portuguese Jew, but others claim he was of royal Greek birth. Saint Germain was an accomplished spy and had visited many of the courts of Europe. He spoke many languages, and was sent on secret diplomatic missions by Louis XV of France. In 1762 Saint Germain lived in Germany, and taught the young Cagliostro many occult secrets. In the *Memoirs of Cagliostro*, Saint Germain was the hero. Cagliostro credited him as the greatest and wisest of teachers. No doubt Saint Germain paved the way for the young prophet at the court of Louis XV of France. Cagliostro attempted to hide Saint Germain's true identity by referring to him as Althotas. The two men traveled together and studied hidden knowledge of practical occultism. They went to Arabia, Persia, Egypt, and finally to Malta. There they curried the favor of the Grand-Master of the Maltese Order—Pinto. The Grand-Master was completely infatuated with alchemical experiments and astrological forecasts. He soon gave Cagliostro funds and letters of introduction to the great houses of Rome and Naples.

Cagliostro had supporters while in Rome, so was soon established as an "Empiric-Physician and Astrologer" and retailed specifics for all the diseases and weaknesses of the flesh. Money flowed in and he lived in luxury. He met the young and beautiful Lorenza Feliciani and quickly married her. The couple traveled to Venice, Sardinia, and Spain, but in each place Cagliostro's rogueries forced them to leave in haste. From Lisbon, they sailed to England, and in London the Comte sold love-philtres, elixirs of youth, mixtures for making ugly women beautiful, alchemistic powders, and charms, naturally deriving a large profit from the trade.

Princes, Bishops, and the nobility in general were keen to probe the secrets of nature, and alchemy and astrology were the pursuits and hobbies of the wealthy. Yet, the seer soon moved on to France. While in Paris, Cagliostro cast the horoscope of Madame Comtesse du Barry and foretold of the violent death of all members of the Court of Louis, King of France. Again, Cagliostro soon tired of Paris, or Paris tired of him. After further travels on the continent he and his beautiful wife returned to London. During this second visit to London he posed as the founder of a new system of Freemasonry, known as the Egyptian Masonry. It abounded with sensual, magical, and mystical references and rites. Cagliostro was received in the best society and was adored by the ladies.

The usual group of wealthy "high-born" pleasure-seekers flocked to the "lodge." He set himself up as a physician and was credited with a large number of miraculous cures. His methods were a mumbo-jumbo of "laying-on of hands" and hypnotism. For the next few years he traveled and acquired wealth and fame in central Europe. While he was in Germany, as a friend of Cardinal de Rohan, Cagliostro claimed he had transmuted base metals into gold and had found the elixir of life. Returning to Paris in 1785, he was introduced to the court of Louis XVI where he evoked spirit apparitions in mirrors before the court. His beautiful wife appeared only before a very select group in a revealing transparent white costume. All these exhibits added to Cagliostro's wealth, fame, and mystery.

The Egyptian-Masonic rite admitted both men and women and consisted of a mystical-sexual ceremony. The initiation took place at midnight in the full of the moon with the ladies clothed in thin white diaphanous robes. Following various occult oaths and harangues, they disrobed completely and were informed that the Egyptian Freemasonry taught material happiness and spiritual peace and pleasure. The entire ritual ended with an orgy of nude reveling and dancing. As they left the next morning, a pair of garters were given to the men (for their favorite mistress) and a cockade given to the ladies (for their favorite lover).

It was during this visit to Paris that Cagliostro, now calling himself the

"Grand Copt," was implicated in the affair of the "Diamond Necklace." The central actors in this drama were Cardinal de Rohan, grand almoner of France and Archbishop of Strasburg; his mistress, an adventuress known as the Countess de La Motte; Queen Marie Antoinette; and Boehmer and Bassenge, a firm of Parisian jewelers. The necklace was ordered by Louis XV for his mistress, Madame du Barry, but the king died before purchasing it. De Rohan was in disfavor at court, but was duped by the Countess de La Motte and Cagliostro into believing he could secure the patronage of Marie Antoinette and become her lover. The Countess arranged a series of midnight meetings between the Cardinal and Mademoiselle Gay d'Olivia, a poor unfortunate who looked like Marie Antoinette. The meetings were in the private garden of the Palace of Versailles. Rohan was convinced and easily persuaded that the Queen wanted the diamond necklace and would buy it, if he would sign the contract with her. The necklace was delivered, and De La Motte broke it up and sold the diamonds. Then the first installment came due. No payment was made and the jewelers complained to the police. The King ordered the Countess de La Motte, the Cardinal, and Cagliostro sent to the Bastille.

It was Countess de La Motte who charged Cagliostro with the robbery of the necklace and then invented for him a terrible past; calling him an empiric alchemist, false prophet, and a lewd satyr. Cagliostro finally proved his innocence, but he also provided the French public with one of the most romantic and fanciful of life stories in the history of autobiography. Then Cagliostro made the most outstanding prediction or prophecy of all history. Cagliostro, Dame La Motte, Gay d'Olivia, Villette (an accomplice), and Cardinal de Rohan were in a single cell, deep in the heart of the Bastille. Their lives were dependent on the outcome of the trial, but the master charlatan cast their horoscopes. Cagliostro stated Dame La Motte would be branded, imprisoned, and later would escape to England. Her death would be ". . . precipitated in the dead of night, a fall from the window in the third story . . ." escaping from capture for bad debts. And such was the case. She was branded, imprisoned, bribed the guards and escaped to England. On August 23, 1791, she jumped from the third story ledge of her house in London to escape arrest and debtor's prison.

He said Villette would depart the Bastille unwhipt and unharmed and would hang on the gallows of the castle of St. Angelo. Gay d'Olivia, the common street girl would go free and marry. Cardinal de Rohan would live to an old age in safety beyond the Rhine. In each case the prophecy came true! For himself, Cagliostro said, "O, horror of horrors! Is it not Myself I see? Roman Inquisition! Long months of cruel baiting . . . Cagliostro's body lying in St. Leo Castle, his soul-self fled to—whither?"

Although proven innocent, Cagliostro was banished and went to London. While in London his downfall started; he was imprisoned in the Fleet Prison; a French newspaper printed an exposure of his life; and his reputation was lost. On leaving England, he traveled throughout Europe, but was unable to find any rest. He finally went to Rome, with his wife accompanying him. At first he did fairly well, living quietly and practicing occult medicine, then he made his final mistake—he attempted to form an Egyptian Masonic Lodge under the very nose of the Roman Church. He was arrested on September 27, 1789, and tried by the Holy Inquisition. His examination took eighteen months and resulted in the death sentence.

The Pope commuted the death sentence to perpetual imprisonment in the fortress prison of San Leo. His cell was a dried up cistern where he languished for three years without fresh air, movement, or intercourse with his fellow creatures and died March, 1795. Meanwhile, his wife was confined in the Convent of St. Appolonis, where she died in 1794.

Cagliostro was vain, naturally pompous, fond of theatrical mystery and the occult. He was a "little mad" and loved the shameful popularity. He acquired a certain practical working knowledge of astrology and occult science, and possessed certain psychic powers of hypnotism and telepathy. On the whole, Cagliostro was the most picturesque figure in eighteenth century Europe. Was he a charlatan? Or, was he possessed of true mystical power? You must decide for yourself.

Another famous astrologer of the period, Francis Barrett, not only practiced the art, but taught and wrote on the subject. Barrett set up shop in Norton Street, Marylebone, London, in the 1790's, giving instruction in the magical arts. This was a period of revival of interest in medieval lore. Alchemy, astrology and all the rituals of magic were being delved into by the wealthy. Barrett's studio was in an area where artists made their home, and his trade did not seem odd to his fellow residents. Barrett brought to his work a scholarship which was unusual for a practitioner of magical arts. He understood a number of ancient and foreign languages, he translated the ancient books of occult and magical lore unavailable in English, and wrote *Magus* (1801). His book became the source book for students of these ancient works.

Barrett, on the cover of his book, called himself a "student in chemistry, metaphysicks, natural and occult philosophy." He was also credited with the authorship of a work originally published anonymously, *The Lives of the Alchemystical Philosophers*, issued in 1815. However, there is some question as to whether he actually wrote this book. In the book *Magus*, Barrett covered a wide range of magic lore, translating the *Heptameron* of Peter de Abano, a thesis on Cabala, and the magic squares of Agrippa of Nettesheim. He mentioned the Rosicrucians, and "Illuminati."

His scholasticism and adherence to the ancient texts made his book an important reference for students of magical lore. A facsimile edition of *Magus* was republished in 1967, with an etching of the author in the front.

Before closing this chapter, we should discuss three other men whose writings are available to the modern student of astrology. The first of these, Richard James Morrison (1795–1874), inventor and astrologer, is known chiefly by his pseudonym of "Zadkiel." He was born June 15, 1795. He is famous for his devotion during nearly half a century to the science of astrology, for in 1831 he brought out "The Herald of Astrology," which was continued as *The Astrological Almanac* and *Zadkiel's Almanac*. His predictions became known far and wide, selling annually by tens of thousands, sometimes running up to an edition of two hundred thousand copies. Among the other periodicals he edited were *The Horoscope* and *The Voice of the Stars*.

Morrison, who was considered by some to be a charlatan and by others a victim of a distinct hallucination, brought an action for libel against Admiral Sir Edward Belcher in 1863. The Admiral, in a letter to the *Daily Telegraph*, stated that "the author of 'Zadkiel' is the crystal globe seer who gulled many of nobility about the year 1852." At the trial, on June 29, 1863, it appeared Morrison had pretended that through the medium of the crystal globe various persons actually saw visions. Some persons of rank who were present at the seances were called on behalf of the plaintiff, and testified that the crystal globe was shown to them without any money payments. The jury returned a verdict for the plaintiff with only 20 s. damages.

Morrison died on April 5, 1874, after writing many articles and books. Two of these are: *Observations on Dr. Halley's great comet, which will appear in 1835; with a History of the Phenomena attending its Return for six hundred years past* and William Lilly's *Introduction to Astrology; with emendations*, reprinted later as *The Grammar of Astrology*.

Another comparatively modern mystic was Alphonse Louis Constant (1809–1875) who wrote under the assumed name of Eliphas Levi. Levi was born in Paris of a poor family, but the boy was precociously clever and was educated for the priesthood. He was expelled from the seminary for holding heretical opinions, so he never became a priest. The conflict between his orthodox Catholic education and his fascination with magic runs through all his books, although he tried hard to reconcile the two warring tendencies in his thinking.

His expulsion from the seminary suggests that Levi was attracted to occultism at an early age. As a magician he undoubtedly followed his own instructions to know, to dare and to will, but fortunately he did not keep entirely silent. In 1856, he published the two volumes of *Le Dogme et Rituel de la Haute Marie,* his most brilliant book. Wildly romantic, vague and verbose, often abstruse and sometimes patently absurd, it was written with zest and imagination, and a depth of insight into the theory and practice of magic which makes it well worth reading over a century later. His later books are less interesting; they are *History of Magic* (1860) and *The Key of the Mysteries* (1861). Levi made very little money from his books. He earned a pinched living by giving lessons in occultism to aspiring students; he was an imposing figure with a great beard, rather dirty personal habits and a gluttonous appetite.

The learned English occultist A. E. W. Waite, who succeeded in translating the *Doctrine and Ritual,* said that in it Levi revealed the secrets of an occult society into which he was initiated, and was then expelled from the society. He was always more interested in theorising about magic than in actually practicing it. The only magical operation he was said to have performed was one of necromancy, though of an unusually pure and elevated kind. It was the evocation of the ghost of the philosopher and magician Apollonius of Tyana. What is almost certain to strike the reader as the most surprising feature of his books is the unquestioning faith in the importance of the magician's ritual, the uttering of Cabalistic words, the potency of talismans, the complicated and unconscionable business of going through the motions. Thus, although Levi condemns superstitious practices, he claims to have obtained wonderful results with the Tarot cards.

The last of the three, Richard Garnett (1835–1906), English librarian and man of letters, eminent for his work for the British Museum library, was born on February 27, 1835. Garnett was educated at home and at a private school, and in 1851, just after his father's death, entered the British Museum as an assistant in the library. In 1875 he rose to be superintendent of the reading room, and from 1890 to 1899, when he retired, he was keeper of the printed books. He died in London on April 13, 1906. A. G. Trent was his pseudonym.

Since he was interested in astrology, he delved considerably into the tremendous stores of astrological books at the Museum and gave out a great number of old charts. He contributed in 1884 to the *University Magazine,* and in 1894 some of his material was collected into a book called *The Soul and the Stars.* In this book Dr. Garnett stated that the people still need to be taught to regard astrology as a definitely empirical science, because the public has been told for so many years to regard the astrologer as a kind of wizard. He thought the best way to offset this wrong opinion that there was something occult about astrology was to compile statistical data. He himself proceeded to show how he compiled some of this material concerning the planet Mercury and its relationship both to mental ability and to mental instability. In spite of his very sound advice, no statistical group of any consequence was formed in England during his lifetime.

At this point we are now ready for the twentieth century and its remarkable advances in astrology. Modern science has changed its attitude. No longer does the (so-called) scientist scorn or ridicule the astrologer as a quack—instead he now knows there are many strange phenomena not accounted for by the mechanistic world of Descartes.

FIFTEEN

New Trends

It is striking that more than 300 years of experimental science has not succeeded in providing any falsehoods in astrological beliefs. Astrology is a social reality since its forms vary from the crudest superstitions to scientific attempts at connecting the astrologer's art with modern psychological and biological knowledge. In this chapter let us look at (and think about) a few of the varied modern concepts concerning the influences of the heavens. Not so many years ago, any claim that forces from outside our universe could affect human beings and their environment would have thrown scientists into an uproar. To accept such a thesis would be to acknowledge a belief in astrology, and to some scientists, a belief in astrology was like a belief in witchcraft.

Now, however, the climate of scientific opinion is changing and definite evidence is emerging which suggests that what goes on in the heavens may well have some cause-and-effect connection with all of us here on earth. An increasing number of scientists are studying the relationship of stars and planets to man. They are studying the claim that astrologers have the knowledge with which to make accurate predictions of future events on earth.

Some scientists are still reluctant to acknowledge their interest, but one astronomer at a well-known observatory admits he knows how to read astrological tables and cast horoscopes; still, he wants this kept quiet. Yet despite such fears, more and more scientists are willing to speak out for the subject of astrology.

The rebirth of astrology began between the two wars, when it showed up first in the United States, Canada, and England; later it spread to continental Europe. Astrology benefited from the powerful communications media of the modern world; thus today astrology is everywhere. The belief spread out over the planet like a universal language; so, many dollars, francs, lire, and marks change hands every day for horoscopes, books, and astrology magazines. Thousands of people plan their actions in conformity with these astrological directives. Yet no great addition was made to the ancient doctrines. The greatest changes were the inclusion of the influences of the three newly discovered planets, Uranus, Neptune, and Pluto, along with the use of high-speed extremely accurate computers.

It was estimated recently that there are over 5,000 working astrologers in the U.S. alone, who supply about 10,000,000 customers with forecasts. The charge for an individual horoscope varies greatly, from two dollars to several hundred dollars. The clients come from all walks of life: from young girls in search of romance to politicians and business leaders. There is little doubt that astrology today is very much alive, more alive than ever before. Newspaper horoscopes are the most commonly read and followed sources in the modern world. Almost every major newspaper features an astrological column; also there are large numbers of magazines devoted exclusively to astrology, and innumerable periodicals run a regular horoscope feature. These usually are women's magazines, though men read them too!

We see the head of genius upraised above the lot of common men, and our interest is somehow excited. We even see fluctuations in such lives not evident in our own; but living as we do on the surface, and seldom seeing below it, we have no knowledge of the causes which make men great. Balzac said: "To us, indeed, who do not see below the surface of human things, such vicissitudes, of which we find many examples in the lives of great men, appear to be merely the result of physical phenomena; to most biographers the head of a man of genius rises . . . as some noble plant in the fields attracts the eye of the botanist by its splendor."

Since cause and effect are in everything, there must be a cause underlying what men call greatness. To find it may well be to answer many other questions which trouble us. At least, it may give us a measure of understanding of ourselves and so provide an intelligent line of procedure. It is a paradox to some, although it appears to others to be self-evident, that a surer knowledge of physical man leads to a more complete understanding of philosophic and astrological man. In this regard, and especially since it concerns the cause of greatness in man, the study of the system of ductless glands in the human organism may serve as the prime example.

Books both for the layman and for the scientist set forth in a fairly thorough manner the nature of the various ductless or endocrine glands and describe their functions. So much so that individuals have already been classified as thyroid-, pituitary-, pineal-centered, and so on. Mainly, these were cases where abnormality or malfunctioning made necessary special consideration or treatment. What has been incontrovertibly established, however, is that the endocrine glands play a tremendously important part in the growth and development of the individual, governing his attitudes, abilities, and emotions, as well as contributing to his physical normality and determining the rate at which he lives.

Further, it is the action of these glands in concert which accounts for the various results, for the fluid each secretes must be balanced and perhaps mingled with that of every other to be effective in the system. This action is so subtle it eluded physiologists of the past—although repeated references to Descartes' "seat of the soul" and to his mystic concern with the "Third Eye" (or pineal gland) raised the question whether the endocrines might not have once been recognizable factors in accounting for man's behavior. It is possible that some medical papyrus yet undeciphered among the thousands in various Egyptian collections may reveal that the endocrines were known and reckoned with in ancient Egypt. It may even be that Greek philosophic speculation aimed at describing the nature and function of those glands, for the nature of the soul and the manner of its descent into the body received constant and serious consideration.

Weather significantly affects the incidence and severity of disease and alters the success of therapeutic measures. An autonomic demand is placed on the inhabitants in areas where the polar and tropical air masses meet. During the polar infall, there occurs a shift of blood, blood pressure rises, as does the metabolic rate, catabolism preponderates, relative anoxia may ensue, and relative acidosis may result. Acute inflammatory episodes are not uncommon at this time. This phenomenon of polar infall and its physiological result can be disastrous for man, often leading to death if an acute attack of a serious disease was previously worse during the tropical low caused by the diurnal movement of the planets.

The birth charts of musicians, criminals, military leaders, and statesmen reveal greatly dissimilar planetary configurations, and any one chart, when properly erected, will be the same whether the investigator erecting it is favorable to the practice of astrology or not. The evaluation of its specialized pattern is unfortunately a different matter, for that rests upon the integrity and ability of the investigator. The diagnosis of physical symptoms by any two physicians may be different, especially if their schooling was different.

The cause of greatness is in the planetary influences present at birth; they can be considered *prima facie* evidence tending to be substantiated in the later life. Such planetary influences could be compared with medical charts of the basic relationships of the person's endocrine glands. Some medical practitioners, especially those trained in psychiatry or working with the mentally and emotionally disturbed, studied this relationship between planetary influence and behavior, and thereby increased the effectiveness of their treatments. If there is a measurable relationship existing between planetary activity and disease, should it not be equally evident in regard to health? And if these are both included, could not the proposition be theoretically extended to embrace the whole man, of which greatness must be only a part?

In advancing the theory of relationship no radical or extreme ends are being proposed: Endocrinologists are not ready to pronounce the final word as to the exact nature of these several organs or their definite purpose in the human system. No more can astrologers state with finality the particular planet influencing any one gland. They ascribe to certain celestial bodies an influence, little suspected and sometimes disputed, on the structure and nature of the mental and physical man. Endocrinologists, as well, ascribe to certain little-known physical organs a hitherto unsuspected importance in the functioning of the mental and physical man.

If both were to join forces in their study, it is possible that not only the cause of greatness might be found, but also the cause of many aspects of human behavior. For reasons which are related to the positive connection existing between the constitution, health and mental genius, a good aspect of the moon and sun at birth indicates a positive coordination between the organic and the functional. When a predisposition to illness, either mental or physical, is shown in the natal horoscope, the particular illness may often be determined by the Sign in which the malefic planets occur. This is due entirely to the effects of these heavenly bodies on the tiny endocrine glands. These endocrine glands are a team of tiny architects for the body of man. They are under the absolute control of the pineal gland. Thus we are not at all mystical when we call them the "sculptors of the soul." These endocrine glands are structures which spread tiny qualities of powerful hormones throughout the body and regulate its functions in both sickness and health.

The influence of the tiny endocrine glands is most clearly seen in the personality of the individual. They are a structure and system which express man's ultimate behavior. Man is an entity and personality is his ultimate element. But man's personality is not nearly an integration of action and reaction at a fixed time. Indeed it is a mysterious basic element which operates on the astro-physical plane.

We must study man through all of his actions—the material and spiritual, physical and mental. Man is the boundary. Man is that line where

heaven and earth lose their boundaries and merge their qualities. To be
a real person is more than to be just an individual. A person is an individual functioning in a society, endowed with awareness and a certain
element of freedom. It is through the personality that the individual becomes a person. Truly the personality is the totality of the individual
made up of all the traits which constitute each person. This must be so,
just as humanity is the totality of the persons forming the human race.

The endocrines are the key to exploring the secrets of normal and abnormal personality. They guard the development of the astrologically determined qualities and adapt them at every moment to the various stresses
of the real world. The endocrines are the custodian of the personality.
The majority of these tiny glands are stimulated by the pituitary and it
is the pituitary which is controlled by the pineal. Recent studies have
shown this "third eye" is really an intricate and ultra-sensitive "biological
clock," converting cyclic diurnal (astral?) light into endocrine information.

The existence of the pineal has been known for at least 2000 years.
Galen of ancient Rome knew about it, and he believed it regulated the
flow of thought from a storage bin to the conscious centers in the mind.
In the seventeenth century Rene Descartes stated quite flatly that the pineal housed the seal of the rational soul. It responded to the events of the
real world and transmitted the information to the active part of the brain.
Modern science has recently shown the pineal responds and functions
under extremely unusual conditions. It was found that the pineal responded dramatically to naturally occurring periods of light and darkness.
Thus it is now known that lighting cycles are extremely important in
regulating our endocrine functions.

The increase in sunlight during the late winter and spring starts the
breeding cycles in many birds and mammals. The daily rising and setting
of the sun determines many of the rhythm patterns in both man and other
animals. Such daily rhythms are called circadian, which comes from the
Latin and means "about one day." The most important part of the personality is based on this process of action and reaction. It is the daily
systemized way in which man as a whole reacts to light. The structure of
our personality is built on an endocrine skeleton which becomes a link
between the organic and psychic. The regular functioning of such an
endocrine structure determines the character of each person and, most
likely, his actual thinking.

In short, personality and character are governed by the sun and moon.
It is the pineal linked to the endocrine glands which acts as the control
center. The marvelous system of the galaxies of the universe is no more
remarkable than the galaxy of tiny endocrine glands which govern every

function of the human being. The two are interlocked, for man is the microcosm controlled by the macrocosm through the pineal gland.

In World War II the Nazis formed a monstrous alliance with astrology, but the study by E. Howe goes a long way toward separating the truth from the myth. One fact was certain: during the war Hitler's court attached great importance to the prophecies of Nostradamus. Goebbels, the propaganda minister, forced several astrologers to bring out a pro-German edition of the *Centuries* to be distributed among enemy populations. Among these was Karl Ernst Krafft, one of the better known astrologers of those hate-filled days. Rudolph Hess, Hitler's most trusted counsellor, was the main supporter of the astrologers. After Hess's flight to Scotland in 1941, Hitler's rage against him was turned to the diviners, and many of them were sent to concentration camps. Krafft, who was not able to foresee this turn of events, died in a concentration camp on January 8, 1945. The Allies in turn were helped by astrological knowledge to prepare their own version of the prophecies of Nostradamus for use as propaganda against the Germans, or so claimed Louis de Wohl. But according to E. Howe, there was only a slight chance that this was true.

Since the end of World War II, the social problem presented by astrology seemed important enough to professional sociologists for them to make several studies. Who are the people who really believe in astrology? Why do they believe in it? In 1963, the French Public Opinion Institute published the results of their research into the attitudes of the adult population about astrology. They found: 58 percent of the population knew their birth signs; 53 percent of the people read their horoscopes in the papers every day; 43 percent believed astrologers were scientists; and 37 percent believed there was a relationship between the character of persons and the sign under which they were born.

According to the psychiatrist Carl G. Jung, astrology is deeply rooted in the human soul, for the sight of the starry firmament always made men dream, and these heavenly dreams, accumulated over thousands and thousands of years all over the world, left a residue in the total consciousness of the race. These are the archetypes, since the psychological sketches astrologers have been outlining for the past 2,000 years are only a simplified version of modern psychiatry. He went even further and studied the marital happiness of couples born under the various signs. His conclusions agreed, in the main, with those of astrological lore.

The great religious festivities on our calendars all have astrological origins. They are only modifications of ancient solar celebrations: Christmas is celebrated near the winter solstice, when the days which are getting shorter begin to lengthen. The birthday of Christ heralds a new series of longer days, just as the New Year does. Easter, when Mother Nature comes to life after her long winter sleep, is near the spring equinox. Even today the Church changes the date of Easter from year to year, following the phases of the moon, since it coincides with the first Sunday following the first full moon after the spring equinox. Truly then, the sun and moon are still important in our spiritual lives.

Our planet is influenced by the moon in other ways since it affects the weather. The effects of the moon are not only limited to the tides of the oceans. The same gravitational force which acts on the tides draws away and reshapes the higher atmosphere, at the same time it sends us a gamut of electromagnetic forces reflected from the sun. New discoveries are continually being added to the list of the moon's influences on the earth. Just recently, it was found the moon's position in relation to the sun affects the earth's daily magnetic index. As we saw, the belief that the moon plays a role in controlling the weather is very old and widespread, certainly as old as the Chaldeans. Even today people contend that the weather changes when the moon does and remains the same until the moon changes again. It was less than seventy years ago that the meteorologists were convinced of this, for their instruments were blind to any lunar influence. Now they look to astrology for some answers to their problem of predicting the weather.

In the past men conceived the sun to be a perfect sphere, as the golden circle of the Pythagoreans. But now we know that the sun is a star in a permanent state of fiery effervescence. It revolves on itself and it is periodically covered with "spots," those abrupt explosions of boiling gases which are launched into space with massive effects reaching down to earth. One could say the earth belongs within the radius of the sun's atmosphere, since these explosions on the solar surface interfere with the atmospheric electricity of our planet, upset and cause fade-outs in radio reception, and account for geomagnetic storms in the atmosphere. H. Berg and H. Hanzlik found in them the explanation for the sudden changes in our weather which they were unable to explain previously.

We are talking about what the experts call "the passage of a warm or cold atmospheric front." These passages depend on the variation of barometric pressure, and they change wind direction. If the pressure rises, the weather will usually improve; this condition is called by the weatherman an "anticyclone." If the pressure descends, it is likely that it will storm, so this condition is called a "cyclone." It seems the rise or decline in barometric pressure depends on the sudden eruption of sun spots, for when sun spots occur in numbers the weather on land is good, but there are storms at sea. This seems to be true for both hemispheres of our earth.

Not only does the sun influence our weather over long periods of time, it also leaves a definite record on earth. Scientists have discovered a very useful way for establishing the effects of solar activity on temperature and rainfall. This allows them to delve into the past and collect information which can be applied to the prediction of future weather. This method is called dendrochronology, or the study of tree rings. It is known that the number of rings on a cross-sawn tree trunk corresponds to the age of the tree in years. But the size of the rings are not the same, they vary with weather conditions: a warm and wet year leaves a wide ring, while a narrow ring is left by a cold and dry year. It is possible to reconstruct, by means of the width of tree rings, the climate of the past in the area in which the tree grew. The most interesting aspect of this study is that graphs constructed from tree specimens found in different regions of the globe show a close resemblance to each other. This suggests there is such a thing as a "climate of the earth" affected by the sun itself.

In astronomy and astrology a nineteen-year period is a crucial one, for about every nineteen years the sun-moon eclipses occur at the same point of the sky. When an eclipse darkens the sky, about nineteen years (exactly 18.64 years) will pass before the event repeats itself. This period was known to the Chaldeans, who called it Saros and believed its magic powers would cause the end of the world. Although no astrologer shares this ancient belief nowadays, it would be unwise to conclude Saros has nothing to do with what happens here on earth. Le Danois emphasized the great importance that Saros can have on our lives; he claimed that the combined gravitational pull of the sun and the moon acts on the tides, causing widespread disturbances in large bodies of water. This has been shown to hold true for the Nile, for it has shown clear rhythmic variations corresponding to Saros for 4,000 years.

So much for eclipses. Let us go back to sun spots, for in 1951 John H. Nelson, propagation analyst at RCA Communications, was put in charge of a study involving the quality of the reception of radio broadcasts. It was known for some time the quality of radio reception depended on sun spot activity, and especially on the activity of the larger spots. When solar activity was correlated with ease of reception, a factor remained unaccounted for. Nelson thought this could be explained in terms of the heliocentric position of the planets. After many observations he concluded that sunspots themselves are not the full answer to the problems. There is very strong evidence that some other forces are at work and the need for a new approach was indicated. The study of the planets netted encouraging results and showed promise. A technique of this planetary type would enable forecasting to be done several years ahead, since advance planetary movements can be calculated with very great accuracy because they are so rhythmical.

One of the basic and most mysterious properties of life is its dependence on these rhythms. Different rhythms have been found to regulate everything, even man's genius, as mentioned earlier. This is true not only for the life of animals but also for that of plants. It is true not only for the organism as a whole but for each of the separate organs, every cell, and the swirling atoms of which each cell is made. Rhythmic cycles underlie all biological reactions, from the most elementary cellular processes to the complex ones of man as a whole. When seen more closely, the movement of such rhythms appears to be the effect of "biological clocks" which keep time for one's life. Protoplasm has the remarkable inherent ability to structure time into regular periods. When seen in certain familiar instances, such as the rhythms of breathing, heartbeat, or spasmodic nervous discharges, it does not surprise us. But the other thousands of clocks ticking away in nature do tend to confuse us.

It was known for many years that physiological rhythms tend to follow the lead of the earth's environment. Sometimes these rhythms adapt themselves to the periods defined by the earth's motion or its position in space. The three main basic rhythms which we understand are: the daily rhythm, which depends on the earth's turning every twenty-four hours; the twenty-eight day rhythm of the moon's circling around the earth; and the yearly cycle of the earth's trip around the sun. Life is able to follow an environmental rhythm by perceiving the rhythm's by-products, changes in light, temperature, winds, rain, humidity, etc. The effects of the yearly cycle are familiar to everyone: in spring the steady increase in temperature causes blossoms to open and animals to begin their courtship. At winter's approach the cold stops some activities: trees shed their foliage and some animals hibernate.

The daily rhythm is obvious, for most plants and animals follow a twenty-four hour cycle of sleep and wakefulness. But there are variations to this basic pattern, since the cat and the owl are adapted to the darkness. Plants use sunlight as a source of energy, and actively synthesize their nourishment during the day. The twenty-four hour rhythm without a doubt is the most important one affecting earthly life, so it has been well studied by the specialists. Yet there are other cycles, such as the reproductive cycles of many sea animals based on the rhythms connected with the movement of the tides. The rising of the tide depends on the respective positions of the sun and of the moon; when they are in conjunction or in opposition (new or full moon), their gravitational effect becomes additive, producing stronger tides than the ones that occur when the sun and the moon are at right angles to each other. Thus the relative positions of the sun and moon do affect life here on earth.

Two heart specialists reported that for the year 1957 there was a very high correlation between the number of coronary infarctions and sudden increases in solar (sunspot) activity. When a disturbance was produced on the solar surface, this appeared to affect the blood vessels of the heart, causing the formation of clots in individuals predisposed to such attacks. The bloodclots obstructed the coronary artery, often precipitating a fatal infarction of the heart. Earlier two German researchers, G. and B. Dull, in 1934 reported some important statistics on deaths by tuberculosis in Hamburg, Copenhagen, and Zurich, in connection with the dates of violent solar explosions.

Scientists began the study of the effects of these cosmic phenomena on man with great hesitation because they thought they were running the danger of becoming identified with outdated superstitious beliefs. But the progress of science made it inevitable that the question would be framed again; there was no other alternative, since it was obvious the human organism is ruled by external rhythms as well as internal ones. There are seasonal and daily rhythms, of course, but there are also many more mysterious ones.

From the most ancient times, the moon was charged with a disturbing influence on mental stability. "Lunatic" has become a synonym for an unruly spirit or madman. Certainly the staffs of mental hospitals know that the full moon affects their patients' behavior. The Philadelphia Police Department is still of the opinion that many criminal acts of violence coincide with the phases of the moon, with an increase in crime along with the approach of the full moon. These effects of the moon seem to be more pronounced on mental patients and on antisocial persons than on normal people.

A Florida ear-nose-throat doctor found remarkably clear evidence of a moon cycle in bleeding after surgery. This amounted to a great preponderance of bleeders near the time of the full moon and only an insignificant number of bleeders at the new moon. In the interval between the first quarter and one day before the third quarter, eighty-two percent of all the cases of excessive bleeding after surgery occurred. Then, too, the marked similarity between the average length of a woman's menstrual cycle and the period between two new moons has always puzzled man's imagination. Is this just a chance coincidence, or is there a cause and effect relationship involved? Perhaps some day astrology will know the answer. It is not at all unreasonable to assume there are some portions in the lunar cycle when, because of electromagnetic, cosmic or other similar changes, the onset of menstruation would occur. This would vary from one woman to the next. But no one yet has studied the relationship of the phases of the moon, the natal horoscope, and menstruation. This certainly needs to be studied, for astrology knows the date of birth affects the entire life pattern of any person.

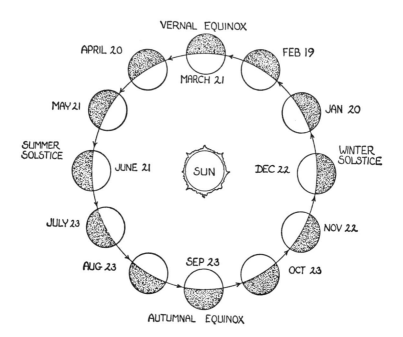

THE SEASONS

Winter Solstice: The noon sun is directly overhead at 23½° S. The shortest day of the year in the northern hemisphere.

Vernal Equinox: The noon sun is directly overhead at the Equator on its apparent migration north. Day and night are equal (both hemispheres).

Summer Solstice: The noon sun is directly overhead at 23½° N. The longest day of the year in the northern hemisphere.

Autumnal Equinox: The noon sun is directly overhead at the Equator on its apparent migration south. Day and night are equal (both hemispheres).

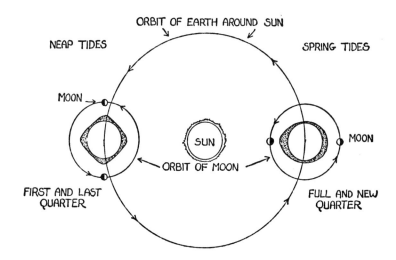

THE TIDES

First and Last Quarter: The moon's attraction works against that of the sun, so the range of tides is decreased.

Full and New Moon: The moon's attraction works with that of the sun and the range of tides is increased.

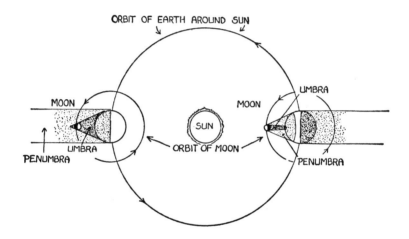

THE ECLIPSES

Total eclipse of the moon: An eclipse of the moon occurs only when the moon is full. The moon usually appears dull red during the eclipse due to the refraction of the red rays of the sun by the atmosphere of the earth.

Total eclipse of the sun: An eclipse of the sun occurs only during a new moon; then the sun is invisible in umbra and partly invisible in penumbra. A total eclipse is visible only in the portion of earth touched by the shadow of the moon (umbra).

Paracelsus and others said man is more than a machine and a biochemical retort; he is more than just an animal for whom life is passively endured. Man feels joy, love, fear, anger, sorrow, and happiness. Man creates beauty to express himself when such expression is needed. Man's body is a physiochemical organism, yet it contains a rational function which is frequently called the mind. Modern man seems at times afraid to trust the mind, its sensations and its emotions. Modern science needs to become less a technological science, and to place more confidence in philosophy and astrology. It needs to study man as a creative human being, a unity, and not merely as a cellular chemical factory or as some mechanical analogue computer. Astrology is possibly the oldest of man's sciences; space travel in this modern atomic age may one day discover that stargazing has a true scientific basis after all.

Glossary

ALKAHEST—a term used by the later alchemists to designate an imaginary substance possessing the power to dissolve all kinds of elements and compounds. The universal solvent.

AMBIENT—that which surrounds, or an enveloping matrix. In astrology the atmosphere enveloping the earth, events occurring in that atmosphere, and particularly the moon which influences all events in this sublunar world.

APOGEE—the position of a celestial body in which its orbit places it furthest from the earth. It is particularly applied to the planets, but in the Ptolemaic system could also be applied to the sun.

ASCENDANT—an astrological term designating any celestial position above the horizon.

ASCENSION—the rising of a celestial body above the horizon.

ASTROLABE—an ancient instrument employed for measuring the angular position of sun and stars, used also to project the celestial sphere on the plane of the equator.

CARDINAL POINTS—the four directions.

CELESTIAL AXIS—the imaginary straight line passing through the heavens and around which the stars seem to revolve in their daily motion. The pole star is the northern end of the axis.

CELESTIAL EQUATOR—when the plane of the earth's equator is extended heavenward to cut the celestial sphere in half, it forms an imaginary circle at this intersection, and this circular line is called the celestial equator.

CIRCUMPOLAR STARS—stars which are so near the celestial north pole or south pole that they never set below the horizon. The further away from the earth's equator one is, the more such stars one sees.

CONCENTRIC—celestial bodies which revolve about a common center, or any orbit around a central point.

CONJUNCTION—when two celestial bodies are seen in the same longitude of the zodiac they are in conjunction. For example, the new moon is always in conjunction with the sun. A conjunction is *superior* when the celestial body is on the side of the sun most distant from the earth, while an *inferior conjunction* is a similar position on the side of the sun nearest the earth, or between the sun and the earth.

CRITICAL DAYS—refers to the belief that certain days are supposed to be destined to bring bad luck.

CULMINATION—the point or time at which a heavenly body crosses the meridian. Also the highest and lowest points of altitude attained by a celestial body in its daily motion across the sky.

DEFERENT—an imaginary circle around the earth traveled by the point which served as the center for a smaller circle known as an epicycle.

DEMONOLOGY—the belief in demons, and the belief in witchcraft.

DIRECT MOTION—the motion of a planet in an easterly direction against the fixed stars as opposed to its apparent daily motion from east to west, due to the earth's rotation.

ECCENTRIC—the circular motion of a celestial body around a center remote from the earth, so that it comes near the earth at one point and at another is far from the earth.

ECLIPTIC—an imaginary circle of the celestial sphere drawn through the middle of the zodiac which marks the apparent path of the sun among the stars.

ELECTIONS OF DAYS—the act of consulting an astrologer concerning the best day on which to initiate a certain act or perform some deed.

EPHEMERIDES, Plural of EPHEMERIS—a diary, an almanac, or a calendar. During the middle ages it was a book of gossip, wisdom, and forecasts. It is also employed in astronomy to designate a set of tables giving the positions of celestial bodies for the various days of year.

EPICYCLE—refers to the motion of a planet in a small circle around a center which itself moves in a circular path around some other center.

EQUINOX—the two days of the year, approximately March 21 and September 22, when the sun crosses or is on the celestial equator. From September to March the sun is seen against the stars below the equator, and during the second half of the year above it.

FREE WILL—the belief of all religions, monotheistic as well as pagan, that man has the freedom to choose, that his mind or soul have some independence and power of their own.

GEMS—believed to have magical powers in healing and in other situations.

GENERATION AND CORRUPTION—according to Aristotle, all earthly or sublunar bodies were composed of the four elements. They were subject to changes either of corruption or generation. Celestial bodies were composed of the primary elements, a fifth substance, or quintessence, and so were not subject to changes of any kind.

GENETHLIALOGY—the science of casting nativities or of elaborating horoscopes. By noting the positions of the planets at the precise moment of a person's birth, astrologers foretell his character and fate. Such forecasts are called horoscopes of nativities.

HELIACAL RISING OF A STAR—when the sun is in a given constellation the stars of that constellation will not be seen, since they are hidden by the sun's rays. As the sun moves eastward out of such a constellation, its stars are seen at dawn. The first time a star is seen after having been blotted out by the sun is called its heliacal rising or its emerging from the sun's light.

HOROSCOPE—the astrological forecast of a person's fate and personality as interpreted from the positions of the celestial bodies at his birth.

IMAGES—special drawings or designs believed to have magical powers.

INCANTATIONS—the uttering of certain words and phrases believed to have great magical powers. They are always spoken in a ritual manner in order to attain an objective.

INEQUALITY IN LATITUDE—the irregular motion of the planets along different arcs of their orbits as measured on their plane of revolution.

INFERIOR PLANETS—Mercury and Venus, whose periods of revolutions are much shorter than that of the earth.

INTERROGATION—the act or practice of consulting an astrologer, medium, oracle, etc.

LINE OF APSIDES—the major axis of the elliptical orbit of the moon around the earth, or a line joining the positions of the moon at perigee and apogee with the earth.

LUNAR CALENDAR—a calendar based entirely on the moon and which has no regard for the sun.

LUNATION—the period of asynodic revolution of the moon around the earth, or from new moon to new moon.

LUNI-SOLAR CALENDAR—one which counts the months from new moon to new moon but adds on extra days, as needed, to keep the months tied to the seasons, or to the tropical year which is determined by the sun. The Jewish calendar is an example.

MEDICAL ASTROLOGY—until about two centuries ago all physicians assumed that the body and its functions were under the influence of the stars and planets. All medical treatment was attuned to stellar and planetary positions.

MERIDIAN, CELESTIAL—an imaginary great circle drawn in the heavens, joining the north and south poles of the sky and crossing both the zenith and nadir. Noon is the moment when the center of the sun crosses this line in the southern sky.

NODES—the points where a celestial body intersects the ecliptic in the course of its revolution around the earth. The two nodes are not permanent against the stars, but slide westward, completing their cycle in 18.6 years.

OCCULT—any quality or property hidden from human eyes or understanding, something concealed or mysterious. The term is not always used in a "supernatural" or magical sense.

OPPOSITION—two heavenly bodies are in opposition when they are 180° apart in longitude. A planet is said to be in opposition when the earth is directly between the sun and the planet.

ORBS—hollow, imaginary spheres postulated by the Greek astrologers as carriers of the planets which were attached to their equators.

PARALLAX—the apparent change in the position of an object when viewed from two different places.

PERIGEE—the point of a celestial body's orbit at which it is nearest the earth.

PRECESSION—the movement of the earth's axis, or the westward sliding of the equinoxes along the ecliptic, completing a full cycle in 26,000 years.

RETROGRESSION—that part of a planet's orbit in which it appears to be moving in a direction opposite to that it previously pursued for a longer time. Normally a planet seems to be moving eastward against the stars. In the retrograde period it reverses its direction and moves westward, then resumes its eastward course.

SIDEREAL DAY—time reckoned by the diurnal motion of the stars, or the time from a given star's crossing of the meridian until its second crossing. Sidereal always means pertaining to stars.

SOLSTICE—the points on the ecliptic where the sun reaches the greatest northerly or southerly distances from the celestial equator. About June 21 and December 21.

STATIONS OR STATIONARY PERIOD—before the planet initiates retrogression it appears to stand still, and before reversing its direction from retrogressive to direct, it also appears to be stationary.

SUBLUNAR—any object or event occurring on earth or within the region between the sphere of the moon and the earth. This region was distinct from that beyond the moon, which was celestial or divine.

SUPERIOR PLANETS—planets having a longer period of revolution than the earth. The outer planets.

SYNODIC MONTH—the month as reckoned by the conjunction of the moon with the sun or from new moon to new moon.

SYZYGY—the two points on the orbit of a planet where it is in opposition and conjunction with the sun.

TREPIDATION—the belief of ancient and medieval astrologers that the eighth sphere, that of the stars or firmament, underwent a slow wavering. Such a motion was postulated to account for the changes in the motion of the axis of the world.

ZODIAC—the belt of constellations through which the sun traverses in its annual trip in the sky. The moon and the major planets also have their orbits in this belt, and the ecliptic runs in its center. The zodiac extends about eight degrees north and south of the line of the ecliptic. The ancients divided this into twelve portions of degrees each and ascribed to them the signs.

Bibliography

Bulfinch, Thomas, *Bulfinch's Mythology*. New York: Thomas Y. Crowell, 1913.

Cavendish, Richard, *The Black Arts*, First American Edition. New York: G. P. Putnam's Sons, 1967.

Christian, Paul, *The History and Practice of Magic*. Vols. I & II. Translated by James Kirkup and Julian Shaw. Edited and revised by Ross Nichols. New York: Citadel Press, 1963.

Claggett, Marshall, *Greek Science in Antiquity*. London: Abelard-Schuman, 1957.

Crow, W. B., *A History of Magic, Witchcraft, and Occultism*. London: The Aquarian Press, 1968.

Dampier, William C. and Margaret Dampier (Editors), *Readings in the Literature of Science*. New York: Harper Torchbooks, 1959.

Dampier, Sir William Cecil, *A History of Science and its Relations with Philosophy & Religion*, Fourth Edition. Cambridge: Cambridge University Press, 1961.

Dreyer, J. L. E., *History of the Planetary Systems from Thales to Kepler*. Cambridge: 1906.

Durant, Will, *The Story of Philosophy, The Lives and Opinions of the Greater Philosophers*, Second Edition. New York: Pocket Library Edition, Pocket Books, 1960.

Farrington, Benjamin, *Greek Science—Its Meaning for Us*. Baltimore: Penguin Books, 1961.

Frazer, Sir James George, *The Golden Bough. A Study in Magic and Religion*, Abridged Edition. New York: The Macmillan Company, 1960.

Garrison, Fielding H., M.D., *An Introduction to the History of Medicine*, Fourth Edition. Philadelphia: W. B. Saunders, October, 1961.

Guthrie, W. K. C., *A History of Greek Philosophy*, Vol. 1, *The Earlier Pre-socratics and the Pythagoreans*. Cambridge: The University Press, 1962.

Jacobi, Jolande (Editor), *Paracelsus: Selected Writings*. Translated by Norbert Guterman. Bollingen series XXVIII, Bollingen Foundation Inc., 2nd Edition. New York: Pantheon Books, 1958.

Levi, Eliphas, *The History of Magic*. Translated with a preface and notes by Arthur Edward Waite. London: Rider and Company, 1969.

Lockyer, J. Norman, *The Dawn of Astronomy, A Study of the Temple Worship and Mythology of the Ancient Egyptians*. Cambridge, Mass.: The M.I.T. Press, Paperback Edition, Aug. 1964.

Major, Ralph H., *A History of Medicine*, Vol. 1. Springfield: Charles C. Thomas, 1954.

Pachter, Henry M., *Paracelsus: Magic into Science*. New York: Henry Schuman, Inc., 1951.

Randall, John Herman, Jr., *The Career of Philosophy, From the Middle Ages to the Enlightenment*. New York: Columbia University Press, 1962.

Robbins, Rossell Hope, *The Encyclopedia of Witchcraft Demonology*. New York: Crown Publishers, Inc., 1963.

Sarton, George, *Introduction to the History of Science*, Vol. I, *From Homer to Omar Khayyam*. Baltimore: Williams and Wilkins, for the Carnegie Institution of Washington (Pub. #376), 1927.

———, *Introduction to the History of Science*, Vol. II, Part I, *From Rabbi Ben Ezra to Roger Bacon*. Vol. II, Part II, *From Robert Grossesteste to Roger Bacon*. Baltimore: Williams and Wilkins, for the Carnegie Institution of Washingtion (Pub. #376), 1931.

———, *Introduction to the History of Science*, Vol. III, Part I, *First Half of the Fourteenth Century*. Vol. III, Part II, *Second Half of the Fourteenth Century*. Baltimore: Williams & Wilkins, the Carnegie Institution, Washington (Pub. #376), Vol. III, Part I, 1947. Vol. III, Part II, 1948.

Seligmann, Kurt, *The Mirror of Magic*. New York: Pantheon Books, Inc., 1948.

Sigerist, Henry E., *The Great Doctors, A Biographical History of Medicine*. Translated by Eden and Cedar Paul. New York: W. W. Norton & Company, Inc., 1933.

———, *Civilization and Disease*. Ithaca: Cornell University Press, 1944.

———, *A History of Medicine*, Vol. II, *Early Greek, Hindu, and Persian Medicine*. New York: Oxford University Press, 1961.

Singer, Charles, *A Short History of Scientific Ideas to 1900*. Great Britain: Oxford University Press, 1959.

———, *A Short History of Anatomy and Physiology from the Greeks to Harvey*. New York: Dover Publications, Inc., 1957.

Smith, Homer W., *Man and His Gods*. Boston: Little, Brown and Co., 1952.

Spence, Lewis, *An Encyclopaedia of Occultism, A Compendium of Information on the Occult Sciences, Occult Personalities, Psychic Science, Magic,*

Demonology, Spiritism, Mysticism and Metaphysics. New York: Strathmore Press, 1959.

Stillman, John Maxson, *The Story of Alchemy and Early Chemistry.* New York: Dover Publications, Inc., 1960.

The Encyclopedia of Occult Sciences with Introduction by M. C. Poinsot. New York: Tudor Publishing Company, 1968.

Thorndike, Lynn, *A History of Magic and Experimental Science,* Vol. I, *During the First Thirteen Centuries of Our Era.* New York: The Macmillan Company, 1923.

——, *A History of Magic and Experimental Science,* Vol. II, *During the First Thirteen Centuries of Our Era.* New York: The Macmillan Company, 1923.

——, *A History of Magic and Experimental Science,* Vol. III, *Fourteenth and Fifteenth Centuries,* New York: Columbia University Press, 1934.

——, *A History of Magic and Experimental Science,* Vol. IV, *Fourteenth and Fifteenth Centuries.* New York: Columbia University Press, 1934.

——, *A History of Magic and Experimental Science,* Vol. V, *The Sixteenth Century.* New York: Columbia University Press, 1941.

——, *A History of Magic and Experimental Science,* Vol. VI, *The Sixteenth Century,* New York: Columbia University Press, 1941.

——, *A History of Magic and Experimental Science,* Vol. VII, *The Seventeenth Century.* New York: Columbia University Press, 1958.

——, *A History of Magic and Experimental Science,* Vol. VIII, *The Seventeenth Century,* New York: Columbia University Press, 1958.

Watson, Robert L., *The Great Psychologists from Aristotle to Freud,* Text Edition, The Lippincott College Psychology Series. Philadelphia: J. B. Lippincott Company, 1963.

Wedeck, Harry E., *Treasury of Witchcraft.* New York: Philosophical Library, 1961.

Index